# Also available at all good book stores

9781785317927

9781801500630

9781801500067

9781801500937

9781801501149

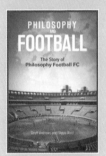

9781801500999

9781801500692

9781801500920

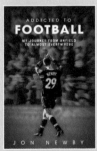

9781801500739

# On the
# Border

# On the
# Border

## The Rise and Decline of the
## Most Political Club in the World

Shaul Adar

First published by Pitch Publishing, 2022

Pitch Publishing
9 Donnington Park,
85 Birdham Road,
Chichester,
West Sussex,
PO20 7AJ
www.pitchpublishing.co.uk
info@pitchpublishing.co.uk

ISBN 978 1 80150 095 1

Typesetting and origination by Pitch Publishing
Printed and bound in India by Replika Press Pvt. Ltd.

# Contents

In memory of my mother, Yael Adar

# Glossary

Ashkenazi – Jew of European descent. Plural: Ashkenazim

Beitar – sport and youth movement of Herut and the
    Revisionist movement

Bibi – Benjamin Netanyahu's nickname

Bibism – the cult of Netanyahu

Hamizrahi – the east stand at Teddy Stadium

Hapoel – sport organisation of the Histadrut (General
    Organization of Workers)

Haredi – ultra-orthodox Jews

Hasbara – Israeli propaganda

Herut – Menachem Begin's party, predecessor of the Likud

Histadrut – the General Organisation of Workers in Israel

Intifada – Palestinian uprising

Kibbutz – a communal settlement in Israel. Plural:
    Kibbutzim

Kibbutznik – member of a kibbutz. Plural: Kibbutznikim

Likud – Israel's main right-wing party, came to power in
    1977

Likudnik – supporter of Likud

Maccabi – sport organisation of the liberal movement

Mahapakh – a revolution, upheaval, turnover but in a smooth way

Hamahapakh (the mahapakh) – Likud victory in the 1977 elections

Mahane Yehuda (Maknneyuda) – Jerusalem's market

Mapai – Workers' Party of Israel, in power from 1948 until 1977, later as Labour party

Mizrahi – Jew of Muslim country descent. Plural: Mizrahim

Mukadisin – Palestinian Jerusalemites

Nakba – the Palestinian Catastrophe, the destruction of Palestinian society and homeland in 1948

Ole – Jewish immigrant to Israel. Plural: Olim

Waqf – the Islamic religious trust that controls and manages Temple Mount

Yerushalmi – Jerusalemite. Plural: Yerushalmim

Yishuv – the Jewish community in Palestine before the forming of Israel

Introduction

# The Navel of the World

*'The air over Jerusalem is saturated with
prayers and dreams like the air over cities
with heavy industry. It's hard to breathe.'*

*Ecology of Jerusalem*, Yehuda Amichai

IN SEPTEMBER 2021 Hapoel Tel Aviv hosted Beitar
Jerusalem for another one of their never-ending clashes of
narratives. Both sets of fans pelted their rival goalkeepers
with items but it was the brutal attack on a young woman
that made the news. The disabled 23-year-old Beitar fan was
deliberately hit on her fragile legs and needed hospitalisation.
However, the attackers weren't Hapoel Tel Aviv fans. They
claimed to be Beitar followers but were, in fact, supporters
of La Familia, the racist organisation that runs the show at
Beitar's matches.

The young woman, among others, was viciously set upon
because she dared to support her team in a crucial match
despite an order from La Familia not to do so.

The reason for the ban on singing was that a Beitar player
named Kamso Mara was warming up. Mara is a Guinean
Muslim and for Beitar ultras it's unacceptable to have such

a player in their team. La Familia are killing Beitar. They're a cancerous body, but see it as a holy mission. In fact, there are a lot of people with holy sacred missions in Jerusalem.

\* \* \*

'Welcome to the Holy City!' said the young clerk at the Jerusalem branch of the Home Office when I moved there in 1989, just before the high holidays. 'No, seriously, you will soon understand,' she added when she saw my bemused face.

She was right.

Almost 30 years to the day of that meeting I returned to Jerusalem to research this book. I've lived in London for over 20 years, since 11 September 2001, but I often come back to Jerusalem, in my writing and in person. The city attracts me for some of the reasons that I love football. It's passionate, unfiltered, dramatic and multi-layered. The story of Jerusalem is the story of the world, wrote Simon Sebag Montefiore in his book *Jerusalem: The Biography*, and the story of Beitar is the story of Jerusalem. To understand Beitar you need to first understand and feel Jerusalem. Then you'll understand how a club that used to have an alliance with Arab clubs in the 1940s has become 'the most racist in the country'.

Legend has it that Jerusalem is the centre of the world. According to the Jewish faith the navel of the world is a huge rock known as the Foundation Stone on Temple Mount. Christians believe it's the Church of the Holy Sepulchre, where Jesus Christ was buried and resurrected. Muslims believe that Muhammad rose to heaven from the same foundation rock. It's an *axis mundi*: the stem through the earth's centre connecting its surface to the underworld and the heavens and around which the universe revolves.

There isn't a place on earth with so many legends to its name. Legends or maybe beliefs, faiths, agendas, narratives, storylines, spins, propagandas, lies, politics or folklore, but when you stand at the Tzahal (Israel Defense Force) Square it feels like you're standing in the centre of the world, or at least the centre of Jerusalem.

Coming from the bustling Jaffa Street there's the breathtaking view of the north-westerly corner of the Old City walls, built from 1537 over four years by Sultan Suleiman the Magnificent. For a better view you can go to the top of Notre Dame Center just down the road, where from the roof you can see the Old City, the domes of the Church of the Holy Sepulchre and the golden Dome of the Rock in Temple Mount just above the holy Foundation Stone. There, the story goes, Abraham was about to sacrifice Isaac, his son, when just in time an angel stopped him. Below, on the side of Temple Mount, lies the Western Wall – the Kotel, the religious focal point of the State of Israel. All of these sites are within a short walking distance of each other.

To the east, the Old City is surrounded by the Mount of Olives and Mount Scopus, plus Israeli neighbourhoods and Arab villages and suburbs. You can even see the infamous separation wall meandering over the hills and the Judean desert. The south is dominated by the large valley called Guy Ben Hinom – Valley of Hinom – the root in Hebrew and Arabic to the word Hell (Geheynom in Hebrew). To the west are major institutes of Israel and in between are many borders, old and new, visible and hidden. In the city of countless communities, you can cross one street and find yourself in foreign, sometimes hostile but very enchanting territory. Some of these area feel like a different country.

Back on ground level lies the area of Musrara, a small neighbourhood that encapsulates the history of the city. It's a wonderful place to get lost in the streets and the stories. The name, meaning graceful in Arabic, is apt as it's mainly two-storey stone houses, cobbled alleys and some of the most beautiful buildings in the city. It started out in the 1880s as a posh residential district for wealthy Arabs, Christians and Muslims, who wanted to have a better standard of life outside the walls of the Old City. Some of the Palestinian elite families lived there until 1948 when the city spilled out from the confinement of the walls to the nearby area. Today Musrara spreads from the Damascus Gate, the main gate to the Muslim quarter and the hub of Palestinian Jerusalem, up the hill behind Jaffa Street and the big city hall, but is divided by a wide road, history, ethnicity and hate.

Nearby on Nevi'im Street (Prophets Street) are the great European strongholds. The name tells you how special this city is as the British called it Prophets Street but not after a single prophet, for fear of causing trouble between religious devotees. In a little plot of land bordering Musrara you can find a great Russian compound with typical onion-shaped domes, French institutes, an Italian colony that looks like it was flown straight from Florence and the beautiful St Paul's Church, a neo-Romanesque gem built by the British missionaries who brought modernity to the city.

In a time when the European powers were competing for influence in Jerusalem, the British, mainly the Anglican Church, tried to win the hearts of the locals in the hope of gaining political power and new believers. The missionaries built St George's Cathedral and a school nearby on Nablus Road, plus a hospital. Like many other compatriots around the world they spread the gospel of football.

Some of the heaviest battles of the 1948 war in Jerusalem were fought around Musrara and they determined the fate of the city. When the war ended, the charming neighbourhood became the border between the newly formed Israel and the West Bank, which was under the rule of the Jordanian kingdom. Walls were erected, with barbed wire stretched between them, and clear warnings of what lay ahead were posted.

The Arab residents left their homes during the war and Jewish immigrants, mainly from Arab countries, were housed in the empty properties. Musrara became one of the poorest and most miserable places in the new nation. Many families had to live in one apartment in unbearable conditions, unemployment and crime were rife and the place became known as cannon fodder to the Jordanian army snipers. Several ugly and large council house blocks were built and were populated with Jewish immigrants from North Africa. That misery became one of the roots of Beitar popularity in later years.

It felt like the end of the world, or at least end of the country. When lines were drawn on the ceasefire maps with a blunt pencil it led to houses divided between countries and a no-man's land in the middle of the historic city. Many games of football were abandoned when balls were overhit and landed behind the walls and borders. In the broken city, simple tasks became an international crisis. On one occasion a UN peace force had to fish out a set of false teeth for an elderly woman who was staying at the French hospital when she dropped them from her window one morning into the separating zone. While the rest of the city and country were recovering from the war, Musrara was left behind.

The great Israeli victory during the Six-Day War in 1967 brought down the border. Jerusalem and the West Bank were conquered by the Israel Defense Force (IDF) and Musrara became safe. However, it was still poor, angry and resentful. Today you can still see bullet holes on the walls and other scars. The place is teeming with paintings of black panthers and graffiti about former Prime Minister Menahem Begin – both are icons of social uprising and class divide.

Musrara was the setting for the rise of angry young men who lived in poverty with their parents who came from the Arab world. They felt that they had been left behind by the Israelis of European origin, and in the early 1970s they demanded equality and justice, inspired by the black American movement of the same Black Panthers name. They shook the country with violent demonstrations until the 1973 war halted their impact, but when Begin became prime minister in 1977 part of the social revolution they demanded came about. Today, the local community centre is holding a photo exhibition on the Black Panthers of Jerusalem, and some street names have changed to the names of the social heroes of the '70s, now a proud heritage of Musrara.

Bordering it are the houses of Meah Shearim, home to ultra-orthodox communities – the Haredi. This run-down, heavily populated area can be hostile. 'GROUPS passing through our neighbourhoods severely offend the residents. Please – stop it' warn the signs. Only 20 metres divides modern Jerusalem from this 18th-century east European *shetl* where 'Zionist' is the worst curse word. There I saw a woman covered from head to toe with layers upon layers of cloth; not even her eyes were visible. It looked like a pile of blankets walking around, lacking any individuality or personality. They are called the Taliban Women, a small cult of Jewish women who cover themselves in shapeless textiles so that Jewish men don't sin in immodest thoughts.

Today Musrara is finding its beauty again at alarming speed. There are so many art schools, civic galleries, photography studios, film and music schools there that the right balance may be lost if one isn't careful. The old block is now home to a violent Hasidic cult led by a convicted sex offender, while other parts of Musrara are living under the threat of Haredi invasion that will change the face of these areas.

I lived there around 30 years ago and enjoyed the trips to little Ethiopia Street and the wonderful area around the glorious Ethiopian church. In the short, narrow street lived Eliezer Ben-Yehuda, the man behind the miraculous revival of the Hebrew language so close to the Haredi heart of the town. Even today some hardliners won't walk in that street because of its once famous resident. Every street has a story, every building a history. So many wars and battles took place in these streets; some are still raging, but without the fire.

I finished my trip in December 2019 with a falafel at the Yemenite Falafel Centre on Nevi'im Street. Motti Maabari, the chatty owner, flirted with the art school girls and handed out pita after pita of warm, full-bodied yellowish falafel during the busy rush hour. There's a waiting time but Motti and his crew ease this with free, fresh falafel balls for the people in the unruly queue. Behind him there's a whole gallery of pictures of famous rabbis of many orders and origins, holy texts and amulets and one framed paper clip from the summer of 2002. There are some droplets of blood on the walls too.

One day a year, on the 21st of the Hebrew month of Av, Motti gives away his hearty falafel for free in gratitude for the miracle that happened there in the summer of 2002. Musain Atta, a 17-year-old boy from Beit Jalla, a Palestinian village near the city, walked that hot day into the little falafel joint and blew himself up with a 4.5kg explosive. Somehow, he was the only one killed, while five Israelis suffered minor injuries. 'He blew up near my son, me and a customer and we all survived by miracle,' said Motti. 'Since then, on the afternoon of that day I make and give falafel for free for the public as a gift for God. So, people can come, eat and say

17

a blessing. What an experience it was.' He used to hold his gratitude feast in the middle of the day but then moved it to the afternoon after many people took advantage of his kindness with one portion after another. Yes, this is a kind and warm-hearted city but it can eat you alive if you're not careful.

This is one neighbourhood with the DNA of Jerusalem all over it. Sit long enough at Tzahal Square and you'll see the world coming to the city – touring, worshipping, adoring and fighting over it. It's within walking distance of the centre of the world and where it all might end – according to apocalyptical beliefs/analytics. A place like this can't produce an ordinary football team and Beitar Jerusalem, the main football club of Jerusalem, is anything but.

Beitar shares the city's DNA. It was forged as a right-wing club during the tumultuous years of the Jewish–Arab conflict, and it attracted fans from places such as Musrara, fired up by social injustice. Beitar enjoyed close relations with Begin's party and is heavily intoxicated by the prayers and dreams in the air.

Jerusalem is the most political place on earth and Beitar is the most political club in the world. This is a story of football as a class war, a political tool, a radicalisation, and racism and its impact on fans who fought against it. If you understand Beitar, you'll understand Israel.

I left Jerusalem after one year. I loved the city but couldn't take it. It was the holiness that got me, the holiness and what it does to the Yerushalmim, to the Palestinians, to the air. It was too thick for me.

'You don't get to choose if you live in Jerusalem, the city chooses you,' I once read.

It's true.

Jerusalem chose Beitar.

# 1

# The Syndrome

*'Jerusalem, Jerusalem, you who kill the*
*prophets and stone those sent to you.'*
Luke 13:34 (New International Version)

THE GOLDEN Gate is the most interesting of the gates of the walled Old City of Jerusalem. It's a double gate on the eastern part of the wall, facing the Mount of Olives and the spectacular Church of All Nations at Gethsemane. It leads directly to Temple Mount and the Church of the Holy Sepulchre further down in the Old City. Legend has it that Jesus Christ entered the city through this gate on Palm Sunday. In March 630, Heraclius, emperor of the Byzantine Empire, rode a horse in front of a parade that marked the return of the True Cross on its way to reside in the Basilica of the Holy Sepulchre.

'The emperor dismounted to carry the true cross into Jerusalem,' wrote Simon Sebag Montefiore in *Jerusalem: The Biography*. 'It was said that when Heraclius tried to enter in Byzantine robes the gate became solid wall, but when he humbled himself, it opened for his imperial procession.'

The ornamented double gate was sealed and reopened by the rulers of Jerusalem many times, but it had been walled up since Suleiman the Magnificent built the impressive and familiar walls of the city in 1541, that we know today. He did it for defensive reasons as the Golden Gate is easy to breach, but many believe it was done for other motives.

According to Jewish belief, the Messiah will arrive at Jerusalem through the Gate of Mercy – its Hebrew name – riding a white donkey, and will enter Temple Mount from the east. That's the reason why it was sealed by the Muslim rulers of the city and a Muslim cemetery was dug around it, in the hope it would stop the Messiah in his tracks. It's worth remembering that Jews, Muslims and Christians believe the Gate to be the setting of the Apocalypse but it's not clear in which order the coming of the true Messiah and the Apocalypse will occur.

Until then, there's no shortage of people with a direct line to God here. This town has seen its fair share of messiahs/false messiahs, and if you walk around enough times, you're certain to meet one or two even today. The coming of the Messiah is a crucial pillar in the belief of observant Jews but also a derogatory term – Messianic – from secular Israelis to the fanatic believers. It's the hope of his arrival by the former and the fear of the consequences of this kind of thought and politics of the latter, which colours the Israeli political discourse.

In 2009 Beitar Jerusalem met their very own messiah. The club has had many saviours over the years but none like Guma Aguiar. Like all other messiahs it ended in a personal apocalypse.

Guma, a warm and charismatic person, came out of nowhere and became the 'king' of Jerusalem overnight in 2009. The handsome 31-year-old drove a flashy car and planned to take over Beitar Jerusalem from Arcadi Gaydamak, the reluctant owner. Guma was doing it in the name of God.

Sivan Cohen of Israeli TV's Channel 10 followed him around and brought us this moving story in a 'Guma Aguiar Superstar' piece.

Born in Brazil to a Jewish mother, Guma was raised in the US state of Florida as a Catholic. A tennis prodigy turned tennis instructor due to an injury, he met businessmen and started to work in the natural gas trading pits of the New York Mercantile Exchange. With this new knowledge, his uncle Thomas Kaplan took him under his wing, looking for investments in gas and oil. Searching in a public library, Guma met John Amoruso, an expert geologist, who explained his theory on drilling in the deep Bossier sands of east Texas. According to *Forbes*, Amoruso was convinced that large quantities of natural gas could be found there because the sand was thick, the very type of high-pressure formation that was conducive to the development of natural gas deposits. Based on this theory, Kaplan set up Leor Energy and installed Guma as its CEO, forming a joint venture with Encana, Canada's biggest natural gas company, and Goldman Sachs.

For months nothing happened; time and money were running out. According to the TV piece, one night the bored young Guma, only 25 years old, was passing time watching TV when he learned about the actions of Rabbi Tovia Singer, founder and director of Outreach Judaism. The organisation is a self-declared 'counter-missionary' organisation 'dedicated to countering the efforts of fundamentalist Christian groups and cults who specifically target Jews for conversion'. Furious, Guma contacted Singer to berate him in the name of Christ, but after five hours of talking, he was convinced to embrace his Jewish roots again. 'I came back home and everybody probably thought that I'm on a crazy drug trip or something,' he said. 'I announced to everybody that I don't believe in Jesus and right away I got on to the wrong foot with just about everybody.'

Guma, however, managed to convince the rest of the family to follow him. Four months later he and Leor Energy struck oil – well, gas actually. It was one of the biggest discoveries in the US in recent years. When Encana finally drilled the field, it found 2.4 trillion cubic feet of gas and the Canadian company bought up all of Leor's assets in the field for $2.55bn in 2007. Guma netted himself an estimated fortune of $200m.

'He felt it was God-sent and I feel the same way,' said Amoruso. 'I felt like I made a huge jump towards God and grubbing and kissing him or her. I felt I've got closer to God,' he testified to Cohen.

Now an extremely rich man, Guma asked his rabbi for advice on what he should do with his life and got his blessing, so Guma and Jammie, a beautiful cheerleader of a wife, moved to Jerusalem. He started donating large sums of money to religious organisations and Zionist causes, among them March of the Living, an annual educational programme that brings youth from around the Jewish world to Poland, where they explore the remnants of the Holocaust. There, in transit between one camp and another, Guma was told for the first time about Beitar Jerusalem, a club in urgent need of a new boss.

So, there you have it: a chance meeting in a tennis court led to Guma working in the New York Mercantile Exchange and a new enterprise with his uncle. His conversion to Judaism resulted in finding a huge gas field and him becoming wealthy. Donating money to charities paved his way to Beitar. Nothing is without a purpose or is accidental in Jerusalem. If you just look at it, you'll see it.

Guma was fun; adored by the fans and loved by the cameras. Before a match against arch-rivals Hapoel Tel Aviv 'a light and smoke show was under way on the pitch' wrote James Montague in *The Blizzard*. 'Dance music thumped out as beautiful Israeli girls danced in the centre circle. On the sidelines Aguiar was jumping up and down to the beat, dancing with a man dressed in a dog suit. Aguiar moved into the centre circle and wiggled his hips in time with the music next to the singer. He closed his eyes, arms in the air and stumbled through the choreography. The dancers didn't miss a beat. "This is Aguiar's night," said Danny Neuman, a Beitar legend commentating on the match for the night. "He has saved Beitar."

"'I want to see the flagship name of Jerusalem, bring some outsiders to Israel to visit and create awareness about this place," he [Aguiar] said. "Raising the profile of Jerusalem would be the most positive outcome. It's torn apart by a lot of conflict. But there are Christians, Jews and Muslims here that love the land they live in. I want Christian and Muslim fans here too."'

Guma danced on the pitch and at endless parties, hugged everybody, gave warm interviews and charmed his way around. He gave $4m to the club and was looking for a great season. 'It's my first time in the Teddy Stadium,' he said to the camera. 'They say, "Are you some kind of Messiah?" I say, "No, I don't want to be associated with a word like that." I have no idea [about the outcome of the Hapoel game]. Only God knows. Maybe he's feeling extra sympathetic to Jerusalem tonight. And if not, perhaps he'll feel extra sympathetic later in the year.' For the first time there was a hint of a different, angry tone to his voice.

Guma immediately stood out in the barren landscape of football club owners in Israel. He wasn't afraid to speak his mind, brought fresh hope to Beitar fans and a sense of relaxed fun for all football lovers. In a short time he became the talk of the town, the man who 'saved the city' as he was introduced at a public event. Even Beitar haters had a soft spot for him.

For the whole time, Guma was embroiled in a bitter legal dispute with his uncle over each share of the Encana deal windfall. Guma demanded some of the $2bn that Kaplan had received and Kaplan counter-claimed that Guma had misspent the company capital. Guma then went on a shopping spree of real estate in the city – a big penthouse in Mamilla with a breathtaking view of the Old City, and a flat with a stunning panoramic view of the Wailing Wall were the star assets. The place at the Jewish quarter in the Old City was a front seat to one of the most important places on earth and he had a Beitar flag on the porch to prove it. 'What do you think, that I'll be in row 56 or something? It's like VIP seats. I want to have these seats if something happens. I pray and hope that I will get the chance to be part of building it [the temple] together with the whole nation or seeing it drop from the sky,' he told a reporter.

'Why don't you live here?' she asked.

'You should try and live here for a week, and when you start talking to the ceiling you'll understand why. When the ceiling starts to talk back, you'll understand why – it's not a place you want to stay in for too long. It's freaks me out.'

Sadly, it wasn't a joke or hyperbole. The ceiling talked to Guma, as did the cobbled alleys in the Old City, the prophets of the Bible, the kings of the Kingdom of Israel and 3,000 years of history. So did the drugs, manipulation, interests and court battles. Guma didn't stand a chance. It took just six months for him to lose his grip on reality. In January 2010 he told reporters of the local *Kol Ha'ir* newspaper that he had released Gilad Shalit, an Israeli soldier who had been held hostage in Gaza. 'I did it to prove that I could enter Gaza and come out alive and that Shalit could come out alive as well,' he said. 'He [Shalit] said that he wants me to tell his family how much he loves them and Israel, and that he hopes this ends soon.'

The next day Guma was sectioned in Abarbanel Mental Health Center in Bat Yam, just south of Jaffa. The sports press had a field day, laughing and making fun of a man having a public meltdown, in a shocking lack of empathy and decency.

After recovering at Abarbanel, Guma returned to Florida to rebuild his life. He cut his ties with Beitar and other Israeli organisations. However, in 2011 it was announced that he had bought a majority stake in the Hapoel Jerusalem basketball team, to which he had donated $1.5m two years previously. On 19 June 2012 he took his 28-metre yacht, TT *Zion*, out of its mooring. According to the US Coastguard's report on the boat's GPS signal, it travelled north-east at before abruptly coming to a halt, then turning and drifting back to the shore. Guma was gone; his phone and wallet were found on board.

Only then did the truth come to light. A jaw-dropping investigation by Nir Shahak for the *Uvda* TV show revealed how badly Guma had been used and abused in Jerusalem. Suffering from a bipolar disorder from a young age, he was fair game in a merciless city. Soon after his arrival many people were aware that there was a new rich guy in town who wasn't careful with his money. He was targeted daily by rabbis and donation collectors and, in most cases, they didn't leave his home empty-handed. He gave $3m to a far-right politician and a militant yeshiva (a Jewish educational institution), and $175,000 to an extreme rabbi who wanted to rebuild the Jewish Temple and who was leading a group of devotees getting ready for the big day, among other generous donations. Some felt it was wrong to obtain money from a person in Guma's condition, but most didn't care. It was just too good an opportunity.

'I left Israel with a really bad taste in my mouth,' Guma told Leah Stern, a friend of the family, in 2012. 'I'm very disappointed. I gave my heart, I gave my bank account. I wanted to make a life there and the second I lost control all backs were turned on me.'

Worse than that, crime organisations tried to swindle him. He was supplied with drugs in order to destabilise him and push him out of control. He was even gaslighted. A team of detectives followed him night and day to drive him into paranoid delusions. The criminals tried to transfer money from his bank account but were stopped by a vigilant clerk at the last moment.

The lovely legend of the big-hearted *oleh* (immigrant to Israel) was instead a horror tale of a helpless victim. Footage of his 'March of the Living' speech reveals his mental state even before he took over Beitar. There he was, in a Holocaust site in Poland, shouting, 'Without the God of Israel we are nothing! How pathetic is that? This [the death camp] is where we belong without the God of Israel.'

And then there was Beitar. The love was genuine, but it was a drug of another kind. Where Guma walked, he was told how great and beloved he was, how he had saved the team, that he was no ordinary citizen. That Beitar was the team of the country, that there was a calling for him to lead Beitar among the nations, that he had been chosen for that role. No wonder that when he took drugs in public and a concerned friend asked him not to do so he said, 'I'm going to buy Beitar. Show me one cop who will dare to arrest me in front of the fans.'

According to a Florida court judgement that found against Guma Aguiar in 2010, 'Aguiar's psychosis manifested itself in both grandiose and paranoid delusions. In the spring of 2008, Aguiar expressed the grandiose belief that he is or could be the Messiah. With respect to his paranoid delusions, Aguiar has stated on multiple occasions that Kaplan was trying to kill him. Aguiar believes that he was poisoned, that he was shot in the back from a helicopter, that snipers were following him and that the medical staff at an Israeli hospital were injecting him with poison in order to kill him. Aguiar's bipolar disorder first manifested itself in 1997 when he was Baker Acted [involuntarily detained as per Florida state law] at a Florida psychiatric hospital for approximately 12 days. At the time, Aguiar was 19 years old.'

Most interestingly, the documents claimed, 'Aguiar experienced the onset of another manic episode in mid-June 2009 and is still recovering from this episode. From approximately June 2009 through January 2010, Aguiar was also psychotic.' It was also stated that Aguiar was abusing 'alcohol, marijuana, Xanax [an anti-anxiety medication], Ambien [a sleeping pill], anabolic steroids and OxyContin [an opiate].'

The Shalit rescue mission wasn't a delusion but an act played out by his guards who had no choice. They drove him to Ashkelon, near the Gaza border, and staged the whole heart-breaking farce for him. 'He was a wounded animal and when the animal is wounded the crow comes,' said one of his bodyguards.

Guma was never seen again. It could have been suicide, accident, murder or faking his own death and starting to live all over again far away from Florida or Jerusalem. There were rumours that he might have gone to the Netherlands, where he had family and friends. In 2018 a rumour was doing the rounds in Israel, spread via WhatsApp: 'Guma Aguiar, who used to be the chairman of Beitar Jerusalem and was reported to drown in a lake near his home in the USA, is alive and was found in a mental institute in Dubai. He is currently on his way back to the USA with his family in a good condition and once he lands he will be quizzed regarding his disappearance.'

Guma Aguiar was declared dead by a Florida judge in January 2015 at the request of his wife and mother. All the family's ugly legal disputes between the mother, widow and uncle were settled and only the memory of a loving husband, father and a fan was left.

'He was a brilliant guy,' says Itzik Kornfien, Beitar chairman at the time. 'He understood very fast what is happening at the club. Usually, it takes people some months and some never get it, but he understood everything, including financial matters, and that turned him on. But when a very rich young man is carried around on the shoulders of the fans, when the whole stadium is chanting his name, it affects people. Even experienced businesspeople. It's hard to stop and it's hard to ignore. It was fun working with him and his ideas were right until the problem sadly began.'

Asked by the Walla! news website whether he thought Guma really had died, Kornfien replied, 'Certainly. He was a reckless thrill-seeker. He took me and friends for an unforgettable spin on this yacht. He sailed on full speed, riding the boat's own wake. At one time the yacht bumped to a huge height and came crashing down. We were all bruised. He was irresponsible on land as well. Driving 100kph in a tiny street with his little kid on his lap, speeding and laughing.'

Guma is one of the many people who have been affected by the 'Jerusalem Syndrome'. It used to be called 'Jerusalem Fever' but in the 1930s it was recognised as a syndrome. It's a group of mental phenomena involving the presence of either religiously themed obsessive ideas, delusions or other psychosis-like experiences that are triggered by a visit to the city of Jerusalem. It's not endemic to one single religion or denomination but has affected Jews, Christians and Muslims of many different backgrounds. Every year about ten tourists are referred to the local mental health institute due to effects of the syndrome. There's also a subtype to the syndrome: those who come with magical ideas of Jerusalem's healing powers.

'Over the years we believed that people came to Jerusalem and got mad here,' said Dr Moshe Kalian, the regional psychiatrist, in an interview to Israel paper *Haaretz*. '... that there is something about the city that makes them go mental here, but our research shows that they come here with history of mental problems and Jerusalem is the stage on which they perform their big play.'

Usually they're referred to Kfar Shaul, a mental health centre in West Jerusalem, built on the ruins of Dir Yassin, an Arab village destroyed in the 1948 war. Usually after a short period of hospitalisation, they're free to go back to their homes.

It had affected visitors such as Nikolai Gogol, and Homer Simpson, when the famous yellow family visited the city, plus numerous ordinary visitors. But maybe to a lesser degree the syndrome has influenced the leaders of the city.

Guma was a tragic footnote in the rich history of Jerusalem and Beitar but he revealed something deep about this environment. If you march through the gates of the city claiming you're the Messiah it will end in tears because the Yerushalmim can spot a fake. When you think you're the voice of history, the leader of the people, the protector of Jerusalem, you're most likely to lose your touch with reality sooner or later. There will be enough people who will make you think you're such but, in the end, reality will catch up with you.

It's not unusual in the football business to get carried away but it's happened in Beitar repeatedly. The city, the status of the club, the fans and constant contact with the owner are making the club prone to the syndrome. Maybe there's a 'Beitar Jerusalem Syndrome'.

# 2

# Mandate

*'The conflict defines Jerusalem, Jerusalem*
*defines the conflict and the future is here.'*

Doron Rosenblum, *Jerusalem's Sorrow*

ONE SATURDAY in January 2013 Israeli football fans woke up to the news that Beitar Jerusalem had signed two Chechen players. With any other team it would be just another news story but with Beitar it was a story that defined the club. The two players were hounded down by some Beitar fans because they were Muslim. A civil war broke out in the stands and spilled out on to the streets. By the end of the season Beitar were a broken club and the two players left for good. Like most stories about Israel, you have to go back at least to the First World War to trace its roots.

The morning of 9 December 1917 was another fateful one in the history of Jerusalem. It all started when a major in the British army, unable to sleep in his tent on the outskirts of the city, heard the rooster call from the village of Lifta, stretched out on the slopes of the mountain ahead. He summoned Private Murch, the officers' cook, to his tent and sent him and another cook to the village to get fresh eggs.

Private Murch managed to find his way to Lifta in the cold mist but there waiting for him, rather than a few hens, was a large delegation led by a man with a big white bedsheet tied to a broomstick. *I Was There*, a magazine of 'Undying Memories of 1914–1918', described the moment:

> 'You are British soldier, are not you?' asked a small man in a black frock coat and tarbush to his head. 'I should say so,' replied Murch.
>
> 'I want to surrender the city, please. Ere are ze keys, it is yours,' went on the stranger, producing a large bunch of keys and waving them before the bewildered Britisher, who now began to think he had fallen amongst lunatics.
>
> 'I don't want your city, I want heggs for me hofficers!' yelled the disgusted cook.

For once in the long and bloody history of wars over Jerusalem, the battle was to surrender.

The local man in the tarbush was Hussein Husseini, the mayor of Jerusalem. During the day and night the Ottoman rulers of the city, including Governor Izzat Bey and the German forces, had left the city towards Jericho. The mayor was ordered to surrender to the British army, which had advanced from the south and reached the Holy City that week.

However, it wasn't that easy. The surrender of an important city like Jerusalem couldn't be accepted by two greasy cockney mess cooks, nor by two petrol sergeants. Next in line were two artillery officers, who also refused the honour but offered to inform headquarters. The mayor offered his surrender to Major-General John Shea, who accepted it in the name of General Allenby, commander of the British forces in the Holy Land. Still there was one more surrender ceremony to be held, this time to Allenby himself at the grand Jaffa Gate at the Old City on 11 December.

The general, under strict orders from the Foreign Office – 'STRONGLY SUGGEST DISMOUNTING!' – walked through the gate and was greeted by the mayor, by now ill with fatal pneumonia. He read his proclamation of martial law in the city, promised freedom of worship to all believers and vowed to keep all holy places safe. The proclamation was then repeated in French, Arabic, Hebrew, Greek, Russian and Italian.

It was all meant to defuse the tense situation and Allenby was not to mention the 'C' word, but when Mayor Husseini finally handed over the city's keys, Allenby is reported to have said, 'The Crusades have now ended.' The mayor and the mufti, both sons of the elite clan of the Husseinis, walked off angrily. Jerusalem has a long memory and the Crusades is one of the ghastly ones in the city's history.

In London, David Lloyd George, the prime minister, was elated. 'The capture of Jerusalem has made the most profound impression throughout the civilised world,' he wrote. 'The most famous city in the world, after centuries of strife and vain struggle has fallen into the arms of the British army never to be restored to those who so successfully held it against the embattled host of Christendom. The name of every hill thrills with sacred memories.'

The *New York Herald* front page read: 'Jerusalem is rescued by British after 673 years of Moslem rule', and the great bell of Westminster Abbey tolled for the first time in three years. Four centuries of Ottoman rule were over.

It was the dawn of 30 years of British rule in Palestine. It brought much-needed modernity to the country, transformed Jerusalem, accelerated the Jewish–Arab conflict and brought the gift of organised football to the country.

Under the Ottomans, the territories known today as Israel, the West Bank and Gaza Strip were all part of the great region of Syria in the empire. Before the age of nationalism, the subjects lived in a rare time of equality and calm. Only six per cent of the population were Jewish but that was about to change.

Jerusalem was, despite its importance, a faraway and neglected city, but towards the middle of the 19th century the great European powers started to compete for influence and build churches, schools and hospitals, thanks to a key change in Istanbul. The Tanzimat-i Hayriye (Auspicious Reorganisation) was a series of governmental reforms between 1839 and 1876 that sought to centralise and rationalise Ottoman rule and capture more tax revenues for the military defence of the empire. The reforms, after years of seclusion, opened the city for foreign powers, who rushed in. It made the city an architect's playground of different styles outside the walls of the Old City and exposed the locals to new influences. Important churches and missions seized the opportunity to convert the local population.

'The Anglican buildings in Jerusalem were based on shapes and design language taken from the motherland and other British colonies,' wrote David Kroyanker in his book *Jerusalem Architecture*. North of Damascus Gate on Nablus Road lies St George Cathedral and school compound, but it looks like a 14th-century English gothic college. The layout is of New College in Oxford and the bell tower is copied from Magdalen College from that same city. The charming atrium is probably one of the first places in the Holy Land where football was played.

As in other missionary schools such as Collège des Frères (established 1892) in Jerusalem, the Friends Boys School (established 1901) in Ramallah, and the Salesian Schools of

Bethlehem and Haifa (1891), football was taught to children. A photo of 1908 of the St George School football team is the earliest evidence of the sport in Terra Santa. In 1909, the St George team travelled to Beirut and defeated the team of the American University of Beirut, one of the best in the region.

At the same time, Jewish pioneers from Russia brought the game to Jewish cities and settlements. There was no league, but the game was played by Jews and Arabs and some well-known people too. Mustafa Kemal Ataturk, father of modern Turkey, was stationed in Sarona, a German Templer colony in Tel Aviv, before the First World War and learned to play football along with his soldiers on the sandy grounds. It led to good relations with the Jewish clubs and discharge for their members from the dreaded draft to the Turkish army. Amin al-Husseini, son of Arab Jerusalem aristocracy and later the Grand Mufti of the city (the Islamic religious authority) and leader of the national movement, played against students of Bezalel, the Jewish art school.

In 1906 the Rishon Lezion-Yafo club was formed in Jaffa as a Zionist gymnastic club. In 1912 it became Maccabi Tel Aviv, named after Judas Maccabeus, a rebellious hero, leader of the Maccabean Revolt against the Seleucid Empire (167–160 BCE), and established itself as the prominent force in Israeli sport to come. A year later, Zvi Nishri, founder of physical education in the Jewish community, published a 23-page booklet about the principles of football with an offensive 2-3-5 formation and diagrams of the offside law. It was a huge leap forward as it was the first book in Hebrew about football and Nishri and his contemporaries had to coin from scratch many terms that are still in use today, such as 'nivdal' for offside.

Hebrew, a holy language for centuries, had become a living and evolving phenomenon. 'The precise moment, maybe, when Hebrew came back to life happened when the first boy whispered to the first girl after a hiatus of 1,700 years "I love you" or when the first girl whispered to the boy "I love you" – in Hebrew,' wrote the great Amos Oz. Or maybe it was when boys started saying nivdal or keren (corner) or simply kaduregel (football) in Hebrew.

The game gained popularity, although it was played in primitive conditions, but all this came to a halt and gave way to the First World War and political upheaval. During the war the British government promised Hussein bin Ali, Sharif of Mecca, that assistance in the war efforts against the Ottomans would be rewarded by an Arab empire encompassing the entire span between Egypt and Persia, to be led by him and his sons. They also shared with France the same territory in the Sykes–Picot Agreement of 1916. However, this didn't stop the British writing a historic letter signed by Foreign Secretary Arthur Balfour to the heads of the Zionist movement. It became known as the 'Balfour declaration', in which he wrote:

> His Majesty's government view with favour the establishment in Palestine of a national home for the Jewish people, and will use their best endeavours to facilitate the achievement of this object, it being clearly understood that nothing shall be done which may prejudice the civil and religious rights of existing non-Jewish communities in Palestine, or the rights and political status enjoyed by Jews in any other country.

The declaration was published on 2 November 1917 and is considered to be the first act in the Jewish–Arab war. It was followed not long after by actual confrontations. Waves of Jewish immigration, mainly from eastern Europe, arrived, followed by mass purchase of land. Zionism took the shape of a national movement to build a Jewish state in Palestine with key targets of immigration, land purchases, Jewish work and revival of the Hebrew language.

At the same time the national Palestinian movement was established, and clashes began. In 1920 a force of Bedouins attacked the Jewish post of Tel Hai, in the north-west of today's Israel. Eight pioneers died in the attack, including Josef Trumpeldor, the commander of the post. 'It's good to die for our country,' he said in his dying moments, and he became a Zionist hero. In 1934 a statue of a lion roaring in pain by the artist Avraham Melnikov was unveiled in the cemetery where the Tel Hai eight are buried. Melnikov went to Giza zoo in Cairo to study lions and based his piece of ancient Assyrian sculpture on this to great effect. The ground-breaking work, one of the most important in pre-Israeli art, became an instant symbol of the struggle and sacrifice of Jewish fighters.

Other fatal incidents happened in Jerusalem and Tel Aviv under the hapless rule of the British in 1920 and 1921. After military rule a first High Commissioner of Palestine, Herbert Samuel, was installed on 1 July 1920.

In 1923 a mandate from the League of Nations became official in the borders of today's Israel and the Palestinian territories. The new rulers brought cricket, rugby, tennis and football with them, but football was the only game that stuck with the locals. Under the mandate, Jerusalem became an important city again and a governor was installed. General William Borton was appointed as the first governor but within two weeks he collapsed under the burden of the post and of the history. Summing up his ultra-brief tenure, Borton told his successor, Ronald Storrs, 'The only tolerable places in Jerusalem are bath and bed.'

Storrs isn't remembered kindly in Zionist history. 'Being neither Jew (British or foreign) nor Arab, but English, I am not wholly for either, but for both. Two hours of Arab grievances drive me into the synagogue, while after an intensive course of Zionist propaganda I am prepared to embrace Islam,' he wrote in his memoirs. It was an approach that didn't endear him to either side. He was the person whom the Zionists loved to hate. They labelled him 'Pontius Pilate' – a comparison Storrs loved. Above all, he is the one person who gave Jerusalem its look and should be thanked for that. His decree that all buildings in the city should be covered by local stone saved Jerusalem from becoming another charmless place. Tel Aviv has its spots of beautiful old international style (Bauhaus) but it's mainly a blob of unimaginative residential blocks, like most cities in Israel. Storrs made sure that Jerusalem would keep its personality and its aesthetics. The city that had known so many great builders, from the time of Herod the Great and Queen Melisende, stayed solid, heavy and charming.

Storrs was a great civil servant who left a legacy. His advisor, Charles Robert Ashbee, was a prime mover of the English arts and crafts movement of which its founder William Morris said, 'Have nothing in your house that you do not know to be useful, or believe to be beautiful.' Together they cleaned the grand walls of the city from centuries of clutter, revived the markets in the Old City and exposed its beauty once again.

Apart from the regulation that all construction in the city had to use 'native Jerusalem stone', Storrs was responsible for the installation of stately ceramic street name signs, many of which can still be seen on buildings around Jerusalem. He was active in reviving traditional crafts such as glass, textile and ceramics, and he initiated cultural and social projects. He also gave away footballs in police stations in the hope that the officers would play with Jews and Arabs. The idea was that everybody would play the game and expend their stamina on the pitch instead of killing each other. It didn't work but cup competition was formed, followed by leagues, and football became part of life in Palestine.

After recovery from the war and mass deportations by the Ottomans, the Jewish population in Palestine, known as the Yishuv, started growing in numbers and aspirations. The early 1920s saw the forming of Histadrut, the Zionist trade union for workers in Eretz Yishrael (the Land of Israel), but it was much more than that. It was an embryonic stage of a Jewish state. Histadrut was an employer, owner of factories, a defence force and a health organisation, as well as a political institute of the socialist party. Part of its duties was to provide culture and sport to the Yishuv to support physical and mental health in those trying times. The Arabs watched in fear as the Zionist mission was getting bigger and more ambitious and, in many ways, autonomous.

By forming Histadrut, two battle lines became clear. Jews vs Palestinians and Maccabi vs Hapoel – the sport section of the organisation. It was the bourgeoisie vs the workers; literally, Hapoel is 'The Worker' in Hebrew.

Hapoel teams played in red, the blood of humans everywhere; their logo was a boxer within a circle of a hammer and sickle. Hapoel Tel Aviv and Jerusalem players and fans use hand gestures to mimic the logo to this day and to annoy their local rivals. The proud socialist insignia can't hide the fact that Hapoel started life as part of Maccabi. The early political map was divided between socialist, and liberals and soon sport followed suit. The main fault line, says Dr Haim Kaufman, a sport historian at the Wingate Institute, was the workers' demand for clear support from Maccabi leaders in the principle of Jewish work, a main pillar of socialist Zionism. Leaders of the Yishuv and workers demanded the building of a society and economy based on 'Hebrew work', while many landowners preferred to rely on the cheaper Arab workforce and a free market. Maccabi, on the other hand, asked for Hapoel support in the national targets instead of the socialist internationalism.

With more waves of Jewish immigration in the mid-1920s, young men struggled to find work in the tiny market and spent their free time playing football, now a popular game thanks to the Brits and a 1924 visit from the great Hakoah Vienna, the outstanding Jewish football team. Teams were formed in settlements, kibbutzim and even by a temporary Jewish workforce that built the impressive First World War ANZAC cemetery in Beersheba in the south. Hapoel principles were to 'keep the worker healthy and to enrich his free time', and the aim to create sport for the masses not just champions sat well in Histadrut ideology.

Hapoel was first formed as a group inside Maccabi in 1923 and Hapoel Haifa was the first team to operate. In 1924 Hapoel left Maccabi for the first time, had some troubled times and formed again in 1926, this time successfully. The flag clubs were Hapoel Haifa and the newly formed Hapoel Tel Aviv, and they received significant reinforcement a year later when the Allenby Club from Tel Aviv left Maccabi under acrimonious circumstances and joined Hapoel. They left, but not before writing an angry letter accusing Maccabi of having 'a poisonous atmosphere of professionalism and commercialisation of football'. The Allenby players called for the abolition of the 'possibility of receiving fixed salaries for a game without being a productive force for the building of the society, people and the land'.

Pre-Israeli football now had a key ingredient: bitter rivalry. All it needed now was structure, and if there's one thing the British imperialists were good at, it was that. They may have left a fine political mess in the region (although it was mainly the Zionists' and Palestinians' work) but they gave Jerusalem its looks and a cradle for football. In 1921 a British club from Jerusalem called Sport Club organised the first cup matches, and in 1922 the RAF Fliers team from Ramla won their first cup, followed by five more. By 1927 five Jewish teams were taking part in the competition but the British teams were too strong for the Yishuv clubs.

Things were about to change when in 1926 High Commissioner Lord Herbert Plumer decided there was no need to keep such a big force 'in the quietest place in the Middle East'. The RAF Fliers went back home with the cup and Palestine was left mainly with a police force to keep it safe and calm. With a much smaller pool of players, the British army teams became second best to the Jewish clubs and the cup final of 1928 was played between Hapoel Tel Aviv and Maccabi Jerusalem. In front of a crowd of 6,000 fans, Hapoel won 2-0 but the cup was shared between the two clubs due to Hapoel selecting an ineligible player.

It was a momentous event in the history of football in Eretz Yishrael; for the first time a Hebrew club, well actually two clubs, had won a tournament in the most important sport.

More good news soon followed when the Palestine Football Association, or Eretz Yishrael Football Association, was formed and accepted into FIFA. After a failed attempt to get on to the Olympic Committee, Maccabi and Hapoel put their differences aside and cooperated in a bid to join the international governing body in 1927.

It wasn't easy, because in order to join FIFA, the bidders needed to get the support of its current members. One nomination was received from Austria, with the help of the great Hugo Meisl, the Jewish manager of the outstanding Austrian national team. The second crucial nomination came from a much closer country.

Josef Yekutieli of Maccabi was the driving force, and thanks to his personal connections in Egypt after organising several tours for Maccabi Tel Aviv, he received the much-needed official request from the already established neighbours to accept the new member to FIFA.

Still there was another key issue: the Palestine FA had to represent all people in Palestine – Jews and Palestinians. Getting Hapoel and Maccabi on board was hard enough but finding Arabs to support the move was harder. Yekutieli again used his widespread personal network to speak to and persuade Mussa Al Turi, a high-office Palestinian from Jerusalem, to get the representative from Arab Sports Club of Jerusalem, Ibrahim Nusseibeh, to take part in the first meeting and sign the official founding document. It worked and the Palestine FA was accepted to FIFA in 1929.

Nusseibeh, however, never took any part in the new body, which became the de facto Yishuv football association. The symbolism is clear: football was and is a valid prefigure of the politics in the country.

The joy, however, was short-lived, as the country was rocked only months later.

3

# Holy Wars

*'The past is never dead. It's not even past.'*
William Faulkner

JERUSALEM WAS cursed by an eternal sanctity more than any other city in human history. It started when a big rock was blessed as the Foundation Stone of the world and later when the two Jewish temples were built on top of it. After the second temple was destroyed by the Romans in AD 70 and most Israelites were scattered around the empire, the desire to return to Jerusalem and rebuild the temple became the cornerstone of Jewish life. 'Neither Athens nor Rome aroused so many passions,' wrote the author Elie Wiesel in an open letter to Barack Obama in 2010. 'When a Jew visits Jerusalem for the first time, it's not the first time, it's a homecoming.'

The rise of Christianity in the 4th century had put the city in the spotlight again. In AD 326, Helena, mother of Emperor Constantine the Great, visited Jerusalem and revolutionised its status. Constantine was the first Roman emperor to convert to Christianity. He played a crucial role in the proclamation of the Edict of Milan in AD 313, which declared religious tolerance for Christianity in the Roman Empire and led to the spread of the religion.

Helena, a septuagenarian, was on a mission in the Holy Land to make the new faith more accessible and more tangible. Yisca Harani, a Christianity scholar, explained on Israeli TV broadcaster Kan about the history of the Land of Israel:

> There were forces who understood that in order for that religion to reach the masses, not as a story which passes from father to son, or from a priest to his flock, it needs to be a living thing that you can touch and feel. A thing that is real and proven. For that there is a need to go to the place, to tell the tale, build a building and prove the story by the place.

The place was the site of Christ's crucifixion and burial. Constantine knew it was under a pagan temple, which was then demolished by his mother and purified by a bishop. The empress built the Church of the Holy Sepulchre on Golgotha hill not far from Temple Mount. The basilica would be the finest in the world with 'the most beautiful structures, columns and marbles, the most precious and serviceable, ornamented in gold'. Christendom now had a focal point.

Helena was also searching for the True Cross, the one Jesus had been nailed to. Hundreds of people were quizzed, and one Jew named Kyriakos – 'Of the Lord' in Greek – who knew where the cross was buried was left until last. After a week without food and water and probably under torture he gave away the location. Helena, the first archaeologist of the land, dug at that location and exposed not one but three crosses, a wooden plaque that read 'Jesus of Nazareth, King of the Jews', and the actual nails. One of the crosses was the one true one and two were the crosses of the thieves who had been crucified next to Jesus.

But which one was the True Cross?

David Newhouse, the Latin vice-patriarch of Jerusalem, says that a funeral procession was passing nearby. The dead body of a young man was laid on each of the crosses and he came back to life after laying on one of the crosses. Alternative versions claim it was a dying woman or an injured man who sprung back to a clean bill of health. In any case, the most important relic ever had been found.

This was on 14 September, which became the day of the Feast of the Exaltation of the Holy Cross and, by coincidence or not, the Jewish Day of Atonement. Helena sent part of the cross to her son, together with the nails, which he set into the bridle of his horse for some reason. 'Until the fourth century the cross is not a symbol,' says Harany. 'There is no object that is adored until then. The True Cross that resurrects the dead and heals the infirm becomes a statement about the credibility of the story, its meaning and placing the holiness. The cross becomes *axis mundi*.'

Saint Helena moved on to find and confirm biblical locations from Capernaum on the shores of the Sea of Galilee to the Church of the Nativity in Bethlehem. The Land of Israel has become Terra Santa and a pilgrim's destination where churches, monasteries and hostels were built during the prosperity it brought. In Vartan's Chapel, deep beneath Jerusalem's Church of the Holy Sepulchre, there's a basic but moving stone etching of one pilgrim, a boat reaching the shore with the words 'Domine Ivimus' – Lord, we have arrived.

Islam's connection to Jerusalem, al-Quds ('the Holy One') in Arabic, is based on one vague passage in the Quran: 'Praise be to Allah who brought his servant at night from the Holy Mosque to the remote Mosque, the precincts of which we have blessed.' According to the faith, the Prophet Muhammad was miraculously transported from Mecca to Jerusalem, and it was from there that he made his ascent to heaven. On this nocturnal journey, astride the miraculous human-faced and winged beast, Al-Buraq, they stopped in Jerusalem and the horse-like creature was tied to the Western Wall, known as Al-Buraq in Arabic.

On the way to heaven with angel Gabriel, Muhammad met all the other prophets who preceded him, such as Abraham and Jesus. Islam linked itself to the traditional holiness of Jerusalem in Christianity and Judaism and integrated this legacy into its own religious system. 'Islam inherited from Judaism and Christianity stories, ideas and the linkage to Jerusalem,' says Harany. 'In the most simplistic way: Muhammad learned among other things from Jews and Christians that Jerusalem is a place that you must adore. Without, it won't work.'

The event that decisively affected and changed the status of Jerusalem and influenced its consolidation as the third-holiest city for Muslim devotion was the conquest of the city by the Khalif Omar in AD 638. After refusing to pray in the Church of the Holy Sepulchre he went looking for the famous Foundation Stone. The khalif used the services of a converted Jew, who took him to Temple Mount, which since Byzantine times had been used to commemorate Christianity's victory over Judaism. There among the temple's ruins and burnt remains, garbage heaps, foxes' dens and parliaments of owls, he was shown the rock. Soon a footprint of the prophet was found on it, Al-Aqsa Mosque (the Remote Mosque in Arabic) was built nearby and the little city in the Judean Mountains grew there and then into godhood for all three Abrahamic religions.

You can feel this if you take a tour in the Kotel Tunnels. Almost 500 metres of the impressive wall are hidden beneath the Muslim quarter, and the tunnels follow it through a dazzling labyrinth of subterranean synagogues, old streets, aqueducts and the bedrock of the city. There you can get close to the Foundation Stone without getting to Temple Mount, watch women pray while school classes sing their way, and guided tours struggle to advance along the narrow paths. 'Legend has it the Divine Presence has never left the Kotel,' said the guide, but some fanatics beg to differ. For them the wall is just a replacement for the real thing. The desire to rebuild the temple, or at least pray there in mass numbers, could spark a global conflict.

Above, the city is having a quiet day. Israelis and Palestinians sit shoulder to shoulder in the legendary hummus joints of the Old City, and the hawkers are selling shmonzes, tchotchkes and cheaply produced orientalism for the hordes of tourists. Camels, hamsas (hand palms) jewellery, shofars (ram horns), crowns of thorns and jingoistic T-shirts, Israeli or Palestinian and some in Hebrew, Arabic and English, all wait for the right buyer. In a tahini factory the mills are grinding sesame seeds in a wonderfully aromatic warm cloud. Children are going home after a school day, while underneath them the tunnels are hiving with life, holiness and politics, not just in the Old City. There's a heavenly Jerusalem, an earthly one, and an underground Jerusalem, in real life and metaphorically.

The walk ends right at the first two stops of the Via Dolorosa at the foot of Omaria madrasah, and a flight of stairs leads to the school and Haram al-Sharif – the Noble Sanctuary in Arabic – in other words, Temple Mount. The original stairs were taken to Scala Santa in Rome by Saint Helena herself and the devotees climb them on their knees. According to Roman Catholic tradition, the Holy Stairs are the steps leading up to the praetorium of Pontius Pilate in Jerusalem on which Jesus Christ stepped on his way to trial during his Passion.

There, still blinded by the harsh light of Jerusalem even in December, I saw a man in a down jacket carrying two big wooden crosses on his shoulder, walking towards Damascus Gate in front of puzzled tourists. He looked more like a courier on a pre-Christmas run than a pilgrim, yet some viewers crossed themselves.

There, in a tiny spot, the three religions meet, not always in good faith as the opening of the tunnels in 1996 led to widespread confrontations between Palestinians and the Israeli army.

Not far away is the Austrian Hospice where you can have coffee with apple strudel and go up for a rooftop view of the Old City and the golden Dome of the Rock. Your heart will miss a beat in front of the scenery and, if you're lucky and it's sunset, as it was when I was up there, the last rays of the sun will bounce off the dome like a bow of burning gold. This will be more than one heartbeat missed.

But where there's holy there are holy wars, some by sword, others by words. 'Jerusalem is not mentioned once in the Quran'; 'There were no Jewish Temples on Haram al-Sharif'; 'There is no historical evidence,' say scholars and politicians, while the seculars watch, a bit amused. There is a constant battle over history and narratives and who has God's word regarding the ownership. Academics and politicians try to show that Jerusalem isn't an organic part of the Quran while the Palestinian Authority and the Waqf (the Islamic body that controls and manages the current Islamic edifices in the Old City) are trying to erase any Jewish connection to the city.

In his essay *The Meaning of Jerusalem to Jews, Christians and Muslims*, Professor R.J. Zwi Werblowsky, Harany's father, wrote:

> Islam, therefore, provides us with perhaps the most impressive example of how a holy city can acquire a specific holiness on the basis of what – to the unbelieving outsider at least – is mere legend, superimposed, no doubt, on an earlier, traditional, sanctity of the place. Whereas in the case of Christianity historic facts (i.e., the life and death of Jesus) created religious facts (e.g. the resurrection and ascension), and both combined to create 'holy places', the Islamic case is the exact opposite. Beliefs and piety created religious facts and these, in their run, produced historic facts which, for the contemporary student of religion, culture and even politics, must be deemed, to all practical intents and purposes, as real as any other kind of 'hard' fact. Certainly, in Islam, which does not make the distinction between the religious and the secular (including the political) spheres in the way Christianity has made it, religious facts have implications which legitimately spill over into the political sphere. This remains true even where the religious dimension is subject to abuse and manipulation by purely political interests.

Suffice to say it doesn't matter at all. 'A prayer in Al-Aqsa Mosque is worth 5,000 other prayers,' a British Muslim told me during another boring Arsenal match. 'I cannot tell you how important it was for me to be there,' he added. Try telling a man weeping into the Wailing Wall that it's just the outside wall of the platform that carried the temple. Or explaining that the story of Helena and the True Cross was a later invention to a worshipper in the Cappella delle Reliquie at the church of Santa Croce in Gerusalemme in Rome. Historical evidence or not, it won't make any difference to their devotion.

'In Jerusalem,' wrote Father Jerome Murphy-O'Connor, author of an archaeological guide to Jerusalem, 'the prudence of reason has little chance against the certitude of piety.'

\* \* \*

The conflict has religion at its heart, which makes it much harder to solve. It all came to a head in the summer of 1929 and the epicentre was the Kotel. Unlike the big plaza of today, at the time there was just a tiny alley surrounded by Arab homes. After a year of tension following the Yom Kippur prayers of 1928 when a divider between Jewish men and women was installed, a move that the Arabs saw as a threat to Al-Aqsa Mosque, the city was on tenterhooks. On the ninth day of the Hebrew month of Av, a day of fasting and mourning of the destruction of the temples, a group of Beitar youth marched to the wall with flags, while shouting, 'This is our wall – shame on the government.' The touchpaper had been lit. Beitar's first appearance on the national stage was unforgettable.

Two days later a football match was played on the Maccabi pitch in the west of the town, not far from where the cockney cooks received, well sort of, the surrender of the city. According to the Jewish paper *Doar Hayom* a group of boys were playing football when a gang of Arabs from Lifta attacked the players and crowd with batons. A 17-year-old Jewish boy was stabbed and later died. Another version says that the ball being kicked into a tomato field belonging to a local Arab was the cause for the riot and stabbing. Whatever the reason, it led to violent attacks all over Jerusalem and Palestine. Some 133 Jews and 116 Arabs died in what's known as the Tarpat (1929) riots by Israelis, and Thawrat al-Buraq – al-Burak Uprising – by the Palestinians.

The worst and most traumatic events happened on 24 August in Hebron, when Arab mobs attacked the Jewish quarter, killing men, women and children and looting Jewish property. They killed 67 Jews and wounded 58, with some of the victims being tortured and their bodies mutilated. It brought the end to hundreds of years of Jewish life in the holy city in which the Cave of Patriarchs is the believed resting place of fathers and mothers of the Jewish people, including Abraham. The Arab name of the place, Al-Haram al-Ibrahimi – Sanctuary of Abraham – tells of the complexity of the impressive building and city. It's home to an important mosque as Abraham is a revered figure in Islam too. For centuries the two communities had lived side by side, until the massacre.

In Jaffa, a Jewish fighter and Hapoel Allenby player, Shimha Hinkis, killed an Arab family of seven in an act of revenge. He was sentenced to death but it was changed to 15 years in prison. In 1935 he was released as part of a general pardon. He was the guest of honour at a match between Hapoel and an Egyptian team upon his freedom and was described as a hero by mainstream press.

Dr Hillel Cohen, author of the book *1929, Year Zero of the Arab–Israeli Conflict*, told Israeli paper *Haaretz*:

It was a rupture of Jewish–Arab relationship.
1929 is an overload of myths and fixations ... in
my book I show the similarity between the two
people. The mechanism and the self-perception

51

and mainly the emotions are alike. There is a love to Temple Mount and desire to show that it belongs to one side, there is a competition for the love of God, and confrontation between Ismail and Isaac for the love of Abraham and the battle for the Cave of Patriarchs. The emotions come from the same place: national pride, love of the homeland and devotion to the holy places. But also fear, loathsome towards foreigners, sense of superiority and desire to rule. It's the same motivation and same patterns of thinking.

Beitar, the organisation behind the march to the Kotel, was the youth movement and later the sporting section of the nationalistic Revisionist Movement that became Herut and later Likud. Led by Ze'ev Jabotinsky, a man of words and a polymath, it was the vocal opposition to the dominant stream of socialist Zionism.

Jabotinsky was a writer, journalist, author and translator of classic works such as Edgar Allan Poe's *The Raven*. In a superb and fluid translation, the Raven's 'Never more' quote becomes a call for independence; it's clear which one. He called for a harder line against Arab violence and against the appeasement policy towards the Brits. He supported the building of a Jewish army, called for a Jewish majority in the land and opposed socialism.

Jabotinsky never had a role in the Jewish bodies of governance. Throughout his political activity he was in the shadow of David Ben-Gurion, the leader of the Yishuv, and his most important contribution to Zionism was an essay called 'The Iron Wall' published in November 1923, in which he wrote:

As long as the Arabs feel that there is the least hope of getting rid of us, they will refuse to give up this hope in return for either kind words or for bread and butter, because they are not a rabble, but a living people. And when a living people yields in matters of such a vital character it is only when there is no longer any hope of getting rid of us, because they can make no breach in the iron wall. Not until then will they drop their extremist leaders whose watchword is 'Never!' And the leadership will pass to the moderate groups, who will approach us with a proposal that we should both agree to mutual concessions.

Then we may expect them to discuss honestly practical questions, such as a guarantee against Arab displacement, or equal rights for Arab citizens, or Arab national integrity. And when that happens, I am convinced that we Jews will be found ready to give them satisfactory guarantees, so that both peoples can live together in peace, like good neighbours. But the only way to obtain such an agreement, is the iron wall, which is to say a strong power in Palestine that is not amenable to any Arab pressure. In other words, the only way to reach an agreement in the future is to abandon all idea of seeking an agreement at present.

'The Iron Wall' became the pillar of the Israeli policy, says Amir Fuchs of the Israeli Institute for Democracy and an admirer of Jabotinsky:

Ben-Gurion adopted the ideas of the Iron Wall and it made its way to the Independence

Declaration of the State of Israel. There is a liberal core to his writing and call for equality for the Arabs. His liberal principles all but disappeared from the right apart from a few but in the centre and Zionist left you can see his finger prints.

Jabotinsky brought the term 'Hadar' to his movement. The insufficient translation is pathos and style, but the true meaning is being a gentleman, a democrat and fair play. How much of those the leaders of Herut and Likud had is open to discussion. Supporters can swear that this is a major part of being a Likudnik but others can claim that even at best it was just an extremely thin veneer over ruthless and discriminating policies. However, it can be both, as in the case of Menachem Begin, the future prime minister.

Jabotinsky wrote his famous essay during a tour of the Baltic countries and, while in Riga, the capital of Latvia, he met Jewish students. He talked about preparing the Jewish youth as a military force who would accomplish the national desires in the Land of Israel as their destination. He left a lasting impression and, days after the meeting, Beitar was formed by the boys. The name was a tribute to Josef Trumpeldor who died at Tel Hai and a name of an ancient Jewish stronghold in the great rebellion against the Romans. Beitar's symbol was a menorah, the seven-branched candelabra used in Jewish worship since ancient times, on the background of the map of the great Israel – the Land of Israel as promised by God, which includes Israel and the east bank of the Jordan River. Less controversial were the walls of Jerusalem on top of the crest, and together with the menorah they were part of the Beitar Jerusalem sign for many years to come.

Football under British Mandate was gathering popularity despite constant bickering. The tension between the Yishuv and the British led to violence on the pitch when representative teams met. Internal fights between Maccabi and Hapoel led to a suspension of the league in 1931, not for the last time.

The first champions were the British Police, who won the double in 1932, the only non-Jewish team in a league of nine. With an ever-decreasing pool of British players to choose from, it was also their last title. Hapoel and Maccabi Tel Aviv shared the championships from then on during the Mandate years.

In 1936 a new club was formed in Jerusalem by a group of enthusiastic revisionists in a small house on Ethiopia Street. This was Beitar Jerusalem, founded by David Horn, an idealistic young man who in 1934 at the age of 18 climbed to the top of the German consulate and removed the swastika flag. Horn looked for young Beitar members and gathered a team that played on a nearby pitch nicknamed the Bananas Pitch, on the historic Hanevi'im Street. The boys cleared rocks and stones from the pitch and played friendly matches against other Jerusalem teams of all origins.

So close to Prophets Street, there were some foretelling signs. One of the players, Haim Korfu, was later a minister for Likud, others were members of the Knesset, and a third, Asher Benziman, was the first fallen member of Irgun, the military wing of the revisionists, in an attack on the building of the British police in the Russian compound in the centre of the city in 1944.

It's doubtless, however, whether even a prophet of Moses's status could see the future of Beitar Jerusalem as a leading club in Israeli football. Beitar struggled in their early years, then folded but were re-formed in 1942.

It was hard enough to make it as a non-Maccabi or non-Hapoel club, and 1936 was a bad year to form a football club too. The country was engulfed by violence again and the repercussions were historical.

4

# Outlaws

*'Here is a place whose atmosphere is peace.*
*Where political and religious jealousies can be*
*forgotten, and international unity be fostered*
*and developed.'*

From Lord Allenby's YMCA dedication address,
Jerusalem, April 1933

JULIAN THE Hospitaller is the tragic patron saint
of hospitallers and hotelkeepers, and during the British
Mandate he had the honour of having the most striking
street named after him. Julian Way was the road on the
westerly parallel ridge to the Old City – above the Valley
of Hinom, the place the Moloch, a deity to whom parents
sacrificed their children, was worshipped, and in front of
the city walls, in perfect view of Jerusalem's mountains.
Today this view is obstructed by many buildings, unless you
can afford a room in the majestic King David Hotel (prices
start from around £350 a night), but a short walk to the east
reveals the stunning vista.

Opposite the King David Hotel is another of the city's
landmarks, and aptly another great hotel. Jerusalem's

YMCA is perhaps the most beautiful of its kind that the Christian organisation owns. Designed by Arthur Loomis Harmon, architect of the Empire State Building in New York, it was opened in 1933 after seven years of work. It has a tower, 50 metres high, which dominated the highly competitive skyline of the city for decades, and two domes by its side. The three come together to symbolise the unity of soul, spirit and body, together with the Holy Trinity. The highly decorated complex is home to a hotel, concert hall and indoor swimming pool, and is saturated in religious symbols. A five-metre, six-winged angel hovers in the middle of the stone tower and behind this, for 58 years, was the city's main football ground.

At the time it was a small pitch with two cement stands near the touchline. The iconic tower loomed over it, supplying a dramatic background to modest football teams. The players enjoyed the facilities in a location that bettered any football ground in the world. Matches were played there from 1933 and for a while Lord Allenby's wish was fulfilled. It was a place where Jews, Arabs and British players and teams played football together and against each other.

Julian Street became the hub of British rule in Palestine. The head offices of the Mandate enjoyed the spectacular view and facilities of the King David Hotel from 1938, in addition to the other buildings on the street, including the YMCA. On holidays the road was decorated with Union flags but ironically this location played a key role in Beitar Jerusalem's history.

The football scene in Jerusalem developed differently to the one in Tel Aviv. Maccabi Jerusalem, established around 1911, was the first and the senior Jewish football club of the city and one of the first in the country. Together with Maccabi and Hapoel Tel Aviv, Maccabi Petah Tikvah and

Hapoel Haifa, it was one of the leading clubs of the Yishuv. At first Jerusalem was a home to several clubs but a Hakoah Vienna visit in 1924 drove a unification move. Hakoah played at the Katamon pitch near the enchanting German compound against the British police and army teams, and beat them, to the delight of the Jewish high commissioner Herbert Samuel, who told Yishrael Got, coach of the Maccabi team, 'The Jewish boys gave a hell of a beating to the English, maybe you can do the same in Maccabi.'

Got cherry-picked the best players in Kadima and HaZvi (known as 'The Gazelle') and brought them to Hashmonai Jerusalem – Hashmonaim was the Jewish dynasty that ruled Judea in the 2nd century BC. Maccabi Hashmonai Jerusalem played on a pitch on the outskirts of the town near Lifta and came up against stern opposition of the Jewish orthodox population, who were appalled by the thought of Hellenistic activity taking place in the open on the holy day of Sabbath in the Holy City. A pashkevil (pasquil), a poster placed on a public wall in the Haredi zone, called for a strike in the community and added, 'To plea the Holy One blessed be He, in synagogues and houses of study to cancel evil bad hardships.'

The hardship wasn't cancelled and the fight for the Sabbath in the Holy City has continued since then.

Hashmonai went on a tour of Egypt in 1927 and it was then that the close relationship between Yekutieli and the Egyptian FA was formed, which played a crucial part in the successful application of the Palestine FA. Hashmonai won the cup in 1928, together with Hapoel Tel Aviv, long before the Beitar Jerusalem football team was formed. They also had the honour of playing in the first official league match in November 1931 against Hapoel Jerusalem, who received an 8-0 thrashing by Maccabi.

A slow decline had started during the 1930s, which cost Maccabi its place in the local hierarchy. At first, Maccabi Hashmonai weren't tied to any political inclination and had many socialist members. After the great Maccabi-Hapoel split, sport became more political and jingoistic and those members felt unwelcome at the club and turned to Hapoel Jerusalem. Maccabi Jerusalem, says Israeli football historian Omer Einav, suffered from a lack of resources and the fatal blow was the opening of the YMCA and its football team. He explained:

> The other clubs in the city were poor and miserable and suddenly they had to compete with a club from a palace that had a pool, tennis courts and a proper football pitch. If you were a young man from an elite family, there was only one place to go to. During that decade everything in Jerusalem was in the shadow of YMCA. They gathered players from everywhere while Maccabi were slowly declining, and the papers kept writing pieces on how to save the local football.

In 1937 Maccabi's name was changed to Bar Kokhba, a false messiah and leader of a doomed rebellion against the Romans in the 2nd century, in a similarly doomed attempt to revive their fortunes. The desperate nationalistic stunt didn't help and was followed 81 years later by a similar pathetic spin, this time involving Donald Trump. The club changed its name again in 1946 to Maccabi Jerusalem but it didn't matter anymore, and Maccabi languished in the lower leagues until its closure in 1961.

It left a perfect gap opposite Hapoel for Beitar but before the latter's emergence in the middle of the 1940s the country was rocked again, in 1936. With ever-increasing Jewish immigration, now around one-third of the population, tension was growing. Tel Aviv flourished and became the first city of the Yishuv, while the Nazis' rise in Germany made Palestine a desired destination for many European Jews fearing for their lives. The Palestinians understood that they were losing their homeland.

In April 1936 the first wave of bloodshed hit the streets of Jaffa and Jerusalem. It was to be known as the Great Arab Revolt, which lasted for three years and had a crucial impact on the 1948 war that led to the formation of the State of Israel. In the first year alone, 3,000 attacks on Jewish and British targets were carried out and a general strike was called. The revolt was mainly against the British, while the Yishuv let them deal with it while building a military power and national institutes.

In 1937 the revolt took a turn for the worse for the Palestinians. An internal war broke out between the two leading Arab families, the nationalist Husseini and moderate Nashashibi, which fractured Palestinian society. Killings and revenge attacks plagued the Palestinian people and leadership that took over the national fight. The British, after heavy losses in 1928, brought in reinforcements and brutally turned the tide, crushing the uprising. More than 200 Brits, 400 Jews and about 5,000 Arabs died during the tumultuous three years up to March 1939.

Just six months later the world was thrown into another war. However, after the initial economic shock, it turned out to be a prosperous and calm time in Palestine. For a brief period there were fears of a Nazi invasion, first from the French, rulers of Syria and Lebanon, after Germany had occupied France. The fears of annihilation of any Jewish existence had resumed during the early success of Germany at the battles in North Africa but the British victory in the Egyptian desert in the second El Alamein battle in November 1942 removed the threat. The country became a base for British operations, football was played and Maccabi and Hapoel Tel Aviv shared the league titles during these years. Meanwhile, in Europe millions of Jews were murdered and died in the forests, ghettos, slave labour camps, death marches and gas chambers. There was nothing the Yishuv could do while their brethren were being wiped off the face of the earth, apart from three days of mourning. Life and football just went on.

The Holocaust has had an everlasting effect on Jewish and Israeli life. The loss, personal and national, was beyond comprehension in every walk of life. From the tragedy of lives lost to the enormity of the genocidal crime, it had huge repercussions for the conflict and later the State of Israel. The meeting of the mufti, Hag Amin al-Husseini, with Adolf Hitler on 28 November 1941 in Berlin was a low point for the Palestinian leadership that turned a vicious, religious and national conflict into a poisonous one. Al-Husseini asked Hitler for a public declaration that 'recognised and sympathised with the Arab struggles for independence and liberation, and that would support the elimination of a national Jewish homeland'. At the Nuremberg trials, one of Adolf Eichmann's deputies stated that al-Husseini had actively encouraged the extermination of European Jews.

One can learn about the depth of the tragedy when looking at the extermination of Jewish football. The great middle-European school of football in Austria and Hungary was headed by Jews, who spread their new ideas around the world, from Italy and France to Brazil, Argentina and Uruguay. Italian football was blessed by a generation of Hungarian managers who transformed it before the war, the two outstanding ones being Árpád Weisz and Ernő Egri Erbstein. Weisz won the Scudetto with Inter Milan in 1930 and twice with Bologna in 1936 and 1937. He, his wife Elena, son Roberto and daughter Clara were all gassed at Auschwitz in January 1944. Erbstein was sent to forced labour in Hungary during the war, a task that most Jews didn't survive, but thanks to an officer who knew him he managed to escape, together with the great footballer Béla Guttmann. Erbstein built the Grande Torino team that dominated Italian football after the war but was destroyed in the Superga air crash in 1949.

Weisz and Erbstein were just two of the countless Jewish managers, players, directors and fans who suffered the Holocaust. If you know where to look you can still see the evidence of pre-war Jewish life and the loss of it in cities such as Amsterdam, Prague and Vilnius. For example, there's a red line of bricks in the plaza near the Amsterdam Opera, which was the outline of a Jewish orphanage. World football has the same ghosts of enormous contributions cut short and grey emptiness at the heart of it. On the banks of the Danube near the Hungarian parliament in Budapest there's a memorial to the Jewish victims. It's a row of steel shoes, like the ones those people had before they were pushed into the river. A pair or two of old-fashioned football boots wouldn't look out of place there.

At home there was a dilemma: what do to with the British. In May 1939 a White Paper was published regarding British intentions in Palestine. In a stunning reversal of policy after previous decisions, the paper called for the limiting of Jewish immigration to only 75,000 over the next five years and provided for limitation on sale of land to Jews. It seemed to guarantee an independent Palestine with an Arab majority and an end to hopes of a Jewish state. Zionism hence saw the British as an enemy, but they were fighting the Nazis. Ben-Gurion, treading a fine line, proposed a complex political path symbolised by a catchy line: 'We shall fight with Great Britain in the war as if there were no White Paper, and we shall fight the White Paper as if there were no war.'

The Yishuv military forces, the Haganah (defence) and the Irgun-Hebrew Organisation (short for Irgun Zvai Leumi – National Military Organisation) were the mainstream. The latter was formed by Beitar members and revisionists in 1931, who were fed up and frustrated with the official line of restraint and splintered off from the Haganah with 1,500 men in 1936. They answered Arab attacks and atrocities with their own atrocities against Arab civilians and attacks on British forces.

The policy of reciprocating violence with violence or the biblical eye for an eye set them apart from the Haganah. They agreed a truce with the British but in 1940 a group headed by Avraham Stern – Yair by his *nom de guerre* (war name) – formed a new underground group in protest – Fighter for the Freedom of Israel – better known as the Lehi from its Hebrew initials, or the Stern Gang by the British. Some of the actions of the two groups had the foremost influence on the conflict and intertwining football scene.

On 1 December 1943 Menachem Begin was appointed as the commander of the Irgun. 'I fight; therefore I am,' was his motto. As Allied victory in the war became more likely, Begin declared war on Britain in September 1944. The Irgun attacked police stations in Jerusalem. In the attack on the main police building at the Russian compound, one of the Irgun fighters, Asher Benziman, was wounded and died of his injuries the next day. He was part of the first Beitar Jerusalem team of 1936. The frustration arising from the

British blockade on emigration while the Jews of Europe were being slaughtered and dying in their millions brought the crisis to breaking point, and in November that year the Lehi killed Lord Moyne, minister resident in Cairo.

Eliyahu Bet Zuri, one of the two assassins, said during his trial, 'Thousands of my people have drowned in a sea of blood and tears but the British captain didn't pick them up to his ship. The British stood on deck watching indifferently while my people drowned. And had few of them made it ashore he – the British – pushed them back to sea for them to sink into the abyss.'

The assassination sent shockwaves throughout the Middle East. Some historians believe it prevented an early founding of the State of Israel with recognition of the great three powers as early as 1945. Winston Churchill, the British prime minister, said:

> If our dreams for Zionism are to end in the smoke of assassins' pistols and our labours for its future to produce only a new set of gangsters worthy of Nazi Germany, many like myself will have to reconsider the position we have maintained so consistently and so long in the past. If there is to be any hope of a peaceful and successful future for Zionism, these wicked activities must cease, and those responsible for them must be destroyed root and branch ... In Palestine the executive of the Jewish Agency have called upon the Jewish community and I quote their actual words, 'To cast out the members of this destructive band, deprive them of all refuge and shelter, to resist their threats, and to render all necessary assistance to the authorities in the prevention of terrorist acts, and in the eradication

of the terrorist organisation.' These are strong words, but we must wait for these words to be translated into deeds.

These words were indeed translated into deeds and for three months the Yishuv was on the verge of a civil war. It was known as the Saison, the hunting season, in which the Haganah hunted the Irgun members. The Haganah forces abducted Irgun fighters and handed them to the British police. Irgun people were fired from their jobs, their children were denied schooling and the Yishuv hit the Irgun financially. Begin called for his faithful to keep up the fight against the British but not to retaliate against the Haganah in order to prevent civil war. The Saison, and another known as the Little Saison in 1947, strengthened Ben-Gurion and his party's dominance and prevented a power struggle when Israel was formed.

It was put to a test when Begin and the Irgun brought a shipload of weapons on board *Altalena*, a 5,000-tonne ship named after Jabotinsky's *nom de plume*, in June 1948, just two months after the declaration of independence. Ben-Gurion demanded that all weapons be transferred to the newly formed IDF but Begin insisted that 20 per cent of it should be given to the Irgun's units in Jerusalem, where they were still independent. After a ten-hour battle near the Tel Aviv shore, *Altalena* was hit by a cannon (operated by a future member of Israel's national cricket team and a professor of English literature) and burst into flames. Twenty Irgun members and five IDF soldiers were killed during this traumatic event, which led to a deep chasm in the Yishuv and Israeli life for generations and bitter resentment in the political sphere. It shaped the Herut party members' and Beitar football club fans' psyche and identities as persecuted underdogs for years to come. This was easily translated to zeal and passion.

Football, naturally, was part of the turbulent times. The 1940s saw the rise of the Beitar teams in Jerusalem and Tel Aviv. Beitar Jerusalem was reformed in 1942 but because of a boycott by Hapoel and Maccabi, who tried to stop Beitar's development, they had to play only locally against British, Arab and Armenian clubs. Still, Beitar Jerusalem were good enough to reach the final of the Jerusalem Cup, a local tournament where they were due to play against the Paymasters – the Mandate Tax department. 'Then the first sabotage by Hapoel Jerusalem happened,' testified Shmuel Kirstein, the director of Beitar, years later. 'When it was obvious that Beitar will win the cup, they stopped the games and the cup stayed in Tel Aviv.'

Many Beitar games were against British army teams, and they served two purposes: physical activity for soldiers and gathering information on the Beitar members. All was put to use in October 1944 when 251 Beitar members, including footballers and club founder David Horn, were deported to detention camps in Kenya. There they continued playing football and one of them, Eliezer Spigel of Beitar Tel Aviv, was very good. 'One of the soldiers, a captain, said he could arrange for me to go to England and play there. I told him I wouldn't go, they wanted us to be far away but I had to return to Israel first,' he told *The Blizzard*.

In Tel Aviv, Beitar Tel Aviv gave Maccabi and Hapoel a run for their money, which quickly led to action from the powers that be. Beitar Tel Aviv won the cup in 1940 and 1942, the second victory a 12-1 record beating of Maccabi Haifa. Then after Beitar played in Cairo against an Egyptian team in 1943, they were suspended for six months for violating some minor rule but mainly for disturbing the order of things. Beitar protested and claimed it was a political decision, but nothing helped. They conceded 11 technical defeats and still came back for the rest of the season. With 11 victories and one draw there's reason to believe they could have won the league that season but for the suspension. But worse was yet to come.

Another sign of strength was the festive matches against Hajduk Split of the free Yugoslavia near the end of the war. Under the orders of its leader Marshal Tito, Hajduk Split toured the Middle East to promote free Yugoslavia. On 5 May 1945, three days before VE Day, Maccabi Tel Aviv played against Hajduk and lost 7-2. 'It was our first meeting with free Europe,' wrote the emotional leading sports reporter Nehemiah Ben Avraham.

Hajduk's second match was against Beitar Tel Aviv, who were strengthened by two Beitar Jerusalem stars, Simon Alfasy, and the boxing champion Asher Barnblum. After an unforgettable first half Beitar led 4-1, and eventually won the match 4-2. The mood was less ceremonial this time. Beitar played with a big menorah (candelabra) on their shirts, while Hajduk's had a red star. The banter, reported the press, was on the same lines – one Split star called a Beitar defender 'you fascist' and received the reply 'you communist'. Hajduk went on to beat the British army team 3-2 and won another two matches in Egypt by scores of 6-1 and 7-1. Beitar were the only team to beat them.

That same year the league was divided into two regional divisions; Hapoel Tel Aviv won one and Beitar the other. The decisive match between the two was never played. It isn't clear why but for the fuming revisionist it was just further proof of the systematic bias against the Beitar clubs and people. 'That is most likely the reason,' says historian Omer Einav. No champion was declared that season, but when a similar situation happened in 1939, Maccabi Tel Aviv self-declared themselves as the champions elect and still count that season – the whole ten matches! – as a proper title.

The league was in hiatus for one year due to Hapoel and Maccabi having another one of their kerfuffles, and Beitar Tel Aviv started the 1946/47 season, the last one before the war, in brilliant form. Beitar were undefeated on their return to the league after their outrageous suspension in 1943, and when it looked as if they were on course for their first league title they suffered another blow, this time from the Palestine FA and British.

On Monday, 22 July 1946, seven Irgun members dressed as waiters entered the King David Hotel, the southern wing of which housed the Mandate Secretariat and offices of the British military headquarters. They left six milk containers in the basement. Inside were 350kg of explosives that brought down the western half of the southern wing of the hotel. Ninety-one people, including British, Jewish, Arabs and tourists, died in the terror attack. It was open war now between the two extremist organisations and the British forces.

Almost a year later, on 8 August 1947, High Commissioner Alan Cunningham outlawed the Beitar movement – including the sports teams – due to its connection with the Irgun. In June of that year, Beitar Tel Aviv were top of the league with 43 points from 24 matches (out of 26) and Maccabi Tel Aviv second with 40 points from 23 matches. For some unknown reason the league was stopped and later a British ban was implemented. It was a bitter end to a run of 36 undefeated matches for Beitar but solidarity with them was out of the question and the FA ruled that all their remaining matches would be deemed 3-0 defeats. However, one of the matches was against a team that had folded, so was called a scoreless draw. Therefore, Beitar Tel Aviv ended the league season with 44 points.

Maccabi won the first of their three remaining matches 9-1 against Hapoel Rehovot. The penultimate match was a derby against Hapoel, which would guarantee them the tainted title in the sweetest way. It went down in history as 'the boxing fight'. Two players were sent off after a fist fight and were suspended for three months, a pitch invasion was cleared and Maccabi won 3-0. They then won their last match, which was played in September, and they farcically won the title.

*Sport Haboker*, a Hebrew sports paper, didn't mince its words when it described the sham:

> This week the league was completed after the unnecessary stop last season. It was ruled that each team played 26 games, but this table doesn't reflect the status of the league and it was finished in an artificial way and this is why it is not valid … when we come to sum up the division games we have to rely on the situation at the end of the league when each team had two games to play. Beitar Tel Aviv was top of the league after not losing one game on the pitch. That team showed in many games including the decisive victory against Maccabi that it is a worthy winner of the title.

Nothing helped – Maccabi Tel Aviv won the ill-gotten championship in a way that became a pattern of the club. Beitar Tel Aviv and Beitar Jerusalem formed new teams called Nordia, after Max Nordau and also a Tel Aviv neighbourhood and a revisionist stronghold. Nordau was an important Zionist leader who advocated the concept of 'muscular Judaism' – moral and corporeal ideals that, through discipline, agility and strength, would result in a stronger, more physically assured Jew who would outshine the long-held stereotype of the weak, intellectually sustained Jew.

On 15 November 1947 Nordia Jerusalem beat Hapoel Jerusalem in the first-ever derby between Beitar and Hapoel in the city. It was a small piece of history but nothing compared with the monumental event that happened two weeks later.

## 5

# Us or Them

*'It's us or them. This is a war for life or death:*
*Either we come out of the war victorious, or*
*we all die.'*

Abd al-Qader al-Husseini, January 1948

THE BRITISH Mandate started with a botched surrender of a desolate mayor, two cockney cooks and bell chimes at Westminster. It ended in a whimper when on 14 February 1947 the British government announced that it would refer the Mandate of Palestine back to the UN. Fed up with the loss of British lives, the cost, with no realistic chance of a solution and with the its empire shrinking, it was time to call it a day.

An 11-member Special Committee on Palestine was set up and arrived at Jerusalem that summer. It met the Yishuv leaders but the Arab Higher Committee, the body representing the Arabs of Palestine, boycotted the meeting, demanding declaration of an independent Arab Palestine. It was, not for the first time nor the last, a shocking error of judgement, for with the absence of an Arab voice the Jews put forward a strong case for partition.

The committee indeed recommended a partition of the land, with Jerusalem and the holy places under international supervision. It was brought down to the General Assembly in Lake Success, New York for a vote on 29 November 1947, with a two-thirds majority needed to pass the proposal. All over Palestine and the Jewish diaspora people gathered to listen to the radio together, following the count. In a tense session that every Israeli is familiar with, the delegates were asked one by one, and gave their votes, while people tried to calculate the percentage. The result saw 33, including the Soviet Union, voting for, 13 against and 10, including Britain, abstaining. It was enough to carry the motion. The dream of a Jewish state in the historic land looked to be within reach.

Amos Oz, the celebrated Israeli author, wrote in his masterpiece *A Tale of Love and Darkness* about that night:

> Then there was dancing and weeping in Amos Street, in the whole of Kerem Avraham and in all the Jewish neighbourhoods; flags appeared, and slogans written on strips of cloth, car horned blared, shofar blasts sounded from all the synagogues, and Torah scrolls were taken of the holy ark and were caught up in the dancing … Kiosks and bars opened all over the city and handed out soft drinks and snacks and even alcoholic drinks until the light of dawn, bottles of fruit drink, beer and wine passed from hand to hand and mouth to mouth, strangers hugged each other in the streets and kissed each other with tears and startled English policemen were also dragged into the circles of dancers and softened up with cans of beer and sweet liqueurs, and frenzied

revellers climbed up on British armoured cars
and waved the flag of the state that had not been
established yet, but tonight, over there in Lake
Success, it had been decided that it had the right
to be established. And it would be established 167
days and nights later, on Friday, 14 May 1948,
but one in every hundred men, women, old folk,
children and babies in those crowds of Jews who
were dancing, revelling, drinking and weeping
for joy, fully one per cent of the excited people
who would spill on to the street would die in the
war that the Arabs started within seven hours of
the decision.

'The masses were dancing in the streets,' said Ben-Gurion
years later. 'I couldn't dance. I knew that we were to face a
war in which we will lose our finest sons.'

The war started the following morning. At the beginning
it was limited to sporadic attacks on the roads and Jewish
areas, but it soon escalated, and within two weeks 74 Jews,
71 Arabs and nine Britons had been killed. A full-blown war
between the Arabs and Jews was raging and by February the
death toll was 1,060 Arabs, 769 Jews and 123 Brits. It didn't
take long for massacres and atrocities by both sides to take
place, each avenged by a fresh one. It was then that Abd
al-Qader al-Husseini, the leader of the Arab forces in the
Jerusalem region, nephew of the mufti, son and grandson of
Jerusalem mayors, terrorist and a charismatic leader, said, 'It
is inconceivable that Palestine will be for the Arabs and the
Zionists together – it's us or them. This is a war for life or
death: Either we come out of the war victorious, or we all die.'

The Arab strategy was to attack the road to Jewish
populations and to lay siege, another in a long history, on

Jerusalem in order to choke it to surrender. The winding road from Tel Aviv to the city passed through 30 miles of Arab territory in control of the 1,000-strong Jerusalem Brigade of the mufti's Holy War Army. It was a long and narrow road surrounded by hills and mountains in which the Arab villages controlled the high ground and harboured fighters and men ready for the call. Jewish Jerusalem was starving for food, munitions and manpower. Water usage was strictly limited and Jewish neighbourhoods were shelled. The 100,000 Jews in Jerusalem were reduced to eating mallow leaves and waiting for the next supply of rice and flour.

One of those families was my mother's. Living in the leafy West Jerusalem area of Beit Hakerem, the whole family took part in the war effort. Her father was away in Europe, working in the Jewish refugee camps, teaching Hebrew; her mother cooked for the soldiers and took part in watching over Arab parts of the city from the rooftop. My mother, Yael, was in the radio centre of the Haganah just outside Jerusalem. Ora, her older sister, was away in the besieged Negev. Her younger sister Shlomit, who stayed at home, said:

> Everybody did his share. At high school we helped build barricades at the German colony from rubble after the fights. I watched over Katamon with my mother in what I thought was boring and pointless activity but turned out to be helpful for intelligence. We felt the siege and shortage of food, gas and water. Every drop from a rare shower was used again to wash the floor and water the vegetables in the garden. Every arrival of a convoy was a major event and we ran to collect food.

Our home was searched once by the British police looking for weapons and they left without finding a thing. Only a day later I saw a local Haganah officer taking away a pistol from its hiding in the closet, of which I knew nothing. Our home was hit by bullets and once hit by a mortar shell fired from Nabi Samuel. Your mother, who was on leave, and I were sleeping when a huge noise and a cloud of dust woke us up. The shell entered from the kitchen window, hit a pot of spaghetti and broke the bathroom wall. It didn't explode because somebody forgot to unscrew the fuse cap and it was still there by the toilet until the bomb squad took it away. It could have been very different.

That generation of Yerushalmim never forgot those days. My mother couldn't stand to see a waste of water for the rest of her life. The acute shortage left a memory that you could still sense many years later when the city and Israel enjoyed prosperity. I remember one day before a snowstorm passing with a colleague from the local paper near Berman Bakery and seeing a long and unusual queue. 'Pfffff,' I snorted. 'What's the worst that can happen with a little bit of snow? No need to panic, it's not the siege all over again.'

The day after, the blizzard arrived, trees fell, roads were blocked and some places ran out of food. I stood corrected.

In response the Jewish forces sent convoys on to the treacherous roads. One disaster followed another – convoys were ambushed, trapped and torn to pieces; men, supplies and arms were lost in the early months of 1948. The price almost brought the Yishuv to the brink. The Arab threats of annihilation of Jewish existence or at least a takeover of

Jerusalem looked plausible. 'If Jerusalem will fall, the rest is not important,' said Ben-Gurion. Long after the prosperous days of the Mandate, even the celebration of 29 November looked to be from another time.

'Look, here our bodies lay, in a long, long row,' mourned Haim Gury, the poet of the war generation about the loss of an entire elite Haganah platoon of 35 men in a battle south of Jerusalem.

In another song, 'Bab el Wad', he wrote about the fight to keep the road to Jerusalem open.

The tide, however, had turned in the spring; the unification of all the Jewish forces followed by an operation to open the road to Jerusalem and holding key points in the city in preparation for the British exit in mid-May eased the pressure. By now it turned out that the Arabs' numeric advantage of two to one in the population sizes wasn't replicated in the battlefields, where the forces were even. There were some crucial differences though; the Jewish forces were united, organised, mobile and had much better intelligence, while weapons trickled from abroad. The Arab forces were based on local ties, which meant they could get big forces from villages and towns for a short period but not fight an all-out war. The Haganah could send units to where it needed, while the Arabs were confined to one region. The damage from the Arab fight against the British and inner factions of 1936–39 gave the Yishuv the upper hand.

The road to Jerusalem today is wide and becoming wider constantly. Mountains are razed to the ground to make way for new motorways and the dramatic impact has been lost. And yet it's easy to spot the history. A passenger can still see the skeletons of the 1948 armoured cars, now revered national relics, just before the road rises to the mountains, or the sharp metallic monument to fighters of the road to Jerusalem a few kilometres from the city. The strategic hill of Castel, 779 metres high, just before the big drop, and the last climb to the city, holds its own story. Once a Crusaders' castle, it became an Arab village and a key point in the battle. Some historians will even go as far as saying that the whole war was won or lost at that point, now adorned with Israeli flags all year round.

Castel dominated the road. It was easy to shoot from the fortified position at the convoys or to launch attacks from there. The Haganah made it a priority to get a hold of it during the operation to open the road and break the siege at any cost. On 2 April 1948 the Haganah took over the Castel and the news reached Abd al-Qader al-Husseini, who was in Damascus pleading with leaders of the Arab League's military committee for support. Husseini realised that Castel's capture by the Jewish forces was liable to unravel his primary strategy: tightening the siege of Jewish Jerusalem until it surrendered.

The Arab representatives in Damascus rejected his request with a mixture of disdain for his military ability and the belief that, in any event, the regular Arab armies that would intervene in the next stage of the war would succeed in recouping everything that was now falling to the Haganah. Daniel Rubinstein, in his illuminating book *The Battle on the Castel: 24 Hours that Changed the Course of the 1948 War Between Palestinians and Israelis*, describes how the tense discussion concluded with a dramatic statement by al-Husseini: 'History will judge you for abandoning Palestine, you and those who are behind you I hold responsible. I will capture Castel and die, I and all my fighters, and history will record that you – criminals and traitors – abandoned the land.' After the meeting, al-Husseini told his friends, who were waiting outside, 'We can go and have a good time in Iraq, or we can go back to Palestine and die for it – we will go back to Palestine.'

Al-Husseini left Damascus and joined his forces near Jerusalem. In the first stage of the fighting, he stayed in his command post in the quarry below the hill. But when his troops' assault was repulsed, he left the post and joined his fighters in the village at dusk on 8 April 1948, where he was shot and died of his wounds on the battlefield. It was the beginning of a crucial day that changed the history of the region.

Shocked and angry at their adored leader's death, over 1,000 Arab fighters stormed and regained the Castel to retrieve his body, causing heavy casualties to the Haganah force. On 9 April the state funeral of al-Husseini was held at Haram al-Sharif, a sign of his status and their admiration. Over 50,000 people followed him, including the armed forces.

The Castel had fallen without a fight to the Haganah but although the Arabs were able to build a great surge of military power and take over the Castel, without proper organisation and leadership, they couldn't hold on to it.

As al-Husseini was being buried, fighters of the Irgun and Lehi jointly attacked the village of Deir Yassin, just west of Jerusalem, where they committed the most notorious Jewish atrocity of the war. The numbers are heavily disputed, but most historians think that around 110 villagers were murdered that day. The survivors were then paraded and mocked in trucks through Jerusalem until their release.

Arab vengeance was swift. On 14 April a convoy for the Hadassah Hospital on an enclave on Mount Scopus was ambushed, with 77 Jews, mainly doctors and nurses, slain and their bodies mutilated. The gunmen photographed each other with the corpses before the macabre pictures were mass-produced and sold as postcards. A beautiful street in Musrara is dedicated to the 77 victims among countless monuments to many other soldiers and civilians in Jerusalem.

However, Deir Yassin was a pivotal event in the war. Since the events of 1929 and 1936, each side claimed to be the victim of crimes and atrocities, and on the receiving end of injustice while plotting a bloody revenge. The Arab media used Dier Yassin to amplify Jewish atrocities and horrifying versions of it were published to major effect. The Hadassah massacre was forgotten, while Dier Yassin became part of the Palestinian psyche. It wasn't the first time they had done this but this time it backfired in horrendous fashion for the Arabs. The psychological impact on the Arab population was devastating. By March, 75,000 Arabs had left their homes. Two months later 390,000 had gone. 'The legend of Dier Yassin was worth half a dozen battalions to the forces of Israel. Panic overwhelmed the Arabs,' boasted Menachem Begin, the Irgun commander.

That week, a main Arab offensive near Haifa was repelled; the winds of war had changed direction. The mixed cities of Jaffa – where from a population of 70,000 Arabs only 3,000 were left – Tiberias, Safed and Haifa saw their Arab residents flee to neighbouring countries or Arab-held territories in Palestine by May. Some thought they would be back with the Arab armies soon, some left fearing for they lives, and others were chased away and ordered to leave. The result was the same. The first part of the war had been won by the soon-to-be Israelis. Their independence war was the Palestinian Nakba – catastrophe. Without strong leadership, panic took over to give birth to the Palestinian refugee problem. By the end of the war the numbers stood

750,000 people. The key point wasn't that they had fled or been expelled but the refusal of Israel to let them back to their houses. The war was fought in towns, roads, mixed cities and remote settlements but, just as importantly, on the demographic front.

Taha Muhammad Ali, who lost his home in Saffuryya in Galilee after fleeing to Lebanon and then lived in Nazareth under the new status of Arab-Israeli, wrote in his poem *There Was No Farewell* about the traumatic night when he became a refugee.

On 14 May in Tel Aviv Art Museum, David Ben-Gurion declared the formation of a Jewish democratic state called Israel. The next day, at the port of Haifa, the Union flag was taken off the pole and folded. The British Mandate was over, and the second part of the war had started. The armies of Egypt, Jordan, Iraq, Syria and Lebanon invaded Israel, hoping to commit genocide and liquidate the Jewish population to carve territories for themselves. Yet again, the Arab forces were each to their own, while the IDF became stronger, better equipped and more determined. In some battles in Jerusalem, the way to the city and to the south against the invading Egyptians, the need for fresh men was so urgent that new immigrants, some of them Holocaust survivors, were taken to the killing grounds only days after reaching Israel. Some died there in the country they had hardly lived in.

The victory came at a painful cost. Almost 6,000 Israelis died during the war, one per cent of the population. The Jewish quarter in the Old City was lost and so were the holy places. In the south, Israel advanced all the way to the Red Sea and took over Beersheba and the Negev desert. Only the West Bank and Gaza Strip were kept under Arab rule – Jordanian and Egyptian – and became the home of many of the refugees. By December 1948 the war had ended, and Israel had 78 per cent of the Palestine Mandate, without the West Bank and Gaza Strip, with a big Jewish majority of 700,000 to 150,000, greater than anyone could have hoped for before the war. Jerusalem became a divided city and the capital of the new State of Israel.

\* \* \*

Football and the conflict became entangled from the very start. Maccabi Petah Tikvah's full name is Maccabi Avshalom Petah Tikvah, named after Avshalon Gisin, a former officer in the Turkish army and part of the Yishuv defence force, who got killed in the 1921 riots by Arabs from the local Abu Kishak tribe. Seventy years later, Morad Abu Kishak from the same tribe played in the team.

Football was used for propaganda and inspiration. Hakoah Vienna's visit had been hailed as a Jewish triumph. The editorial in the *Haaretz* newspaper in 1924 said:

> For the diaspora on the banks of the Danube Hakoah were a full revolution, like the first plough in the hands of a Hebrew farmer ... There is a place of glory for the owners of Hakoah who freed themselves from the shame of diasporic slavery and raised the flag of revival and national independence.

It led to tours of Jewish teams abroad and the foundation of the local FA and the Palestine national team. The team photo, with a big P on the shirts, is used on Twitter spats by pro-Palestinian groups as proof of a Palestinian state and history; little do they know it's actually a Zionist team.

The 1948 war took the lives of many players. Two from Hapoel Jerusalem and ten from Maccabi Tel Aviv fell, including the biggest star to die in the war. In the heart of Jaffa there's a street and a little square where stands a sculpture of a footballer volleying a ball. The street is named after the player immortalised by the work of art – Nathan Panz – of Maccabi Tel Aviv, Beitar Tel Aviv and the Irgun.

Panz was born in 1917 in Vitebsk, then in Russia and now in Belarus, and emigrated with his family to Tel Aviv in 1921. He stood up as a great footballing talent from an early age and played with the senior team of Maccabi Tel Aviv when he was just 16. He joined the team's USA tour in 1936 and scored 22 goals in 11 matches, leading to offers to join clubs in New York and Chicago, but he preferred to return to Tel Aviv. In that year he led the team to its first title and a year later at the age of 20 he became the captain. As the star of the league, he also took part in the matches against Greece in the 1938 World Cup qualifiers.

Panz was a big star in a little town. Yosef Merimovich, a Maccabi player in the 1940s and later manager of the team and Israel's national team, told *Haaretz*, 'Panz was an excellent, unstoppable player with great dribble and technical skills. He could shoot with both feet and defenders couldn't cope with his shimmies. He was an idol of the youth due to his honesty, integrity and leadership.'

That integrity led him to a major confrontation with the Maccabi board over the rights of the young players. Panz was asked to apologise but refused. This was followed by a move to Beitar Tel Aviv, then in the second tier, and the golden age of the team began. After winning promotion to the top league, Beitar Tel Aviv had a successful run in the cup competition and met the British Army 17th Battery in the semi-final in downtown Haifa. It led to one of the most bizarre matches in local cup history.

According to *Haaretz*, at the 20-minute mark Beitar scored a goal that was disallowed. Panz protested, stood in front of the referee and asked, as the captain, for an explanation. This didn't go down well; two British officers came on to the pitch and manhandled Panz away to a room nearby where he was kept under the watchful eyes of British paratroopers armed with bayoneted rifles. Beitar refused to continue the match and the referee was about to suspend it but eventually it was resumed.

Beitar won the tie and, according to one story, Panz was released after a short time and rejoined the match, even being the best player on the pitch. According to a much more heroic version, Beitar won with a goal after 115 minutes following a shot from 40 metres by Verner Caspi. Jubilant Panz broke away from the guards and joined the celebrations.

In any case, Beitar made it to the final where they met Panz's old club Maccabi, beating them 3-1. Panz scored one goal and won the cup for the first time. Two years later Beitar won it again after thumping Maccabi Haifa 12-1 in the final.

In 1947 Beitar Tel Aviv were on the verge of winning their first title but under the orders of the British rule all activities of the Beitar movement became illegal and the team had to cease its activities. Many of the players resumed playing under the name of Nordia but Panz refused to take part in what he saw as a sham. He rejoined Maccabi Tel Aviv and played while fighting. He joined the Irgun, collected donations and visited fellow members who were under arrest. He also took part in guard duties and attacks, during one of which he raided a British army train full of weapons and munitions near Pardes Hana, then returned to Tel Aviv for a match in which he scored the winning goal.

Following the outbreak of war in 1947 the local league was suspended but seven clubs from the centre played in a makeshift competition. Near the end of April 1948, Maccabi and Hapoel met for a Tel Aviv derby. Panz scored the equaliser in a 1-1 draw, his last goal. On 28 April 1948 he joined the Irgun forces in an attack on Arab Jaffa. In the small alley of Manshia, not far from today's Bloomfield Stadium, his armoured vehicle was hit by an anti-tank rocket fired by British forces and he died with two other Irgun members. He was one of dozens of Jewish footballers who lost their lives in the war and thousands attended his funeral.

Another star to lose his life in the war was Arab Zaki al-Darhali, who was killed in the bombing by the Lehi of the Social Services Center (Saraia) building in Jaffa. The *Falastin* newspaper published the news of this incident and mourned his death on the front page. Panz and al-Darhali played against each other on at least one occasion and died in the same city.

Arab Jaffa was surrounded two weeks later and most of its residents left the city. Yafa became Yafo and later joined Tel Aviv as a major city of Israel. Today 18,000 citizens of Jaffa are Arab and, despite rapid gentrification, the old conflict is still noticeable. The Arab street names were replaced in 1948 by Hebrew ones or just numbers, and calls to rename some of them with meaningful names from the Arab and Palestinian cultures were mostly turned down (apart from 14 streets). This led to a guerrilla naming warfare when Hebrew names were displaced by homemade signs.

When I visited the place, a short distance from the bustling tourist attractions of Jaffa, which were packed to the rafters on a sunny Friday, a flock of geese was keeping an eye on the statue. In the little garden opposite the square, a stunning black-and-blue rooster was parading with his hens. Near the blue sign in Hebrew and English telling the name and story of Panz, a green one was displaying a call to repent before Allah.

The past is never dead. It's not even past.

And yet, in 30 years of conflict up until 1948, whenever it was relaxed enough, Arabs and Jews played together and against each other. The main animosity was kept for the rulers and their presumed biased referees.

In Jerusalem the discrimination against Beitar from Hapoel and Maccabi led to the formation of local leagues and a coalition of minorities between them and the Arab teams against Maccabi and Hapoel. Between the violent events, national aspiration, religious devotion and the wars were also players and fans who wanted to play and watch football. They wanted to support a team and to identify with it, sometimes in order to forget the situation, sometimes to emphasise it. For where there's life, there's football.

# 6

# Scapegoat

DURING BIBLICAL times in Jerusalem the great priest (Cohen Gadol in Hebrew) picked two goats for a ceremony held on Yom Kippur, the Day of Atonement. One goat was sacrificed at the altar at the temple and the other one was sent to the desert for its final journey, following the scripts of Leviticus (16: 8–10):

> And Aaron shall cast lots upon the two goats; one lot for the Lord, and the other lot for the scapegoat. And Aaron shall bring the goat upon which the Lord's lot fell, and offer him for a sin offering. But the goat, on which the lot fell to be the scapegoat, shall be presented alive before the Lord, to make an atonement with him, and to let him go for a scapegoat into the wilderness.

At the cliffs watching over the wadis of the Judean Desert, about 12km from the city, the outcast animal was thrown to its death, thus absolving the Israelites from their sins. That was the scapegoat.

The custom ended with the demolition of the second temple but the term in Hebrew and English survived, meaning the practice of singling out any party for unmerited negative treatment or blame. The most famous artistic expression of the biblical command is a painting by the English pre-Raphaelite painter William Holman Hunt, who took goats to the brutal conditions of the Dead Sea and produced two paintings of the subject. Hunt, born in 1827, lived on Hanevi'im Street for two years and visited the region many times. Like many of his compatriots in Jerusalem he was an early-day pre-Zionist and believed that the return of Jews to the Land of Israel was the first step before the apocalypse and the promised kingdom of Christ – that Jesus himself was the ultimate scapegoat scarified for the sins of humanity. More than 150 years later you can still feel those notions in the streets – the one about being the scapegoat and the other one yearning for the apocalypse to come.

\* \* \*

Beitar Jerusalem played their first match as an Israeli team on 17 December 1949, away against Hapoel Ramla, from an old town on the coastal plain built in the 8th century by the Umayyad Arabs, and which served as their capital. Most of the Arab population from Ramla and nearby Lod were expelled during the 1948 war but some returned and the Arab population in both cities grew over the years. The two Jewish–Arab mixed cities were the focus of violent clashes between the communities during the events of 2021.

Beitar won the second-tier match 8-0 during a much-disrupted season. It was the only match of Beitar's first four scheduled that was actually played. The first Beitar match in the capital of the newly founded state was played in January 1950. The old pitch in the north of the city near to the Shmuel Hanavi neighbourhood was now a no-man's land between Israel and Jordan, surrounded by wire fences, minefields and lines of ugly cement walls. Beitar, like the rest of the local teams, played at the YMCA ground not far from the border and looking over to the Old City. Now it's an unreachable enemy territory forbidden for Israelis.

For the first time since the sacking of the city by the Romans in AD 70, the city was under Jewish control but the Old City and the holy places were beyond the reach of the Israelis. For 19 years until 1967's Six-Day War the burden of holiness was partly removed from Israeli Jerusalem, and ordinary lives were lived.

Jerusalem was declared as the capital but was no more than a town at the end of one road, a dead end divided at the heart of the city. Lieutenant-Colonel Moshe Dayan, leader of the Israeli forces, and Lieutenant-Colonel Abdallah A-Tal of the Jordanian Army drew the border towards the end of the war in November 1948, in thick green and red wax pencils over a 1:20,000 map. The result was the Municipal Line that tore Jerusalem in two from today's French Hill in the north to kibbutz Ramat Rachel in the south. The thickness of the pencils and the crude drafting split neighbourhoods, streets, homes and communities apart and formed numerous no-man's lands – deserted pieces of land along the green line. It also gave the name The Green Line to the border, the base of future peace talks between Israel and the Palestinians.

A Jordanian armoured car stood in front of the Notre Dame for 19 years, marking the place where the assault on Jewish Jerusalem was stopped by last-gasp efforts of the fighters asking the Haganah command to bomb their positions in a desperate attempt to hold the line. A handful of injured Haganah fighters managed to stop the vehicle with a Molotov cocktail. That was enough for Ali, its driver. In *O Jerusalem!*, Larry Collins and Dominique Lapierre wrote: 'Disgusted by the turn that the war had taken, he scrambled from his turret, dashed through New Gate and presenting himself a civilian, kept right on going until he reached his Arabian home.'

UN forces had to deal with retrieving lost footballs kicked over by Israeli kids and a lost set of dentures dropped by a woman from the French hospital. Legend has it that the false teeth belonged to a nun from Notre Dame but actually she was just one of the search team and was immortalised in an article by *Time* magazine when she was photographed with the dentures. Mission accomplished and Miriam Saada, the woman staying at the hospital, received her dentures, but if you ask Israelis of a certain age, they'll speak about the nun's teeth.

Tens of thousands of Arabs fled or were expelled from the upper- and middle-class neighbourhoods of Katamon, Talbia, Baqua, Ein Karem, Musrara and Lifta, leaving their homes and belongings behind while thousands of Jews left Sheikh Jarrah, Silwan, Gush Etzion, the part of Hanevi'im Street near Damascus Gate, and painfully the Jewish quarter in the Old City. Seventy-three years later those homes at Sheikh Jarrah would be the centre of another eviction that turned into a bloody and violent conflict yet again.

Musrara was cut in two. Like other places in the city, it was given a Hebrew name – Morasha – which nobody used and it never stuck. Huge cement walls were erected in between the beautiful small homes, and the charming streets became over-populated dwellings for newly arrived families in huge numbers, mainly from Morocco. East-facing walls were reinforced in fear of Jordanian sniper shots and mortar attacks, and wire fences were stretched near the new border. The no-man's land became a swamp and home to jackals, foxes and storks but that didn't stop the more adventurous boys taking short trips to the other side.

Israel was living in a heady mix of triumphalism, relief and ecstasy, combined with bereavement over the war's dead and victims of the Holocaust. Streets were named after the fallen, their sacrifice and heroism. Deep ideological debates followed every decision and a sense of the historical days was mixed in with the unending grief of the bereaved families. One per cent of the population died in the war, over 60 per cent of European Jews perished in the Holocaust and not many homes were spared the pain.

The Israeli right was incensed that Ben-Gurion left the Old City and the holy places to the Arabs, calling it treason and demanding it be taken back at the first opportunity, but most Israelis lost the taste for more fighting and were eager to rebuild their lives. The zeal turned quickly with the morning-after-the-night-before awakening. Israel had to overcome much more mundane challenges. None of its neighbours recognised the new state or its borders. The full-blown warfare was replaced by sporadic terror attacks, reprisals and new challenges.

'The euphoria was short-lived,' says Shlomit, my aunt. 'There was an urgent need to build a state. However, it wasn't the utter disappointment of today. Back then there were hopes, beliefs and a need to deal with the mass waves of immigration.'

The city divide was clear. Although Maccabi Jerusalem was still active, the fans belonged mainly to Beitar and Hapoel. Haim Baram, a journalist and son of local Mapai kingpin Moshe, was a football-mad child and Hapoel fan. In his memoir *Red Yellow Black*, he estimated that Beitar had 90 per cent of the fans in those early days. The key was partly geographical – Beitar had the north and centre while Hapoel were stronger in the south of the city but mainly along the line of social class and origin. Hapoel were Ashkenazi (Jews of European descent), close to Mapai and established, while Beitar were Mizrahi (Jews who came from the Muslim world), poorer, more traditional and nationalistic. Hapoel were Haganah people who followed the socialist and secular mainstream politics of Ben-Gurion, while Beitar's base was the old Irgun and Stern Gang fighters who had stayed loyal to Begin, now a part of the small opposition.

Israeli football in the 1950s was political, corrupt, violent and important. The early days reflected the young country's baby steps. Football was still under the control of Maccabi and Hapoel, very much Tel Aviv- and Yishuv-centric. Only in 1971 did a team from outside the Tel Aviv region win the title and the Israeli FA favoured the already established teams. Hapoel Be'er Sheva was the major team of the key town in the Negev in the south but its application to join the Israeli FA in 1954 was rejected, saying the city was too far away and the roads were dangerous. We (I'm Be'er Sheva born and bred) had our final laugh years later. Beitar and Hapoel Jerusalem both started life in the second league and soon found their *raison d'être* in local rivalry. It wasn't unusual; Israeli sport was still controlled by the old power struggle and the second season was called off due to other issues between Hapoel and Maccabi. In Jerusalem it seemed it was the beginning and end of all things.

According to Haim Baram, and Meir Gabay, the author of the wonderfully biased official history book of the club, *I Love You Beitar*, the derby was the most important match of the season. Gabay, a seventh generation in Jerusalem and part of a family of Irgun fighters, was the Jerusalem reporter of the influential *Hadshot Hasport* (The Sports News) daily paper. He never hid his loyalty to Herut and its team, unlike many other Beitar fans who worked in Histadrut organisations and factories. For them, Beitar matches and goals were the only legitimate outlet for their views. 'Every time one of them celebrates a Beitar goal he gets his revenge on his Ashkenazi bosses,' wrote Baram about Beitar fans working for a Histadrut organisation.

They were the lucky ones; other right-wing Israelis were refused work because of their political affiliations. There were people who were 'one of us', that is, socialists who got their jobs with a wink and a nod of the head, while there were others who were rejected endlessly. 'The numbers of fans grow rapidly,' wrote Gabay. 'The daily struggle against the Mapai's establishment led to discrimination and rejections from work opportunities. While Hapoel and Maccabi teams enjoyed state funds, the proud members of the team and the fans had to fight the hostile and alienated establishment.'

The first derby was on the eve of the war, on 15 November 1947, when Beitar was still under the guise of Nordia. The team, led by Simon Alfasi, won 3-1 in the historic match at the Shmuel Hanavi (Prophet Samuel) pitch against favourites Hapoel, who lost two of their players in the coming war. In January 1950 they met again and Beitar were victorious once more, this time 4-1. 'The fascists won in Spain but it won't last forever,' concluded *Davar*, Mapai's paper. Before the second derby of the debut season, Moshe Baram spoke to the terrified players.

> Don't you forget that you are the flag-bearers of the organised workers in the city. The 'Begininstic' Fascism is raising its head in the eternal capital of Israel but we should not surrender any front so what has happened in Spain won't repeat. Maybe Beitar has the majority of fans for the time being and they will rule the stands. But you are not

alone. The pioneers of the kibbutzim will follow
you. I bless you in the name of the workers of
Jerusalem.

Beitar, playing under the Irgun emblem of the great Israel
map with both banks of the Jordan River, won 3-1.

After a hiatus of one year due to the Hapoel–Maccabi
bickering, animosity resumed in January 1952. Hapoel,
still searching for their first victory against Maccabi, used
desperate measures and moved the home match from
the YMCA to Rehovot, a small town south of Tel Aviv
where Baram Senior had hoped they would enjoy a more
supportive crowd than in Jerusalem. 'A discussion was held
at the Kremlin about how to break the Beitar successions
of victories,' wrote Gabay. 'In an unprecedented step and in
order to prevent the arrival of many Beitar fans the match
was moved to Rehovot. The plot failed as the fans still made
it to the ground.'

Hapoel won for the first time, 4-1, and Gabay wrote
wryly in the official book, 'The one who surprised in a
shocking display was Fadida, Beitar's goalkeeper that after
the game, how interesting, never set foot again in the YMCA
and disappeared from the football landscape.'

Beitar's chairman, in contrast, didn't hold back after the
game and told his players that they 'turned in Jerusalem,
the blue and white city, to the red Moloch. The snitches,
the ones who gave our best boys to the Anglo-Nazi army
are celebrating today. Those that murdered our brothers on
the *Altalena* are happy today. You have failed the menorah.'

In the 1953/54 season the derbies became even more
important when Beitar were on the verge of a historic
promotion to the first division. In the first match Beitar
won 3-1, and on the eve of the second meeting Hapoel's

goalkeeper was beaten up by Beitar fans near his home in Nachlaot, the picturesque historic alleyway area near the city market. Things weren't much calmer at the YMCA. 'The referee works in the Histadrut' was one of the angry calls of the fans. In a previous match against Maccabi Petah Tikvah, Beitar scored from a penalty after a foul by the visitors near the halfway line. Nobody even dared to protest as the ref and Petah Tikvah players knew it was the only safe way home.

In the second derby Hapoel won 2-0, which put Beitar's promotion at risk. However, in the last match of the season Beitar beat Hapoel Rehovot 2-1 to clinch promotion. 'Evel Bahistadrut' (mourning in the Histadrut) was the cry at the stadium, and then at King George V Street and finally at Strauss Street in front of the local branch of the Histadrut. Years later, when I was living in Jerusalem, the veterans of those battles still shivered in disgust and hate when they recalled those words. The first Jerusalem club in Liga Alef was Beitar.

The *Herut* newspaper gushed all over its front page and published a special editorial: Tens of thousands of sons of Jerusalem saw in Beitar the return of the glory of Jerusalemite sport. Sons of the capital of all classes and walks of life saw Beitar as their apostle and its victory as theirs. Those who felt from short distance the passion of the people, who followed the games in the last season will know best the meaning of Beitar for the youth of the capital and the size of the contribution of Beitar in defending the capital's honour.

Not every year such out of proportions sporting events take place. After two decades, Beitar has joined the family of Liga Alef teams. On this day of celebrations of Beitar's promotion – long live

the capital city of Israel! – long live Beitar! – long
live the national sport!

The joy and pathos were short-lived. Beitar had a team based
around the 1940s heroes but Simon Alfasi, the player of
whom Menachem Begin said 'one goal by him is worth a
thousand speeches by me', was 32 years old and the club was
relegated after only one season in the top tier. In that season
Beitar had their first encounter with Hapoel Tel Aviv, their
nemesis to be. Both matches ended in respectable 1-1 and
2-2 draws.

The second match took place in Jaffa, in the Basa
stadium. Hapoel legend Yaakov Hodrov, the best goalkeeper
of his generation, maybe the best Israeli keeper ever, said
before the match that Beitar weren't good Bab el Wad, i.e.
outside of Jerusalem. When Alfasi scored an outstanding
equaliser with a 20-metre volley, he turned round to the
national keeper and said, 'Hey Hodrov, we passed Bab el
Wad ages ago,' and a narrative was born. Plucky Beitar vs
condescending Hapoel of Tel Aviv. It would shape Israeli
football for years to come.

Baram also tells of a match against Hapoel Hadera in
1955 in which the visitors led 2-0. Beitar's hardcore fans
refused to accept the scoreline and started pelting Haim
Levin, Hadera's teenage goalkeeper, with stones and threats.
The game, writes Baram, should have been stopped but the
farce went on. Beitar equalised but even one of their players
found it unacceptable. Asher Bernbloom, the right-winger, a
member of the Irgun and well-known Herut pedigree family,
stood up in front of the south stand and demanded they stop
the violence. Bernbloom, second best only to Simon Alfasi
in the team of that generation, was also a famous pugilist,
champion of Israel and a man you shouldn't ignore. However,

the leader of the hardcore group – the word ultras wasn't in use yet – stood up and shouted to the player, 'Don't be a gentleman at our expense, Asher.'

Bernbloom backed down, the game was resumed and Beitar won 4-2.

It wasn't the last time the fans intimidated teams successfully. Time and time again Beitar supporters were rewarded for their violence. While one can claim that Baram was biased, Gabay doesn't paint a much different picture in his book: 'YMCA was not just a bastion that visitors found it hard to get points but also a dangerous pitch to come to in fear of the local fans. As the road to Jerusalem rose to the hills you could sense the trepidation among the players.'

Those fans had a dilemma in the penultimate matchday of the 1957 season. Hapoel Jerusalem were flying high with a realistic chance of promotion while Beitar hosted Hapoel Hadera, one of Hapoel's rivals. Hadera led 2-0 after 24 minutes, but Gabay and Baram tell a different story in their books regarding the rest of the match. Both describe a growing unrest in the crowd but Baram wrote that it was the Beitar fans who couldn't stomach the shameful display of their heroes:

> I squeezed into the south stand which was purely Beitar. They did support Hadera but the way in which the game was fixed cause, a growing anger that became a clear outrage. Ten minutes until the end, with the score 3-1 to Hadera, the Beitar maneuverers became unbearable and hundreds of fans stormed the pitch and brought the game to an end. This was the first and last public act by both sets of fans.

Gabay, who covered the match for his paper, had a different view. He wrote that Beitar played well, that it was Hapoel fans in the south stand, and that after 80 minutes 'Hapoel people used a clever and original ploy. A mysterious hand threw a large number of coins onto the pitch. Many kids and youths ran onto the pitch to collect the money and after them the rest of the fans.'

This story tells mainly about the standards of the young Israeli footballers and the sheer hate and passion between the two Jerusalem clubs. The battle was never confined to the poor pitch near the Old City – it was kept alive in the workplaces, political rallies and history books.

It was one of the most shameful Saturdays in local football history. Hadera were awarded a 3-0 victory, and two other matches for the league leaders were cancelled altogether. Hapoel Kfar Saba beat their rivals 12-0 while Maccabi Rehovot won 11-0. It was all too clear to see that the season was fixed and based on corruption and political motives. The solution was to hold a mini-league between the top five clubs. Beitar were the sixth. Hapoel were promoted eventually, and rage ensued.

Hapoel Jerusalem became a member of what's now called Liga Leumit (National League) and kept that position while Beitar languished in the second division for 11 costly years. To make things worse, Beitar finished the following season first but were denied promotion because of the same malaise of corruption and unsporting behaviour of many clubs. Promotions were called off to the despair of fans.

The problems were prominent but Israeli football established itself as an important social institution. The government promoted the matches against a strong Yugoslavia and USSR as a national event. Players had to change their names to Hebrew ones and they met Jewish supporters in

Moscow before the match in 1956 as proud representatives of the Jewish people. 'Body culture – a guarantee for the people's health' was the slogan in the Ramat Gan Stadium for the replay, which the Soviets won 2-1. More than 50,000 fans squeezed into the stadium and saw an Israeli goal by Nahum Stelmach. His header, which beat the great Russian keeper Lev Yashin, was celebrated as a national triumph, but sadly the news film crew missed it when they focused on the Mapai leaders in the front row. One newspaper reported that the Israeli goal caused a Zionistic resurgence among Russian Jews and the match became a source of pride for many years.

Football was a great tool of acclimatisation. You didn't need to have great Hebrew, or many friends in the new land. If you supported the local team, you had a common goal for 90 minutes and felt a sense of belonging. 'My father emigrated from Romania in the 1970s,' Ariguy Berger told me. 'People made fun of him at work, in the army. He didn't understand a word but when he went to see Hapoel Be'er Sheva he was one of them. They all wanted and cared about the same thing and understood each other.'

It was that way in the 1950s and still is today. While Hapoel and Maccabi Tel Aviv and later Hapoel Petah Tikvah got all the titles, Hapoel Jerusalem became a member of the top league and grew stronger. Beitar were stuck in the second league but the zeal was burning even brighter and became the foundation for much later success and everlasting troubles.

# 7

# Status Quo

NEAR THE town of Beit Shemesh, nestling in the Judean Mountains, stands a big rock with a little curved niche in the centre of it. Today it's hard to find the rock among the wild foliage, but from 1950 until 1967 it was a holy place – the Rock of Destruction. The Ministry for Religious Affairs set its status in stone in a big ceremony in 1950. Road signs help worshippers locate it and before long it was associated with traditions and costumes.

Legend has it that the big rock was meant to arrive at the under-siege Jerusalem during the revolt against the Romans. The man who carried it was a strong hero, a direct descendant of Samson – the greatest biblical hero.

Following a call to strengthen the fortifications of the walls of Jerusalem, Samson carried the stone, but when he reached that hill, he saw pillars of smoke rising from the ransacked city. Heartbroken, he collapsed and the rock killed him at the spot where he's still buried. A martyr of Jerusalem who earned recognition almost 1,900 years later.

The legend sounds right. Samson used to live in the area and was known for his rare strength and affairs with local women, but the tale was born during the British Mandate by Dr Ze'ev Vilnai, the great scholar of Eretz Yisrael geography and sites. He was guiding a tour when he was asked about the stone – actually part of the remains of an olive press – and came out on the spot with the lovely tale. The story became part of local folklore and later came to serve a need in the new state.

In his book *Love Thy Country*, Vilnai wrote:

> The director general of the Ministry for Religious Affairs declared the Rock of Destruction as a holy place and invited honourable delegates for the event. At that occasion he told the legend that I concocted as a tradition of times gone by. He didn't mention my name of course and didn't find the need to invite me to the sanctifying ceremony of the rock that thanks to me has become a holy site.

For 19 years Israeli Jerusalem developed without most of its holy places. The Wailing Wall was near the border but also deep into Jordanian territory and so was the Cave of the Patriarchs in Hebron and Rachel's Tomb near Bethlehem. But even during that rare lull, Jerusalem couldn't escape its holiness. The people and the state were craving for places to worship and came up with new ones. The most important site was Mount Zion, just outside the south-west corner of the Old City. This dazzling cluster of holy sites was the nearest point to the Wailing Wall and the only top-tier holy site in Israeli hands. It became a viewing point for VIP visitors to the Old City and Temple Mount as a substitute for the real thing.

All over Israel and Jerusalem, caves, rocks and tombstones suddenly turned into divine locations with a relentless energy. Today only Mount Zion retains its significance, and when

I visited it in December 2019, it was almost as busy as the most important sites inside the walls. No wonder; the spot is a house for King David's tomb, which is holy for both Jews and Muslims. Christians believe that the Last Supper happened in a nearby hall and the whole site is dominated by the huge dome of Dormition Abbey, where the Virgin Mary fell asleep for the last time before her assumption to heaven. The place is bustling with wide-eyed Christian pilgrims and orthodox Jews mixing in the narrow alleys before and after their rituals. The best way to relax after a visit there is to follow the great walls all the way to Jaffa Gate into the open, green and calm national garden. It's truly one of the best walks any city can offer.

Since the visit of Saint Helena, the city has become accustomed to the dynamic of sanctification. It came to answer religious, political and economic needs. The last place to receive the status of a Christian holy site was the Garden Tomb just north of Damascus Gate, where, the Protestants claim, sits the true site of Christ's crucifixion. The site, an old burial cave, was made famous by Major-General Charles Gordon (the one of the Khartoum glory). After his visit, Gordon suggested in his book, *Reflections in Palestine*, a different location for Golgotha. It lies north of the traditional site at the Church of the Holy Sepulchre and is now known as 'the Garden Tomb', or sometimes as 'Gordon's Calvary'. A quarter of a million worshippers visit the place every year.

In the west of the city, watching over the forested mountains, Israel has its secular holy sites: the military cemetery at Mount Herzl, the national memorial centre near it, and Yad Vashem, the Holocaust Memorial Museum, established in 1953. Today the place is home to a moving and overwhelming exhibition about lives lived and lost in the

Jewish communities of Europe. At the start of the museum one can read a quote by the Jewish German writer Kurt Tucholsky: 'A country is not only what it does but what it tolerates.' Among the horrors, there's a final room dedicated to life right after the war, and among the items there's a lovely simple poster of a black-haired footballer with a Maccabi logo on his shirt from the Föhrenwald displaced persons camp in Bavaria. At the camp on one Saturday in 1947, tells the poster in Yiddish, there will be a football match of Maccabi Föhrenwald in Liga Mastershaft (Championship League). For where there's life, there's football.

\* \* \*

December 2019: Beitar Jerusalem are playing at Teddy against humble Hapoel Hadera. It's a mild night for a Jerusalem winter and when I left my digs I had a look at the famous market of Mahane Yehuda, a mandatory stop for TV crews when doing a piece about Beitar fans. The place was full of tourists and locals but only a few yellow-and-black scarf-wearing Beitar fans. Some young men with angry yellow sweatshirts adorned with the initials LF had their last bite to eat before heading south to the Teddy Stadium. The atmosphere wasn't building up.

The place to meet the supporters before a match is the big Malha shopping mall near Teddy. It was packed with Beitar fans, coming from all over Israel, Hapoel Jerusalem basketball fans whose team was also playing that evening in the nearby arena, and large numbers of shoppers, many of them Arabs. All were relaxed and ignoring each other.

Supporters made their way to the west stand but you could hardly guess there was to be a match there that evening. Just opposite, near the east stand, you could sense some football energy. Big groups of young fans with all the La Familia insignia were getting ready, preparing their drums and flags and getting inside after a police search for pyros. A man with a big kippa and long side curls was handing out tiny books of Psalms. 'My brother, Psalms for the successes of Beitar?' he asked every passer-by but me. I made eye contact and passed near him twice. Nothing. I do look like any other middle-aged Israeli but he could see I wasn't one of them.

Inside a dusty and windy stadium, about 6,000 fans saw a 2-0 Beitar victory. One of the people present was a Hamas member on a reconnaissance mission before a planned attack on a Beitar match. He was caught eventually and the mission never happened as the place was well protected.

While the east stand was in good voice and singing mainly about Hapoel Tel Aviv (the 'communist pigs'), it was an underwhelming event. I remember Saturdays with 12,000 to 18,000 fans filling the smaller versions of Teddy. I recall the passion, zeal and loaded atmosphere. I didn't experience any of it this night. It was a lacklustre affair and in hindsight it has only seemed worse since. A dreary dry Monday night in Jerusalem. After the match some Beitar fans attacked Hapoel fans and stole their gear. I guess I wasn't the only one who got bored.

\* \* \*

To understand the rise and decline of Beitar one needs to understand the city and Israel. The years between 1948 and 1967 were a period of quiet growth for the capital but the early days of the new state had profound ramifications. The orthodox autonomy was born then along with the great social tensions that still haunt Israeli society. They all played a part in Beitar's trajectory.

The international border was removed after the Six-Day War in 1967 but Jerusalem is still a city of borders. Some are clear and others are unseen but easily felt. The Mahane Yehuda market, now a hub of restaurants and pubs, sweet stalls and bakeries, is metres away from one such border. It's midnight and I'm having a beer with my old friend Yossi Gabay at a pub that belongs to a local rapper. Yossi is an eighth-generation resident of the city, a former Beitar player, once a marketing director of the club and a well-connected guy. We worked together during some phases of our lives and I've learned to trust his instincts.

'Over there,' he points to the north over the light railway line of Jaffa Street, 'is a different world.' Around us there's music, lights and people who are young and alive, an enclave. And over the tracks is Haredi Jerusalem. It used to be a non-religious area; my maternal grandparents were both teachers at the nearby Lemel school. The beautiful neo-classical stone building with an iconic clock with Hebrew letters at the top is now a yeshiva deep inside the autonomy. Lemel school, which was at the front of the languages war between Hebrew and German, is now a place where the main tongue used is Yiddish.

Amos Oz, in his travel book *In the Land of Israel*, quoted Dov Sadan, a literary professor and a politician, who said in the 1960s that Zionism was nothing more than a passing episode, a temporary mundane phenomenon of history and politics, but that orthodox Judaism would re-emerge, would swallow Zionism and digest it. 'In these neighbourhoods,' wrote Oz as early as 1983, 'where I was born and raised, the battle has been decided: Zionism has been repulsed, as if it had never been.'

There are whole cities in Israel where the state is watching from the outside while religious leaders call the shots. For them and their followers the laws of the Torah are the ones to obey. Some of the Haredi orders are anti-Zionist and others are just non-Zionist. The founding of the state is a crime against God by the secular Israelis. It doesn't stop most of them from enjoying state budgets but they have their own limited education system. Most don't serve in the army and they have unspoken permission to live their lives and to run their religious affairs in a non-official autonomy.

The special status of the Haredi sector was born in 1948 when Ben-Gurion promised leading rabbis not to draft yeshiva boys to the army, although every young man was desperately needed for the war effort. Four hundred pupils of the Torah and Talmud received an exemption under the condition that they wouldn't go to work but would stick to religious studies. The understanding known as the Status Quo shaped the orthodox world in Israel, had a huge impact on society and the economy of Israel and made Jerusalem into what it is today. A poor, religious city with football clubs where most of their fans don't live in the area. If you passed through the Haredi education system the chances are that you don't have the basic skills to work in modern Israel. In a list compiled in 2019 by the National Statistics Office, 43 of the 100 worst neighbourhoods to live in were in Jerusalem, most of them of the orthodox communities, while 44 of the best were in Tel Aviv.

Like in the case of the Stone of Destruction, religion, belief and holiness are all fluid, political and based on needs. This principle became the keystone of Haredi life in modern Israel. Although most of them don't support the idea of a Jewish state they have learned to enjoy it. The number of yeshiva boys rose more than a hundred-fold, while the exemption from the army caused hate and tension, and the ban on work doomed Haredi families to poverty and a life on state benefits. Every street in the Haredi quarter is recognisable by the small charity boxes hanging everywhere and big signs asking for donations. 'Charity will save from death' is one and another is the much-mocked picture of hungry children saying, 'Mother, you promised a chicken dinner for Shabbat.' It's a show of solidarity and caring for the poor but also a reminder of the result of the Status Quo.

Anshel Pfeffer is a brilliant *Haaretz* political writer based in Jerusalem. He was born to an orthodox family in Salford, where he became a Manchester United fan. He grew up later in Jerusalem where he still lives in the charming German colony. He took his kippa off years ago but still writes about Jewish life in his weekly column. When you write about politics in Israel you're never too far away from writing about Jerusalem and the orthodox. Even more so after the COVID-19 pandemic, which has highlighted the fault lines in Israeli society and the growing problem of the Haredi autonomy, where the law is hardly enforced and the rule of the rabbi is far superior to that of the state. Pfeffer says:

> Ben-Gurion was the one who enabled the autonomy. He came from an orthodox family and estimated that, like him, young Haredi will be taken over by Zionism. He thought that there are only few Haredi Holocaust survivors and it wouldn't harm to give them the Status Quo. However, today they are around 13 per cent of the Israeli population and the numbers are growing. The Haredi public was hit hard during the Holocaust. It's not only the killing and loss of lives but also the loss of their centres. Even before the war the immigration to America or Palestine usually meant becoming secular.
>
> They rebuilt their communities in Israel and they lived in a welfare state, as modest as it

was, for the first time ever. They enjoy modern healthcare and after the Holocaust there was an urge and ideology to make as many children as possible in numbers which were impossible in the past. The Haredis evolved and learned how to live in a Jewish democratic state and we see the results now.

When you walk down Ethiopia Street, on your right is the circular Ethiopian church, with the lion cubs of Judea at its front. Inside, the church is closed to visitors but you can walk around and smell the incense, see the huge drums and enjoy the pastel colours on the walls. A black Jesus welcomes the worshippers and to step inside is to step inside a culture not known to many, but once you step outside you're back to the problems of 21st-century Jerusalem. The place has seen violent fights between different political and ethnic groups of Ethiopian worshippers over power and control, just like their Jewish neighbours.

In the quaint lane, the stone walls are covered with climbing plants but don't let that fool you. No. 11 used to be the Ben Yehuda family home. A plaque commemorating this historical fact has been destroyed numerous times. Some feuds are never forgotten. Some Haredi people will avoid this useful passageway to their shtetl because of the long-gone resident at No. 11. 'The Abomination Lane', they call it. Even the tombs of the Ben Yehuda family aren't safe and were desecrated in clashes during another seasonal clash between the Haredis and the state.

Ben Yehuda was a lexicographer and newspaper editor. He was the leader of the Hebrew revival movement that transformed the language, which for centuries had been used only in study, into a modern spoken language. He spoke with his household members in Hebrew and had to invent many modern words that later became part of the Hebrew dictionary. He fell out with the orthodox Ashkenazi community because of his objection to their way of life, which was based on donations. He called it 'leprosy that corrupts the society'. They never forgave him for that.

At the end of the street, you're standing in front of Me'ah Shearim, the Haredi non-Zionist mass. The walls are covered with big billboards pleading with tourist groups not to enter and calling for women to retain their modesty. For some men even the sight of a secular woman well covered in the Jerusalem winter is too much and they cover their eyes when they see one. The shock and the insult on my European girlfriend's face was painful to watch. Some local women take care to cover themselves absolutely so no body part or shape can be seen by men. Known as Taliban Women, they live under layers of fabric even during the summer. You can hardly tell there's a human being there as their eyes are also hidden behind a dark veil. All this is done so a man won't be tempted and waste precious Torah learning time on immodest thoughts.

According to Ashel Pfeffer:

> The Haredi approach is seclusion, although it's not the classic Jewish way. In many communities Jews lived with ties to the outside world. At the beginning of the emancipation, they had a chance to become a part of the great society but they see it as a threat to the authority of the rabbis. After the Holocaust they rebuilt their communities in the USA and Israel which are a paradise for Jewish life but a threat to theirs so they became even more secluded.

On the first sunny Saturday in April 2021, the COVID-19 lockdown was lifted in the UK and I drove to Stoke Newington's Church Street, a lively, trendy spot that was beaming with life after the dreadful winter. People just wanted to get out, eat out, drink, splash out money and show some skin. Modesty wasn't on the cards. A street or two away the Haredis came back from the synagogue dressed in black and balancing enormous fur hats called shtriemel over their heads. They didn't bat an eyelid when they saw cars driving in front of them. In Jerusalem their brethren will stone such cars.

In London they can live side by side with other people but in Israel it's different. 'I used to live in French Hill,' Yossi Gabay told me, 'and one Saturday I was about to drive in my car with my family and one Haredi came and stood in front yelling "Shaabes" [Shabbat in Yiddish]. I told him to get out of my way and drove but I told my wife that we need to move.'

Pfeffer says:

> The Haredi needs are different. People can share the same space in London but in Jerusalem and other cities the moment a Haredi family moves next to you soon they will be followed by more. It may sound racist but a secular family doesn't have an interest to live next to Haredi. You just know that sooner or later the street will be closed on Shabbat, and battle will start over the community centre, the school and the resources not to mention modesty issues. Today Jerusalem is not just more orthodox, it is also more racist, it's more in the open. You have less people to voice other opinions because they don't live there anymore.

So, what's the future for the city and Israel with such a large sector outside of work and the law? According to Pfeffer:

> There is a paradox. The numbers are growing but the whole structure is based on being a small minority. Once they are a majority there are questions of how they sustain themselves. The outside world is much closer now and they can't enclose themselves now. The minute you are in touch with the outside world, you are not Haredi and I think they will change in a generation.

In 2020 it all reached a critical point. The Haredi, crucial to Benjamin Netanyahu's last desperate stand, enjoyed disproportionate power. State money was poured in to keep the Status Quo, which by then had become a massive burden. While the secular sector was facing the heavy-handed restrictions of the pandemic, the Haredis were practically exempt. The only flights into Israel were from and to orthodox strongholds such as New York, and while schools and universities were shut down, most of the religious education was uninterrupted.

On 30 April 2021 more than 100,000 worshippers made the pilgrimage to the foot of Mount Meron in the north of Israel for the feast of Lag Ba'omer. It's a festival of fire around the tomb of a holy rabbi, which has become a major event in the religious calendar. The small place, which is outside the state jurisdiction, has become a cluster of buildings and alleys of different Haredi orders without any planning, engineering or supervision. When thousands of men left one event, they were funnelled into a death trap. Forty-five believers were crushed and died at the site in the most shocking example of the cost of Haredi autonomy.

The Haredi takeover of parts of Jerusalem has made the city poorer, cost Beitar a decent stadium for decades and changed the demographic of the city. According to the National Office for Statistics, 35.6 per cent of adults living in Jerusalem in 2019 defined themselves as Haredi, 20.5 per cent as religious, 10.2 per cent as traditionalists/religious and 22.2 per cent as traditionalists/not that religious, and only 18.6 per cent as secular. In Israel the number of Haredi is around 13 per cent and the number of seculars is 43.2 per cent. For most of the Haredi population football is a gentile sport and a waste of time. No wonder that Teddy is more empty than full.

# 8

# Dust of the Earth

DURING THE endless election campaign between 2019 and 2021, a tedious existence that was only interrupted four times for an actual election, three prominent right-wing media personalities – Erel Segal, Yinon Magal and Avishay Ben Haim – went to Teddy for a TV piece for Channel 13. The three are known as shofars, in other words mouthpieces for Prime Minister Benjamin Netanyahu, named after the Jewish ceremonial instrument made of a ram's horn, and have worked endlessly to promote Netanyahu and his family for years. They all went to watch Beitar's match against Hapoel Tel Aviv. Easy picking, for any item about social tensions.

Netanyahu himself, not a known football fan, was there with his wife Sarah, an Imelda Marcos type of woman (she was convicted in court for trickery) and son Avner – a genuine Beitar supporter – to collect some love from the fans while Segal, a dyed-in-the-wool Beitar fan, watched the match anxiously.

In the background of the fans singing 'Beitar the flag of the country', Ben Haim exposed his theory: 'Beitar have played a major role in establishing the impossible alliance between second-class Israel and the Likud princes. A unique space where the Mizrahi on the pitch and the stands are not guests but landlords, a space where they feel equal.'

The translation for this word salad has become Ben Haim's flag. For him, Netanyahu is a sacred symbol of Jewish identity treasured by the second-class Mizrahi who are suffering under the Ashkenazi yoke in Israel. If you support Netanyahu, you're second-class Israel, and if not, you're conspiring treason against a beloved leader while Beitar is a potent symbol of Mizrahi empowerment. This half-baked theory was broadcast by the most popular TV channel almost every week for years.

At one stage Segal pointed towards Beitar fans and said, 'About 40 to 50 per cent of them go to the synagogue on Saturday evening while there [he points in disgust to the other side] – if 10 per cent goes it is a generous estimation. That's the story.'

These feelings are reflected in a popular fans' song:

> *Even at the hardest times*
> *I will sing your name in the streets*
> *Yellow in my veins, Beitar forever*
> *See red becomes like a bull*
> *We'll break the sickle with an iron bar*
> *To one commandment I'll adhere:*
> *To wipe the Amalek seed!*

Amalek is a biblical enemy of Israel and there are two commandments that involve Amalek: to remember what the Amalekites did to the Israelites and to destroy the Amalekites utterly.

On the pitch, Hapoel won 1-0. Off it, the elections ended in another deadlock.

* * *

When you walk in Musrara today, among the pretty stone houses and the ugly cement council estate blocks, currently under the control of a fringe Haredi cult of a convicted fraudster and sex offender, you'll see graffiti of black panthers. There's one on a wall near the fabulous neo-classic Anglican St Paul, Church and one in front of the Center for Middle Eastern Classical Music; both are big and bold and ready to pounce. The feline predator isn't the only one to receive the honour. The familiar bespectacled face of Menachem Begin, the former Likud leader and prime minister, pops up in front of a yeshiva and in the lanes.

The Black Panthers were a Mizrahi protest movement that evolved in Musrara and shook the political system in the early 1970s. They protested against the Mizrahi discrimination and let their anger be known in their first flyer, which was distributed in 1971:

> We, a group of oppressed youngsters, are calling everybody who have had enough, enough of not having a job, enough of sleeping ten in a room, enough of looking at the new buildings for olim [immigrants from the USSR], enough of getting locked up in prison and getting beaten every other day, enough of unfulfilled government promises, enough of discrimination, enough of depravation. We protest for our right to be like all other citizens in this country.

Reuven Abergail, one of the founders and leaders, told the *Makor Rishon* newspaper about the reasons behind the Panthers (who took their name from the American civil rights movement):

The immigrants from Muslim countries suffered everywhere but in Musrara it was the worst. The flats were old and cramped, sometimes with 12 people in a room. Lots of electricity and water problems. The worst for us was to see the humiliation of the parents. The only school in the neighbourhood was a Haredi Ashkenazi one and we got there more beating up than education. Many of the kids preferred to roam the streets than to go to school. After the Six-Day War we had good relationships with the Palestinian youth because we lived nearby and we shared the language. The police didn't like those ties and arrested many of us.

To borrow a phrase from the US civil rights leader Jesse Jackson, it was the protest of 'the desperate, the damned, the disinherited, the disrespected, and the despised'.

It was an eruption two decades in the making. After 1948 Israel had the challenge of accommodating mass immigration from all over the world. In just 18 months the population grew from 600,000 to 1.3 million. The first waves of immigrants were accommodated in the empty houses of Palestinians but after a short time those places ran out. The solution was to put the olim in 49 transit camps, no more than cramped tents or basic sheds, on the outskirts of the established cities and towns. There in the horrible living conditions lived refugees from the ashes of Europe and the Muslim world that turned hostile to its Jewish communities.

The budding state was desperately poor after the war and the population boom. Israel had introduced austerity measures and limitations on basic food staples, furniture and footwear. Years later, my parents still told me about the 'horrible tinned snook', a South African fish that was hated in the UK during the war, and in Israel in equal measure.

The horrors of the Holocaust were still tangible. A daily radio programme called *The Search Bureau for Missing Relatives* is an everlasting emotive memory of the 1950s. The broadcast was based on messages from survivors looking for relatives, mentioning their pre-war home and last known information. It led to moving reunions but, in most cases, there was no response. Listening to the programme became a ritual of the new Israeliness when Hebrew-speaking children helped their less fluent parents.

The Holocaust was an unmentionable taboo during the first years. The big change came with the public trial of Adolf Eichmann, who was in charge of the final solution – the mass killing of Jews by Germany and its allies. Eichmann was abducted in 1960 from Argentina where he had found refuge after the war. He was put on trial, which was broadcast to the nation by radio, was found guilty and sentenced to death. The verdict was carried out in 1962. For the first time Israelis listened to the survivors without judgement, and healing could commence.

The mood was very different in 1952 when the Reparations Agreement between Israel and Germany was agreed. Ben-Gurion, ever pragmatic, rose above the emotions to secure Israel's economic future. Facing waves of immigration, the payment from West Germany to the survivors and to the Jewish state helped revive the economy and had a major social impact on society and Beitar.

Begin, who had lost his family in the Holocaust, objected to the agreement vehemently. He delivered a harsh speech during huge and violent demonstrations in Jerusalem in January 1952:

This will be a war of life or death ... You will not vanquish us, because there is no force in the world that can vanquish the Irgun soldiers ... This government, which will open negotiations with the murderers who annihilated our people, will be a malicious government that bases its rule on spear and grenade.

Begin called on citizens to refrain from paying taxes and to engage in civil disobedience, even at the cost of being taken to a 'concentration camp'. He planned violent demonstrations in the centre of the city and near the Knesset. 'When you shot us with the cannon, I gave an order, "No!" Today I give the order, "Yes!"' he said, referring to the threat of civil war during the *Altalena* crisis and the possibility of renewed internal conflict.

Eventually the Knesset, while stones smashed the building, windows and tear gas spread inside, approved the agreement. The money was received by the state and individuals and Begin was outcast as a dangerous populist by Ben-Gurion and his party.

The German money transformed the Israeli economy, helped build a moderate middle class and caused a big financial chasm between Ashkenazi and Mizrahi citizens. They had both arrived at the same time, both being sprayed at the ports with DDT to limit the spread of the insect-borne diseases, all suffering in the transit camps. However, with the German money many Ashkenazi families, usually much smaller than the Mizrahi families, could get a nice flat in the city. Seventy years later some families have a flat or house to pass to their children and grandchildren while others don't. Ashkenazim were also better connected to Mapai and this helped to find jobs and accommodation.

The transit camps were eventually replaced by 26 new towns for the immigrants, spread mainly along the borders, from Kiyat Shmona by the Lebanese border and Beit She'an in the Jordan Valley all the way to the Negev desert. There in the acrid land, in the middle of nowhere, it wasn't the home people dreamed of in the diaspora. In some cases, the olim refused to get out of the trucks. The state official in charge ordered the driver to raise the trunk and the people spilled to the ground like sand. The trauma lasted for ever.

Begin was a political outcast following the riots. 'Without Herut and the communists' was the basic rule of Ben-Gurion's politics. Herut, Begin's party, was in the opposition without any influence or power, jobs to give and budgets but ironically it was the basis of its powers that be.

As frustration grew among the Mizrahi immigrants in the camps, Herut turned out to be their political home. The party and Begin offered them an understanding and acceptance. Herut and the Irgun fighters' dejection from the mainstream led to a union of outsiders. Begin, although a Polish-born Ashkenazi, knew how to approach them. A brilliant narrator, his public speeches attracted huge crowds and built his status as a popular alternative to Mapai, the ruling party.

While the established Israelis tried to mould a new type of Jew – a fighting, socialist, non-religious Israeli – Begin always emphasised tradition, national pride and religious values. With him the Mizrahim could keep their cultural heritage. As early as 1955 Begin had the wisdom to tie the anger, burning insult and feeling of discrimination among the Mizrahim in the camps to the general resentment towards Herut and the Irgun fighters.

When meeting with Mapai leaders in 1957 Ben-Gurion said: 'There are two factors that help Herut's demagogy.

Patriotic slogans about Jerusalem's Old City and bigger Israel and primitive public that you can easily incite against the people who lived here for longer.' In early 1959 the PM wrote in his diary, 'The danger is in some of the Mizrahi groups … the primitive element is easy to manipulate politicaly and socially. Their hate to the Arabs is great and they are enchanted by talks about historical borders [of Israel]. They do not have among them leaders with enough education and culture.'

In 1959 riots broke out in Wadi Salib in Haifa where many olim from Morocco were living in abject conditions. More riots and protests followed all over Israel as the gulf between Ashkenazi and Mizrahim grew. The transit camps were turned in some places to crime-ridden slums and new waves of European immigrants were spared the hardship of those places and sent to much better flats in the city 'fitting their background'.

During the 1960s more and more Mizrahim took roles inside Herut, and Begin led the way to a new version of the Israeli right, away from the liberal secular ideas of Jabotinsky. Professor Amir Goldstein wrote:

> Begin crystallised an ideology that combined nationalism and tradition while respecting religion and its values, institutes and symbols. Begin's narrative was flowing with concepts, slogans and ideas that were close to the cultural perception of many Mizrahi groups. For the majority of olim from Muslim countries religion is the most basic part of identity and they didn't recognise the separation between religion and nation.

In an essay called *Forgiveness*, A.B. Yehoshua, the famous Israeli author, wrote:

> The Mizrahim, mainly those from Morocco, felt that the Labour party asked from them a double demand: not just leave the ways of the diaspora life behind and turn into new Jews but also to convert the Mizrahi culture with another one ... Begin didn't asked them to change. He accepted them as they were.

The early insult has influenced life in Israel ever since. Amos Oz, in his 1984 book, *In the Land of Israel*, described a meeting with Begin supporters after the violent 1981 elections in which Begin used the ethnic card to win the elections from a losing position. 'My parents came from North Africa; all right, from Morocco,' they said to him. 'So what? They had their dignity, didn't they? Their own values? Their own faith? Me, I'm not a religious man. Travel on the Sabbath. But my parents – why did you make fun of their beliefs? Why did they have to be disinfected at Haifa port?'
Another man adds, in sadness beyond all anger:

> The Mapainiks just wiped out everything that was imprinted on a person. As if it was all nonsense. And then they put what they wanted into him. From that ideology of theirs. Like we were some kind of dirt. Ben-Gurion himself called us the dust of the earth. But now that Begin's here, believe me, my parents can stand up straight, with pride and dignity. I'm not religious either, but my parents are; they're traditional and Begin has respect for their beliefs.

Why don't you ask who dragged the Moroccans into prostitution and crime? Why don't you ask who taught the kids, while they were still in transit camps, to make fun of their parents, to laugh at old people, to ridicule their religion and their leaders? Why don't you ask first of all, who taught Mizrahim that money's is the most important thing in life? Why don't you ask them who invented theft and fraud? Who invented the stock market?

In 2017 a TV documentary called *Salah This is Eretz Yishrael* caused a public debate. The creators brought shocking quotes from the state leaders in the 1950s, including Ben-Gurion, who said: 'This is dust of the earth from the dullest, rejected, low and despised countries. The reception in Israel, the discrimination, the cultural wipeout, the funnelling into menial schools and jobs and even a suspicion of mass abduction of babies of Yemenite parents – they all came to the fore.'

'I travel the length of the land and I can tell you that the Mizrahi–Ashkenazi tension is still the most important factor in each general election,' Shalom Yerushalmi, the sharp political analyst, told me when we met in December 2019.

\* \* \*

Ben-Gurion left political life in 1963 and went to live in Sde Boker, a small kibbutz in the Negev, until his death in 1973. Without his towering leadership, people were looking for a new father figure and Begin was the answer for many. Herut was a political outlet for the anger and Beitar was the football branch of the party. Many ministers and even a prime minister and a president of Israel boosted their political career by taking care of the club. Begin, however, was more famous than Beitar and not the greatest football fan. The official Beitar book claims that his visit to the cup final of 1975, Beitar's first, was only his second Beitar match. However, in 1959 he wrote a letter to the head of Beitar in Jerusalem asking about the poor state of the youth team of the club. 'This team of ours went at the time from strength to strength and was the glory of the city and the flag of the movement and now is in dire straits,' he lamented.

The 1960s saw Hapoel Jerusalem establishing itself as a top-tier club with a decent stadium. Katamon Stadium was based in the leafy middle-class area of the same name, while Beitar was dwindling in the second tier. The political tension eased a bit and the city grew, thanks to jobs in the civil service and the Hebrew university. It all worked for the benefit of Hapoel, who became more popular in the south of the city. Haim Baram estimates that they closed the popularity gap and had about 40 per cent of the fans in Jerusalem.

That was also when Beitar got their famous yellow colours for the first time. Unlike Maccabi Tel Aviv, who have played in yellow and blue since the 1940s in solidarity with European Jews who had to wear a yellow star under Nazi hardship, Beitar's reasons were more prosaic. Ely Gabay says Yossi, his son, who was in charge of running the team, saw a documentary about the Brazilian national team and their famous kit. He couldn't find such a shirt so he bought yellow fabric and had it made into a football kit and an image was born. The waspish, alarming yellow and black took over the vanilla white and suited Beitar's image as the not-so-nice outsiders. Later this had political connotations.

The club took baby steps towards professionalism. Fans weren't allowed to travel any more to matches on the team bus like they used to do in the early days. A drinking problem of one of the stars was treated, well more or less, when he was promised a free drink for every victory instead of getting hammered on the way to matches.

Beitar didn't enjoy success at that time but the club's image and identity were forged during the lean years. Although Beitar Tel Aviv was the senior and the more successful Beitar club, they never had the same passionate following. In Tel Aviv they had to compete not just with the well-established Maccabi and Hapoel, but they also lost Mizrahi fans to Beni Yehuda and Shimshon, two small clubs in Mizrahi neighbourhoods. In Jerusalem, Beitar had only Hapoel as a rival and there was another factor: in Jerusalem everything is more direct, harsh and concentrated. Like stock after long simmering, the conflict in Jerusalem is reduced and packs a punch.

The insult was the fire that was kept stoked by politicians but not without a basis. *Saadia: Roots to the Homeland* was an official short film made by the state in 1951 and reflects the attitudes at that time in a terrifying way. The film, shot by the IDF and director Ze'ev Rav Nof, tells the story of Saadia, a child from Yemen who meets Rutty, a young female soldier, in an army educational base. Saadia is portrayed as a primitive boy who can't eat properly and smokes at the age of 11. 'In the name of the world of light,' says the voiceover, 'Rutty is getting down to Saadia, the dark world of the transit camp. Rutty will share her light with Saadia, elevate him to her stature and bring him into her world. And there she'll be light for Saadia as well. This is the integration.'

Shalom Zecharia was the boy who played Saadia. On 6 June 1967, the second day of the Six-Day War he fell in the fight at the Hill of Evil Counsel, overlooking the city, one of the first battles in Jerusalem during the war. A war that led to the most profound change in Jerusalem's history and status in our lifetime. Nineteen calm years changed dramatically overnight to the volcanic Jerusalem we know today. A year later Beitar won a promotion to the top tier and both city and club started the modern age.

# 9

# The Seventh Day

*'There are decades where nothing happens;*
*and there are weeks where decades happen.'*

Vladimir Ilyich Lenin

ON THE façade of the Church of the Holy Sepulchre, on the right ledge above the square, a wooden ladder has stood for almost 200 years. It doesn't have any religious significance, but it's there every day, and when for some reason it isn't there, it's newsworthy.

One legend among many tells that the Immovable Ladder adorned the façade after 1838 following a violent clash between Greek Orthodox and Armenian priests in the holy church. At the height of the fighting the Greeks locked the Armenians inside their chapel. They had no other way of getting food but to open the window and, using the ladder, to drop a bucket from the ledge and bring up the supplies. The dispute was resolved but the ladder became part of the furniture, folklore and the status quo. An edict issued by the Ottoman Sultan in 1757 and reaffirmed in 1852 is an understanding among religious communities with respect to nine shared religious sites. The decree defines exactly which parts of the church belong to which group, a subject that has been the source of great controversy over the centuries and contributed to the Crimean War. And yes, the ladder is mentioned there.

One can mock the priests who have a fist fight at the church but actually, most of the time, the peace among the six different sections who live together in such close proximity is a kind of miracle. Not far from there, the Jews have their own disputes at the Western Wall between the orthodox, who have run the place since 1967, and group of progressive women who want to pray at the site in their own way. Every inch matters in this tiny piece of land.

Jerusalem is a place that changes slowly, unlike Tel Aviv and its trends. You can find your favourite restaurant 30 years after you had your first kube soup in Jerusalem. It will be served by the daughter of the man who served it to you the first time, but it will be the same soup. In Tel Aviv it's most likely that your favourite place has changed hands, name, type of food and has probably been demolished to make way for a posh glass tower.

In June 1967 Jerusalem saw the biggest change in hundreds of years during the brief period of the Six-Day War and the following weeks. That war is my earliest memory. It's not an uncommon story among Israelis for their first memory to be a war. I remember the adults filling up sand bags in Beersheba in preparation for Egyptian air raids that never came. In fact, the enemy aeroplanes never took off.

On the morning of 5 June 1967, the Israelis attacked and demolished the air forces of Egypt and Syria. The war that all sides were gearing up towards for months was practically won in one hour. On the ground the IDF had crushed the Arab armies and, in the meantime, Israel had sent a message to Hussein, King of Jordan, to stay out of it, but to no avail.

When Jordanian forces opened fire along the city line, the war had arrived in Jerusalem.

On the morning of 7 June, after three days of heavy fighting, the Old City was under Israeli control for the first time. 'Temple Mount is in our hands,' radioed Motta Gur, the commander of the paratrooper forces, and the blue-and-white flag was raised over the Dome of the Rock but was taken off after a short while. At the Western Wall the paratroopers stood for one of the most iconic photos in Israeli history. You could feel the history come into being in front of your eyes.

After six days of fighting Israel took over Jerusalem, the holy places in it, Hebron and Bethlehem and the entire West Bank. In the north, Israel conquered the Golan Heights from Syria and in the south the IDF defeated the Egyptian army and took over the Gaza Strip and the whole of the Sinai Peninsula all the way to the Suez Canal. Israel found itself with a mini empire.

The euphoria on the seventh day was intoxicating. From the brink of annihilation, so people thought, to glorious victory and a return to the birthplaces of the nation. A whole neighbourhood in the Old City was razed to the ground in a matter of days to make way for a spacious national plaza in front of the Western Wall. Above it the control over Temple Mount was handed back to the Waqf (the Islamic religious trust that controls and manages Temple Mount) and Jordan.

In the midst of the celebration, on Friday, 22 September 1967, two paid adverts were published in the weekend papers. One was by the Front for the Complete Eretz Yishrael. Fifty-seven highly influential intellectuals, politicians, authors and poets, from left and right, were the signatories to a stern call to hold the new territories:

The whole of Eretz Yishrael is now in the hands of the Jewish people. And in the same way that we are not permitted to give up the State of Israel, we are under order to hold what we got from her: Eretz Yishrael. We must be loyal to the wholeness of our land, the past of the Jewish people and its future. No government in Israel can forfeit this wholeness.

On the same day 12 unknown people published another, much shorter, advert:

Our right to defend from extermination doesn't
   give us the right to oppress others
Occupation leads to foreign rule
Foreign rule leads to resistance
Resistance leads to oppression
Oppression leads to terror and counter terror
The victims of terror are usually innocent civilians
Holding the occupied territories will make us into
   a people of murders and murdered
Will shell get out the occupied territories now

This debate came to rule Israeli politics and foreign affairs for generations. The old border disappeared. The walls, warning signs and wires were cleared, and Israelis flocked to the Old City and the holy places in bewilderment and shopping frenzies.

A year later, Beitar arrived. The team was promoted to the first division after a season that stretched over two years and 60 matches. The Israeli FA bizarrely tried to fight corruption, violence and a rise in salaries and decided to have the two seasons between 1966 and 1968 played as one.

Then came the pre-war tension, the war and another three months' delay.

It meant another season in the second tier for Beitar but promotion was never in doubt. They had 104 points out of 120 with a goal difference of 161 to 36, without a defeat in the last 32 matches, and 19 consecutive wins. Under the leadership of Leizy and Ruvi Rivlin, sons of a Sephardi elite family who ran the team, Beitar returned to the National League where they would play the might of Maccabi and Hapoel Tel Aviv, Hapoel Petah Tikvah and contest the local derby once again.

The YMCA was full, and although it wasn't the domination of the early days among the local fans, the team gained more and more fans who fell for the passion of Beitar. Ehud Olmert, son of a Herut MP from Benyamina, was one of them. He told me:

> I was a Hapoel Petah Tikvah fan. I adored Nahum
> Stelmach, the team forward, and even wrote him
> a letter. I moved to Jerusalem in my twenties to
> study law at the Hebrew University and then I
> became a Beitar fan. It fitted my ideology and the
> passion of the crowd took me over.

I heard a similar story from Ze'ev, a colleague in the army, a man with a Mapai background and left-wing views: 'Yes, it was unusual at the time but when I saw my first game at YMCA, it was different. I was converted. The excitement, the fanaticism, you couldn't stay indifferent.'

The first season back at the top tier started with a resounding 4-1 away defeat to Maccabi Tel Aviv and more was to follow. The team struggled, the manager was replaced and Beitar lost in the first derby 2-0 to Hapoel and drew

0-0 in the second meeting. The team survived by the skin of their teeth only on the last day of the season, which was remembered primarily for the game against Hapoel Tel Aviv at Bloomfield Stadium in Jaffa.

Over the years Beitar fans had gained the reputation of being the most violent in Israel. The official club book is teeming with press cuttings and light-hearted notes about matches that were abandoned due to a 'rain of stones' and other 'shows of strength' like the one in the 1962/63 season. Beitar, when still in the second league, hosted Hapoel Holon. After a 1-1 draw the fans stormed the pitch and chased the referee, only to hit Beitar's keeper by mistake and break one of his teeth. Points were deducted, matches had to be played away from the YMCA, but nothing changed. It became part of Beitar.

The two most shocking riots occurred away from Jerusalem. On 14 June 1969 Beitar played at Bloomfield Stadium in Jaffa, Israel's best ground. Bloomfield, a no-frills stadium with 22,000 seats and steep cement stands that hugged the green pitch, was a pleasure for players and fans. It was home for most Tel Aviv teams and usually two successive matches were played there each Saturday, the nostalgic double bill. However, the owner of the stadium was Hapoel Tel Aviv and the Histadrut, with all the emotional baggage that comes with it.

Beitar, still in a relegation battle, arrived with masses of fans for an unforgettable event. Ahron Lahav, of *Davar*, the Mapai newspaper, wrote: 'A tornado storm hit Bloomfield Stadium yesterday. Hundreds of Beitar fans stormed the high fenced pitch. They tore, broke and set alight the goal posts for they refused to accept the defeat of their team that may face relegation.'

Hapoel Tel Aviv had on their side the mercurial Ronny Calderon, a maverick of a winger who caught the eye of

# ON THE BORDER

Rinus Michels of Ajax and was invited for trials at the great Amsterdam club, but then led a life of self-destruction and crime. A moment before it all imploded, he made Beitar a laughing stock and scored in the last seven minutes with a rocket, according to Lahav, leaving his marker, Shimon Charnucha, looking puzzled and hopeless.

Hapoel had tried to save some money and didn't hire adequate police protection required for such a match and, according to Lahav, 'It cost them dearly.' Twelve minutes into the second half, Hapoel scored the second goal and hell broke loose. Lahav wrote in archaic style:

> Some Beitar fans didn't approve the joy of some Hapoel fans at the VIP stand, and they went into action. The high fence between the stand-dwellers and the pitch gave way and dozens of crazed fans charged in desire to lynch the referee, the new Oleh, Issyk Cohen. They shouted at him, 'You are a dirty Jew; pity you didn't stay in Siberia.' At the same time other fans on the terraces were busy launching every available object like bottles full of juice, sandwiches, plenty of fruits and vegetables towards whoever they suspected of being a Hapoel fan. The stadium in Jaffa soon looked like a food market.

The match was held up for 30 minutes while police were rushed to the stadium to allow the match to resume. Beitar scored a goal but ten minutes from the end Hapoel scored their third. It led to one of Israeli football's greatest myths. Lahav reported:

> The goal ignited the mad community in gate number 13 but this time they were joined by

132

new recruits who sat behind Beitar's goal. The deranged fans threw big rubbish bins towards the goal and some of them skipped above the fence into the pitch in order to hit one of the stewards who threw the bins back to the stands.

The mayhem didn't stop Calderon, who charged towards the goal. According to Lahav, Calderon was about to score, only for some fans to clear the ball from the goal line. Legend has it, but alas there's no footage, that Calderon was en route to the goal when an armed soldier stood in front of him. The winger nutmegged him, scored and kept running into the players' tunnel without looking back.

The soldier was Gideon Piro, a prominent member of Herut's Jerusalem branch, a 6ft 3in unit of a man. It's most likely that Piro just kicked away the ball in a goal line clearance without any nutmegging, sadly. When Piro was 12, he was placed, armed with a knife, behind a goal in a key game in Raanana. Had Beitar gone behind, he had the task of puncturing the ball so the match wouldn't reach its conclusion and Beitar would avoid relegation. This was written in the *Israel Hayom* newspaper after Piro's death in 2009. The match ended in a 2-2 draw with two balls stabbed.

Back at the Hapoel match, play was resumed with a drop kick that led to a brutal foul by Charnucha, a violent thug of a centre-back, and that was that. The referee and Hapoel players fled for dear life into the dressing room and Beitar fans had to make do with the wooden goalposts and a bonfire on the pitch. Piro was charged with violent conduct but escaped justice after Cohen, the poor referee, testified that he had saved him that day. Benny Piro, Gideon's brother, told *Israel Hayom* that the truth was different: 'Don't forget that I was a football referee myself. Cohen did me a favour and saved my brother.'

Beitar's image was cemented on 6 April 1974 during the second leg of the State Cup semi-final against Hapoel Petah Tikvah, the old powerhouse of Israeli football during the early 1960s, winners of five titles in succession. In the first match at the YMCA, the visitors won 1-0. But the match in Petah Tikvah, near Tel Aviv and in a small stadium engulfed by lush orange orchards, is still considered to be the most violent in Israeli football history.

Benny Tavory, then a soldier and the son of a local Mapai politician who four years later became the mayor, remembers the game vividly: 'The atmosphere was mental from the start. Not a spare seat left. I have an Ashkenazi look, and very fast they could tell I'm not a Beitar fan. They were hard core Yerushalmim, and the Petah Tikvah fans were nerds, concert-goer kind of fans.'

Petah Tikvah scored first in the first half but Beitar, who played with ten men from the 33rd minute, scored in the second half and the match went to extra time. Petah Tikvah scored a second goal in the 110th minute and the mayhem started as Beitar fans led by Piro rushed to the pitch.

Tavory recalls:

> By then it was on the verge of explosion. Fights broke out in the stands and Hapoel's doctor, who knew that I'm an army medic, called me to the pitch to help. I just needed to calm down some people, no broken limbs, yet. I went to the dressing room under the main stand and everyone was shaking. Outside, on the bench I saw a friend, Merik Efron, son of a rich revisionist family whose father was a football lineman, sat there and could

hardly breathe after getting beaten up. We took him to the dressing room, but we could have done it only with the help of a burly Beitar fan who shielded us.

Six minutes later Hapoel scored their third goal and the competition was over in every sense of the word. The fences came down and the fans invaded the pitch looking for Hapoel supporters and players. The hunt was on. Eitan Amit reported in *Yedioth Ahronoth*:

> I stood at the Hapoel Petah Tikvah stadium last night and felt sick. I was with the local police commander who had a forehead bleeding after a glass bottle hit him. He was standing there with a handful of policemen trying in vain to stop a crowd of bloodthirsty madmen that charged onto the pitch in order to lynch anybody who stood in its way. I saw one of his men with a hand red with blood from a deep gash caused by a knife.
>
> I saw Yitzhak Visoker, the Petah Tikvah goalkeeper, with horror on his face. He stood in the middle of the pitch and Beitar fans equipped with glass bottles, wooden planks and metal pipes storming towards him. He ran, swinging his long arms to make way. He knocked down one 'cannibal' who tried to hit him with a chair. And another lunatic who raised a bench in front of him, before disappearing into the dressing room while getting hit in the back of the neck by a brick.

Three Hapoel players ran behind one of the goals, climbed the perimeter wall and hid in the orchards for hours until it was safe to come out. According to some reports, a soldier with an uzi machine gun shot a burst of bullets towards them and missed. Another soldier was confronting Gaby Rosendoren, one of the Hapoel players, who said, 'I heard a whistle and I saw a frenzied mob running towards me. I tried to run but they surrounded me quickly. A soldier with an Uzi told me, "We are going to kill you," and then they started kicking me and hit me with a metal object.'

Like in Bloomfield, the goals were set on fire and the stadium was vandalised. In the dressing room the condition of Merik Efron was getting worse and the doctor asked to rush him to the nearby hospital. 'I went out and looked for that big Beitar fan,' says Tavory. 'I found him as he led us to the ambulance parting the sea of rioters like Moses at the Red Sea.'

Four Hapoel players needed hospital treatment after being hit by Beitar fans and players. Eliezer Rivlin, the Beitar chairman, wasn't impressed:

> Since the game didn't reach its conclusion, we will demand that will be replayed. The referee is not telling the truth when he is saying that Beitar fans stormed the pitch. It was the Petah Tikvah fans who wanted to celebrate their goal and then others. Had Petah Tikvah put a serious police force in charge, they would have prevented their fans getting on the pitch. That is why I'm declaring that what Hapoel Petah Tikvah have done to Beitar Jerusalem is worse than a lynch. I'm proud to be Beitar chairman!

For his finale Rivlin added sobbing and tears, to no avail.

The Israeli FA ruled that Beitar should play half a season away from Jerusalem and Beitar became identified with senseless violence. Traumatised, Hapoel Petah Tikvah lost the final to Hapoel Haifa. Both teams came out of the match in tooth and an eye, to quote the Bible.

After their difficult first season, Beitar settled into the National League. The team played in the tiny YMCA, on a poor pitch. In the winter it was no more than a mud bath and not known for great football. In Katamon, Hapoel, under the leadership of Eli Ben Rimoz, a long-haired maverick striker, had their best period, winning the State Cup in 1973 after beating champions Hakoah Maccabi Ramat Gan, the proud carrier of the great Hakoah Vienna name.

In 1970 Israel played for the first and only time in the World Cup finals, losing to Uruguay and drawing twice, against Sweden and finalists Italy. In a foggy YMCA, Beitar at last had had their first derby win in the top division. Ruvi Rivlin promised his players that if they could finish above Hapoel Jerusalem they would go to Mexico for the World Cup and, indeed, Beitar finished fifth, just above their local rivals. It was still a big thing then, before it became the normality.

* * *

Jerusalem saw tectonic changes of its own. With the whole of the West Bank under Israeli control, Israel had burning issues to address and the status of Jerusalem was the most urgent. On 11 June 1967 the government decided to unite both parts of the city and to annex Jordanian Jerusalem, which was just six square kilometres, of which the Old City was one square kilometre. The new annexed territory was 70 square kilometres in total and included many Arab neighbourhoods and villages.

Most of the land was empty and a building frenzy was soon to follow. New big neighbourhoods were built, usually as an Israeli reaction to American or UN pressure or as a punishment to the Palestinians. In *Urshalim*, his indispensable book about modern Jerusalem, Nir Hasson wrote:

> The Jewish neighbourhoods were built as huge architected complexes, not in an organic way but as a dictated policy from above. The new neighbourhoods were laid on the empty hills as one unit. Allegedly there was a consideration in the topography and the heritage of Palestinian architecture; arches and dome elements were incorporated, for example, but the size of the neighbourhoods made those elements no more than an orientalist grotesque. The only rule that was kept rigorously was the one inherited from the British Mandate – the covering of building, in stone. Alas the stone cutting technique has evolved since then and instead of thick stones with yellow-reddish hue that lay spots of shadows on the walls, these were thinly sawn bright white stones. This bright whiteness has become characteristic of the new districts.

The most important decision by the government was regarding the status of 70,000 Mukadisin, the Palestinian Jerusalemites. Unlike the territory, they were just partly annexed. They're residents of Israel but not citizens. They do have a blue Israeli ID card, which makes life easier, and they can vote for the Jerusalem municipality but not the Knesset, while the Palestinians of the West Bank and Gaza Strip were under strict military rule with very few rights. Occupation, in another word.

Palestinians living in Israel since 1948 are full citizens (although until 1966 they lived under military rule), they can vote and get elected for the Knesset and are considered equal by law. While they call themselves 1948 Arabs (1967 Arabs are in the occupied territories), I'll use the common term 'Israeli-Arabs' for two reasons: I think it conveys the special situation better and because the book is written through the lens of an Israeli writer.

The first three years after the war saw violent and non-violent resistance. Seventy-nine terror attacks took place in the city, in which 17 people lost their lives. It sadly became part of living there. Still, those were the days when Israelis flocked to the markets, restaurants and the sites of East Jerusalem. During the summer nights, the old no-man's land between Musrara and Damascus Gate turned into a joint space where Israelis and Palestinians had khaflas – big parties and get-togethers – ate sweet watermelon with white salty cheese, listened to live music and watched kung fu movies.

'It was a culture of cooperation between Jews and Arabs,' says Reuven Abergil of the Black Panthers. 'Between the melons we had the best Arab and Jewish musicians. It was a shared experience but the local municipality and the police didn't like it and shut the huts down.'

Jerusalem grew as the capital of confident Israel and now also the centre for West Bank Palestinians. Hapoel had a purple patch but it was soon about to change. Beitar, the city, the Likud and the Mizrahim was about to take centre stage.

* * *

One of the most mysterious stories of Jerusalem, writes Haim Be'er in his book *This is the Place*, is the legend of the sitting place of the Messiah. Be'er tells the legend of how the

Messiah sits among the poor at the city gate, waiting for the day his service is needed.

Yosef Rivlin, one of the pioneers of Jewish settlements outside the Old City in the 19th century and ancestor of Ruvi and Leizy, claims that he found the place – a holy hill deep in today's Haredi region. It's in a small park near the Histadrut building in Straus Street where Beitar fans celebrated derby victories. The place is known as Nabi Ukasha and you can find a small mosque and imperious old burial place from the 12th century there. Rabbis who knew the secret ways of the Kabbalah used to meet there and pray for the Messiah to come. In 1948, during the height of the siege, they gathered there for a special prayer that led to significant improvement, so goes the legend.

Some Muslims believe that Moses, Jesus and Muhammad are all buried there, a tradition that gave its name to the nearby Nevi'im Street (Prophets Street). Others think that it's the resting place of three fighters from the Saladin army, who fought in the military campaign against the Crusaders in the 12th century. Two olive trees, 800 years old, provide some shelter from the sun during the summer and some much-needed tranquillity. The Islamic buildings have been targeted throughout the years when things have gone badly in the city and country.

Beitar's messiah, a bona fide one, arrived in the early 1970s. His name was Uri Malmilian, a boy from Mamila, a valley in the shadow to the west of the Old City. Before his coming, Beitar wasn't even the first club in the city. When he left the club, it was one of the most popular in the land. For all the bad boy/right-wing appeal, Beitar needed a star player to break through.

Malmilian was born on 24 April 1957 in Jerusalem to a religious family of Kurdish Olim from Iran. He was the fifth child of nine, all living in a four-room flat in Mamila, a crowded area between the city centre and the Jaffa Gate. The neighbourhood, with all its alleys, steps, arches and charm, was demolished in the 1970s, in a typical myopic move by Teddy Kollek, the powerful mayor and builder of new Jerusalem between 1965 and 1993, and the Israeli government.

Today you can find a thriving shopping district there that retained some of the old buildings (actually reconstructed but better than nothing) and a ghastly residential project for the ultra-rich of the world. No more than vulgar orientalism for a limited number of very rich people. The synthetic collage of the ghost quarter, populated for a limited time a year, fancy hotels and huge multi-storey car park at one of the world's most meaningful historical sites, is just one of the crimes committed against Jerusalem since 1967.

Until the summer of 1967, Malmilian played under the watchful eyes of the Jordanian Legion soldiers. In his autobiography *The Boy from Mamila* (written with Ely Azur) he describes one afternoon:

> A whistle of a bullet tore the air followed by a burst of shots from an automatic weapon. I saw people running everywhere looking for a place to hide. I was scared and terrified and I stood by a wall like the adults. When the fire stopped, I saw people running toward a border wall. In the background I could hear a child crying his heart out. A mother said, 'It's Danny, the neighbours' boy. The sniper has injured him.' He was pale and blood was pouring from his leg. He screamed in pain. I couldn't watch it anymore. I ran to my mother and asked, 'Why did they shoot him? Why

can't people live in peace?' My mother stroked my hair and said, 'There are bad people in the world. Watch out for yourself. Don't play by the walls.'

Malmilian grew up in poverty, 12 people under the same roof with all the kids cramming into one room at night. 'The summers were hard but the winters were unbearable,' he wrote. 'We didn't have any means of heating and the winters in Jerusalem were hell. Only later our father managed to buy an oil heater and we watched every drop of oil.'

Although the conditions were harsh, Malmilian grew up in a loving, harmonious home, he said repeatedly. He left school after the eighth grade but the work ethic he received at home helped his long career. 'It was hard but I will always look at it as a beautiful period,' he wrote.

When things heated up around the border, he was told not to play on the street and instead he went to the YMCA up the hill, gave a hand to the kit man and practised for hours. One day a Beitar children's coach named Michel Portal came to look out for talent in Mamila after hearing rumours of a special talent. Malmilian, even then, stayed cool: 'I knew he came to see me but I wasn't nervous. I didn't care where I played.'

Portal was impressed and Malmilian was invited to join the children's team. It all happened just after the war, an event he remembers as a tense period in which he 'didn't kick a ball for six days'.

> YMCA was my second home so I didn't have a problem fitting in. There were days when I took the ball and went there; found a target and aimed at it for hours. Sometimes the goal post was a tree or even just a rock. I kept shooting at it again and

again from different angles and learned how to be accurate. When the YMCA was closed, I jumped over the fence and had a private place to train. Nobody disturbed me.

The history of Israeli football almost changed when young Malmilian later had second thoughts. Like Raúl of Real Madrid and Franz Beckenbauer of Bayern Munich, two legends after fate took them to their clubs, it could have been very different for Malmilian. Raúl was a youth player at Atlético Madrid but moved to Real when Jesús Gil, the all-too-colourful owner of Atleti, decided to shut the youth academy down to save money. Beckenbauer was dreaming of joining Munich 1860 but during a friendly match in 1958 playing for his amateur club against 1860 had to endure physical treatment and even a slap from an opposition player named Gerhard König. Beckenbauer decided to join Bayern instead and transformed the history of the Bavarian giants.

Under the impression of Hapoel's star player Ben Rimoz and the neat football played at Katamon, Malmilian crossed the city lines. A youth coach at Hapoel saw the potential and persuaded Uri to join them but he couldn't foresee the local reaction. He said to Sport 5's *Story of a Champion*:

> When I was 13 years old, I trained at Hapoel for a month. Mamila by then was all Beitar and there was graffiti on the wall: 'traitor'; 'son of a whore'. I was boycotted. Nobody played with me. Nobody spoke with me. I couldn't stand it and returned to Beitar. He who is above deserves a big thanks.

Malmilian was fast-tracked through the youth system and was even asked to play before his 16th birthday, against all regulations. The heads of Beitar applied pressure on the young boy and his father to forge an ID card but both of them, men of truth and values, refused. He made his debut aged 16 and the manager who handed it to him was Emmanuel Schaffer, a key figure in the story of Israeli football.

'I know I'm mad,' Schaffer said to a friend who had asked him why he curses so much. 'You must understand that anybody who was there and survived came back mad. Those who think they are normal, they are mad. We all became mad. Nobody came back from there sane.'

'There' was the Holocaust, the years when Schaffer, a Jewish German-Polish teenager, fled and suffered years of hunger, loneliness and terrible loss. It was a burden he had to carry for the rest of his life, and fame and success didn't make it any lighter.

But Schaffer was a survivor by nature. He managed to see the end of the war and rebuild his life. 'Football was his life,' said Eran Schaffer, his son, in the family house in the affluent Ramat HaSharon, to the north of Tel Aviv. 'Football helped him survive during the war, football helped him back to life and gave him fortune and fame.'

In the summer of 1970, football gave Schaffer his place in history when he led Israel as manager to their first and only appearance in the World Cup finals. It was his proudest moment when Israel played against world powers Italy and Sweden. In many ways he owed that success to the nation that had hurt him so deeply. Football and Germany were the two factors that shaped Schaffer's life and his personality.

Together with his family he moved around Europe between the wars and, as anti-Semitic persecution grew following Hitler and the Nazism rise, the family contemplated emigrating to Palestine. Instead, Schaffer's father chose in 1937 to move to the village of Porohy in Poland, where he had relatives. When the war broke out, the region where the Schaffers were living was under Soviet rule according to the Ribbentrop-Molotov pact that divided Poland between Germany and the USSR. For a time they were safe and Emmanuel was sent to school in Drohobycz, where he lived with his uncle and aunt. There he began playing football with the Jewish club of Beitar Drohobycz.

In June 1941 the war came to the USSR when Germany attacked its former ally. German forces stormed through eastern Europe and millions of Jews fell under Nazi rule, their lives placed in constant danger. Schaffer, who heard rumours of the hardship of Jews in Nazi territories, fled to the east, while his family stayed behind.

'Eddy [his nickname in Germany] escapes behind Russian lines by pure good fortune,' explained an article in *Anstoss*, the magazine of the artistic and cultural programme for the 2006 World Cup. 'For many months he suffered from typhoid, diphtheria and deficiency diseases before finally overcoming them.'

Schaffer, still a teenager, reached Baku in Azerbaijan and later wandered further east to Alma Ata (Almaty) in Kazakhstan, where he worked in a shoe factory producing boots for the armed forces. He escaped the Nazis and the fate of his people but life was extremely hard for the young boy in Stalin's country. There were nights when he had to share a bench in a park with his cousin whom he met there. Many times he went to sleep without having a proper meal and later in life, when he became a successful manager, he didn't forget those days. 'I must have a loaf of bread every day,' he told his players, 'just so that if I die tonight, I won't die a hungry man.'

During those days his personality was forged. His work at the factory hardly made ends meet, but his luck was about to change. One day he saw a woman carrying a bag of fresh pirozhki – Russian pasties. 'The smell must have tortured him,' said his son Eran. He followed the woman and offered her a hand carrying the sack. She agreed, and when they reached her destination, she gave him a pirozhki. The fresh, warm pasty was a rare treat but the young Schaffer was too resourceful to waste it. Despite the huge temptation to devour it, he managed not to eat the pirozhki and instead sold it in the local market for a greater quantity of plain bread. From that day on he waited for the woman every day and helped her in return for one pasty. 'Even early on in life he knew how to survive and how to do business,' said Shoshanna, his widow.

Life became easier when he joined Dynamo Alma Ata, the NKVD (secret police) team and it was then that he received the news from his aunt that his parents and three sisters had been killed in the Holocaust. When the German army advanced east, the Jews in the village were rounded up and sent to the Stanisławów ghetto (today, Ivano-Frankovsk in Ukraine). There they lived in horrendous conditions until they were murdered by German and Ukrainian collaborators in the Jewish cemetery. Tens of thousands of bodies were thrown into mass unmarked graves.

The shock and grief followed him to his final days but Schaffer had found a new purpose in life. With a friend, Zvi Zimmet, he returned to Bielawa in Poland, where his aunt lived, having survived the war thanks to a Polish woman who hid her. There he founded a Jewish football team – ZKS [Jewish Sport Club] Bielawa.

While working as a salesman in a clothes shop, Schaffer honed his skills acting as organiser, coach and player. The team won promotion to the second division of the Polish league but that wasn't the only achievement of ZKS, which was much more than a football club.

According to Zimmet:

> The work we did at the club helped people who had their heads down. It helped them a lot. It was also a social club with dancing and singing in Hebrew and Yiddish, songs that people remembered from before the war. It uplifted the morale and once the gentiles saw a different kind of Jew it changed their perception.

In 1950 the club activity was terminated by Soviet orders and Schaffer, having been called up to the Polish army, decided to emigrate to Israel. With his football connections he got a job in Haifa port and a place on the wing at Hapoel Hanamal Haifa [Haifa Port Worker]. Later he married Shoshanna, a Holocaust survivor from the same Polish village, although they met for the first time in Israel, and moved to Hapoel Kfar Saba. He had a decent career, winning eight international caps before an injury forced him to retire in 1957. The next year he forged a friendship and understanding that changed his life, in West Germany of all places. To go and live in Germany in 1958 was a bold move for an Israeli. 'For him it was the best school in the world,' explained Eran Schaffer. 'He thought that German football after the 1954 World Cup was the best in the world and as a perfectionist he had to go there. He made the distinction between football and the past.'

He still had some difficulties according to his son:

> He once went out with a friend, journalist Yehoshua Sagi, to a German restaurant, and there

was a big queue. He said to Sagi, 'Let's go out of here. I've been made to queue for food by the Germans before; I'm not doing it again.' He found it hard with old Germans – the thought of where they'd been during the war was always at the back of his mind but that was the place to learn football. Weisweiler was the Alex Ferguson of the time. He turned Borussia Mönchengladbach into a European force.

'It always surprised me,' said Amatzia Levkovic, his assistant at the 1970 World Cup in Mexico, 'but he spoke German and adored their football. It was the best school and it was his homeland.'

Germany wasn't just the Fatherland: it was the land that rejected him in the most brutal way and categorised him as subhuman. For Schaffer to be greeted back there was a sign of acceptance and even revenge. His life mission was to present a different image of Jews, and football was his weapon.

He became Weisweiler's friend and was chosen by the rest of the year at the school as one of the two best students; the other was the great Dutchman Rinus Michels. Schaffer had several offers to work in Germany but his family was the priority. Shoshamma said:

He went to visit Recklinghausen where he grew up, and wrote to me that a woman from the Jewish community said that he could live and work in wonderful conditions there. I told him that I would not let my son grow up in Germany and I wouldn't have a German nanny for my son, no matter how much money he was offered.

148

When Schaffer returned to Israel, he rose from coaching the youth team of Hapoel Kfar Saba to become manager of the Israel national youth team in 1964 and, on the eve of the 1968 Mexico Olympic Games, he was promoted to lead the senior team. It was the start of the best two years of Schaffer's career, and the best two years in Israeli football.

Israel began the Olympics with a 5-3 win over Ghana and secured a place in the second round after a 3-1 victory against El Salvador. A 2-0 defeat to the eventual winners Hungary in the third match led to a quarter-final against Bulgaria. Georgi Christakiev scored for Bulgaria after four minutes but Israel levelled through Jehoshua Faigenbaum in the final seconds. Extra time brought no further goals so the match went to the drawing of lots. Bulgaria won. 'I'm sure the two pieces of paper both had Bulgaria written on them,' said Mordechay (Motalle) Spiegler, the Israeli captain, half joking. As a result, Israel missed the chance to win their first Olympic medal.

The match had major implications for Israeli sport and world football. Israel had to wait 24 years to win their first Olympic medals, claiming a silver and a bronze, both in judo, in Barcelona in 1992, while the heads of the Israeli FA, in their frustration, tried to come up with a better and fairer way to decide the outcome of drawn matches. In a letter to FIFA, they suggested a penalty shoot-out.

Schaffer brought his German values, science, systems and demands to the national team and the result was a culture shock. 'We will have three training sessions,' he said to his players in one of their first meetings. 'Three sessions a week?' complained one of the players. 'Even in our team we don't do that.'

'No!' shouted Schaffer. 'Three times a day.'

In broken Hebrew, a language that he never fully mastered, he set rules that stunned the players. Food and fitness were key issues. He controlled their diets, threw away cakes and cream from the tables and checked the players' weights regularly. The stars of the team were outraged but he had history on his side.

Israel, in the years after the Six-Day War of 1967, was a bastion of self-belief and the army was a model for Schaffer as he looked to install the mentality of an elite unit. When Israel reached the Mexico World Cup of 1970 (through easy Oceanian qualifying), Schaffer successfully demanded long periods to work with the players. In the year before the World Cup he had 170 days of training with them, far more than their clubs had.

He galvanised the team with a speech about what it meant to play under the Israeli flag. 'We have the best army in the world,' he said. 'We have the best engineers in the world. There is no reason why we won't have great footballers too. They have two legs as we do, but we have better brains.' One player even volunteered for reserve service on the deadly shores of the Suez Canal when he got back from Mexico.

In Mexico, Schaffer told David Lacey of *The Guardian*, 'Whatever the results, our aim is to prove to the world that what we have achieved in our home with the army we can achieve on the football field.'

His personality also brought crisis after crisis to the team. He was a perfectionist, a demanding man prone to flying into a rage at the slightest provocation. His poor Hebrew didn't help and he used his assistants and some of the players to ease tensions after those eruptions. 'They were all my children,' he said in later life, trying to defend his outbursts. 'We are a team of amateurs,' he told Lacey, 'and that means that I have to be tough. There is no other way. Not all of my players love it but that's the way it is. I would rather be a good coach and a tough guy than a bad coach and a good guy.'

The language barrier and the strict discipline led to some misunderstandings that found their way into Israeli folklore. 'I want to see you tomorrow at half eight,' he said, translating from German, and so meaning 7.30am. One player was up and booted by 4am. The players he took to the World Cup weren't the best in Israel but the ones he could work with and whom he deemed dedicated enough for the mission. The sensitive, lazy and unfit were left out. 'He picked the most reliable rather than necessarily the best players,' the goalkeeper Yitzhak Visoker told the Israeli journalist Uri Misgav. 'He saw us as his soldiers and he wanted only those he could count on. What was great about us was that we completely agreed with his German approach.'

That meant man-to-man marking, attacking full-backs and operating as a unit with a workrate never previously seen in Israeli football. Only two players had creative licence: playmaker Gyora Spiegel and Russia-born winger Motalle Spiegler. Spiegel, a member of a football dynasty, was wonderfully talented but was also slow and not keen on running up mountains, and was the hardest player to fit into Schaffer's spartan style. Spiegel told Misgav:

I found the fitness sessions hard not just because of the difficulty but also because nobody bothered to explain why it was so important. I rebelled and had lots of discussions with Schaffer and it wasn't pleasant. I really struggled with the long-distance runs. I was way behind and didn't make a real effort to catch up with the rest. I asked him to tell me why it was so important but he didn't like it because it would have broken the distance between us. In the end he just used to say, 'Shut up and do as you're told.'

Those were the years when the relationship between Schaffer and his old mentor, Weisweiler, became closer. Borussia Mönchengladbach took their winter breaks in Israel and, in February 1970, played against Schaffer's Israel. At half-time Borussia, inspired by Günter Netzer, led 3-0. 'Eddy,' asked Weisweiler, 'shall we keep on playing like this or should we drop down a gear?'

'I told him to keep on playing like this,' said Schaffer. 'I wanted the players to know what they were up against in Mexico.'

Drawn in the same group as Uruguay, Sweden and Italy, Schaffer feared a series of heavy defeats. He brought a lieutenant-colonel from the Israeli army to work on fitness and took the team to the heights of Ethiopia, Switzerland and Colorado in preparation for playing at altitude in Mexico. Alamosa in Colorado was, according to David Primo, a tough defender, 'a satanic hell hole, a shitty miners' town up in the mountains'.

Amid the turmoil, players and coach found a way to work together. Spiegel said:

> We heard him but did things our way. On the pitch we played as we thought we should do and usually it worked. Motalle and I understood that in football you need moments of spontaneous inspiration and unexpected moves. I used to leave myself some space, to keep some energy so that in the decisive moment I'd be sharp enough to score or give the crucial pass. Schaffer wasn't stupid: he

saw that and shut up. He gave a little, we gave a little and met each other halfway.

On 2 June 1970 Israel played their first World Cup match, in Puebla against Uruguay. Goals from Ildo Maneiro and Juan Mujica didn't tell the whole story. Uruguay were comfortable 2-0 winners and Spiegel and Spiegler didn't wait long to voice their opinions. 'We are strikers, not centre-halves,' they told Israeli TV and began crisis talks with Schaffer.

Israel looked like they didn't belong in the World Cup. 'Israel intended to rely on set pieces, corners and free kicks but against the tall Uruguay defence that availed them little,' reported *The Guardian*, but the newspaper also had positive words about the manager: 'Schaffer's fierce urgency of manner has been welcome effervescence in the pervading moroseness of the group. He has communicated a great deal of it to his players, many of them pitifully innocent of the simplest tactics of modern professional football.'

The team was on the back foot, timid and passive. It was their worst performance under Schaffer and he blamed the Israeli FA who hadn't let him travel and spy on the South Americans. 'I saw Sweden and Italy and I knew what was in store for us. I didn't see Uruguay, so they were unknown and that's why we lost,' he said.

Five days later in Toluca, Israel faced Sweden. It was one of the most violent and brutal matches in World Cup history, with both teams exchanging kicks, elbows and grapples. It suited the Israelis and, with their nine fighters and two artists, they took the game to Sweden. Tom Turesson scored in the 54th minute (from an offside position, claimed Schaffer) but two minutes later Spiegel found Spiegler, who equalised with a beautifully struck shot from 20 yards, Israel's first-

ever goal on the world stage. Back in Israel it was hailed as
a historic point won.

Against Italy, the European champions, Israel looked like
a different team. If initially the players couldn't believe they
were sharing the same tournament stage with Pelé, Moore
and Müller, and against Sweden they came to 'kick the hell
out of them' as one player commented, against the team of
Riva, Rivera, Mazzola and Faccheti, they came to play. 'We
played in a smart way,' said Spiegel. 'It wasn't just being back
in our box. We played slowly and held the ball. We made it
to the halfway line in 20 passes. They were used to a much
faster pace and it rattled them.'

Italy had two goals disallowed and hit the woodwork but
Spiegler also had a golden chance saved by Enrico Albertosi.
Physically, the Israeli amateurs held their ground in Toluca
and both teams were happy to hear the final whistle. After
Middlesbrough in 1966 and their shock defeat by North
Korea, the Azzurri didn't mind how they got out of the
group. Italy made it safely to the second round and later to
the final, while Israel left Mexico with two points and a
decent performance. In Israel, the results were received with
joy. A piece in the *Maariv* newspaper said:

> There is no doubt that yesterday we made history
> in world football. We took a point from a superb
> Italy and we finished our performance at the
> World Cup with an achievement we didn't dare to
> dream of: two draws against the lions of the group
> … You should have seen our players, all of them
> bar none. How they battled, how they fought and
> how they threw themselves to the ground when
> it was the last option. And for this I have two
> words: Well done!

'Everyone should play according to his abilities,' Schaffer said. 'When you play against a similar team you can attack like we did against Ghana [in 1968]. When you play against the mighty Italy you need to be tactically disciplined.'

The players were given a vacation in Acapulco, $100 as a bonus for their efforts, and Schaffer fulfilled his life's ambition to represent Israel on the world stage, but the euphoria was short-lived. A bitter dispute with the Israeli FA, who demanded that players be called to the national team on the basis of the political affiliation of their clubs, led to Schaffer's resignation a few months later.

The team of 1970 is used as a weapon in the ongoing squabble between Ashkenazim and Mizrahim. The most successful team was mainly Ashkenazi, despite the Mizrahi majority among players in the league. But when Schaffer worked with Malmilian he didn't care where his parents were born. He had done it like that for two reasons: the rare talent and his work ethic. The boy had them both in abundance. 'He brings colour to the game. Every team needs a talisman, a creative playmaker,' Schaffer said at the time.

Meanwhile, Beitar were still obsessed by the local rivalry. When Hapoel faced relegation and had a do-or-die match, Beitar fans filled Katamon in hope of *Schadenfreude*. Hapoel won and celebrated in front of the frustrated Beitar supporters. When Hapoel Jerusalem were about to finish second during another season, Beitar fans demanded that their players give away a match against Hapoel Tel Aviv so Tel Aviv would finish second instead of the nearby socialists. This time Jerusalem lost and their fans celebrated it. It was about to change very soon. Although the hate for Hapoel Jerusalem is still a key element, the hate for Hapoel Tel Aviv would become the dominant one. And besides, after 30 years, Beitar and Malmilian started to fight for trophies of their own.

## 10

# O Clouds Unfold

'MAHAPAKH,' ANNOUNCED Israeli state TV on 17 May 1977 at 10pm. The word had been invented a minute before by Haim Yavin, the channel anchor, when he received the exit poll result for the ninth Knesset. It means a revolution, upheaval, turnover, but in a smooth way. On that day Israel had its first democratic overthrow of the old guard. The Likud, a joint list comprised of Herut, the Liberal party and some smaller parties and headed by Menachem Begin, dethroned Labour after three decades in power. Begin became prime minister for the first time, a role he held until his resignation due to his mental state in October 1983. It was a much overdue change; Labour was riddled with corruption, a sense of entitlement and staleness. The anger following the failure of army and government in the Yom Kippur War in 1973, the Mizrahi issue and a string of corruption cases, as well as the forming of a new centre party that shifted votes from Labour, brought 29 years of socialist power to an end. The word can be used in any context but hamahapakh (the Mahapakh) means the first and most important one in 1977.

Football provided clear signs that a big change was in the making a couple of years earlier. In 2017 the state bestowed on Uri Malmilian the great honour of lighting a beacon at the Independence Day Ceremony on Mount Herzl, one of the nation's most revered occasions. Asked what his greatest moment was, Uri replied, '1977, hamahapakh.'

Malmilian wasn't the first to draw the line between Beitar Jerusalem's success and the Likud rising. It's hard to quantify its contribution but no one can dispute the symbolic connection.

Ronny Deon is a well-known Jerusalemite football journalist. He used to walk the lines at YMCA Teddy in a purple crushed-velvet suit, reporting for radio and the written press. Deon, a Hapoel Jerusalem fan and son of the former chairman of the club, had the unenviable task of reporting at the time about the changing of the guard. He wrote for Beitar's official book about the 1970s and '80s. Always the professional, he did the job with full integrity.

'You can divide the history of Beitar and football in Jerusalem in two: before and after Uri,' he says. 'He transformed the team from a bunch of warriors to one which plays attractive and technical football.'

You can pinpoint the moment it happened – one week in the autumn of 1973. Just before the start of the league, Beitar and Hapoel met for a two-legged cup tie. In the match at Katamon, Beitar won 2-1 and Malmilian scored the first goal, a curved shot from a tight angle. 'The fans actually carried me on their shoulders all the way from Katamon to YMCA,' he recalled later. 'It was an eruption of joy. We thought we would get thrashed but it turned out to be a turning point.' In the return, 16-year-old Malmilian ran the show and Beitar won 1-0.

Only days later, on 6 October and during Yom Kippur, the armies of Egypt and Syria attacked Israel. The post-Six-Day War hubris gave way to shock, grief and anger after 2,656 soldiers fell in the war Israel wasn't prepared for. The six years' euphoria changed to bereavement and self-doubt that never disappeared from the Israeli psyche. When football was resumed, Beitar beat the much-depleted Hapoel side 5-1 in the league. 'Those three games changed football in Jerusalem. Beitar was from now on the front foot,' says Deon.

It wasn't so straightforward though. In 1975 Beitar had to play most of their home matches away from Jerusalem as a punishment for the Petah Tikvah riots. Without a home and income, the club struggled and the team was involved in a relegation dogfight. Somehow Beitar made it to their first cup final and, in front of a rare appearance by Begin, lost 3-1 to Hapoel Kfar Saba. Worse was to follow as the team lost the crucial do-or-die match against Hapoel Tel Aviv at YMCA. The team was relegated back to the second division and players were afraid to leave their homes, says Deon.

But then the Knesset intervened. Two junior Knesset members, the late Yossi Sarid of Labour and Likud's Ehud Olmert, both heads of the Sport Committee, asked the FA to freeze the relegation due to corruption and suspicious results. 'We recommended to freeze it because we found unacceptable events and numerous cases of threats and thrown matches,' says Olmert. 'Yossi wasn't attached to Beitar like me but he was decent to understand that there was need for special actions. The FA ignored us at first but then 80 Knesset members signed a petition to stop the relegations and they accepted it.'

There's a lesson here – there are no small roles in life. Olmert and Sarid took a neglected committee and through commitment gained fame and publicity. Begin, however, wasn't impressed.

Olmert said:

One day I went to Begin and asked him to join us. He said, 'Ehud my son, I don't sign petitions.' 'But it is for Beitar, our team, our fans, they will be delighted and they are our voters,' I replied. He looked at me with puzzled eyes and said, 'Ehud, son, young man, let me teach you something. They will vote for us if I'll sign or not,' and indeed, they have voted for him in 77. I understood that you shouldn't build on the fickle nature of fans. I never did, I never tried to humour them and to look for their affections despite being the person that for many years helped to find the financial support that enabled the club to flourish.

It's a lesson that Arcady Gaydamak, the owner of Beitar, has learned the hard way two decades later – you can't count on fans to vote for you no matter how much money you've poured into the club. Sarid's doings were easily forgotten when he became the prominent voice of the left and Olmert himself won't be welcomed today at Teddy by La Familia, although for many decades he was adored there for good reason.

The 1975/76 season saw Malmilian's breakthrough. In the previous season he had suffered from injuries but now he was stronger, more mature, and with the help of a better team he could show off his talent. Alongside Danny Neuman, creative midfielder and son of famed Zvi Neuman of Hadassah Hospital and the Hebrew University, and Victor Levy, an engine of a player, Beitar transformed from the old hard-working fighters to a team easy on the eye.

Malmilian was a silky player with a rare touch and outstanding reading of the game. Yossi Gabay, seven years his junior, played with him later and is still in awe. He says:

Beitar was a grey team until then. The goals at YMCA were scrambled from inside the box and the team was helped by biased refereeing. It wasn't good football. And then came Uri and Danny, mainly Uri, and you could see a genius on the pitch.

For us he was like Messi today in world football. Something you didn't see before. I played and trained with him and at league games you saw his genius two or three times a match. During a training session we saw it 40 times because each ball went to him. He had eyes at the back and sides of his head. He read four steps ahead of the game. He had a touch, such a lovely feeling, in his foot. He used to put the ball behind the halfway line and ask the keeper where does he want him to send the ball. 'Left post', 'right post', 'middle or sides of the crossbar'. He hit the target seven out of ten times while a good player could do it once. He was a humble and introverted person which made him even more loveable. We used to go to small places like Or Yehuda or Beit Shemesh for training matches against lower-division teams and 3,000 people used to come to see Uri. Nobody promoted those games and still thousands came just to watch him.

During the 1975/76 season Beitar were just behind the champions Hapoel Be'er Sheva, my team. When we won our first title in 1975 it was a highly symbolic event. Although a Hapoel club, the team from the capital city of the south and the Negev desert was different from all previous winners. For the first time a club not from the Tel Aviv region (with the exception of Maccabi Netanya, which is halfway between Tel Aviv and Haifa) had won the league. Be'er Sheva was proper periphery, in the most deprived zone of Israel, a local team comprised mainly of Mizrahi players from a Likud-supporting town. Today it would be called a second-class Israel triumph; then it was huge joy and pride.

On matchday 21 the two teams met at a muddy YMCA and the team from the desert won 2-0. With a five-point lead (and two points per win) and 13 matches to go, it looked like another title for Be'er Sheva. But then they stopped. In the last 13 matches they won only three, one of them a generous 4-0 victory against Hapoel Jerusalem in their penultimate fixture. With one match to play, Beitar closed the gap to only two points before the last day of the season. A win in their final match for Beitar and defeat for Be'er Sheva would have led to Beitar becoming champions.

The odds looked slim. Be'er Sheva were at home to Maccabi Yafo, a small club from Jaffa. After a whole season without a loss at the dusty local stadium nobody thought that the minimum of a draw would be a problem. Beitar went to Bloomfield to play against Maccabi Tel Aviv, who could be relegated if they lost. To make things more complicated, both Beitar and Maccabi had one more match still to play: the cup final.

Rumours were doing the rounds that a deal between Be'er Sheva and Yafo would provide each with a point that would guarantee a title and survival. Another deal was league for a cup – Beitar would lose the league match in return for cup final victory. It wasn't baseless; Israeli football was known to have such deals and Beitar had numerous former Maccabi players, plus nobody thought Be'er Sheva would lose.

To make things kosher, the games weren't broadcast on radio and referees were imported from Europe but, in the end, the teams decided to play in the honourable way. Be'er Sheva's management told Yafo they didn't want to agree to a result, a move that caused anger. Mutzi Leon, Yafo's star player, said, 'Our morale went down but the adrenalin shot up. Who is Maccabi Yafo for them? A toilet! We said, fuck these fucking c**ts and their fucking mothers.'

'We thought we will walk it,' said Alon Ben Dor, of Be'er Sheva and the national team. 'But when we played, we felt heavy and lost our concentration.'

After 17 minutes Yafo won a penalty and converted it. I was there with my brothers and 16,000 fans. I don't think many people were worried yet but that was the only goal scored in the first half. On 51 minutes Be'er Sheva attacked the goal we were sitting behind. As the winger took the ball, we knew what was about to happen: a dive and a penalty. A penalty for Be'er Sheva was a sure thing. Eliyahu Ofer had scored all of his league penalties before. It was his last one and he was about to finish with an immaculate record from 12 yards. He kicked to the left; the keeper stood still. The ball hit the post and was cleared. The sky fell upon us.

According to the press, Be'er Sheva had 47 shots at goal and hit the post once. When the referee blew the final whistle, the silence was deafening. Nobody knew what had happened in the other match. It was 45 years ago but I still remember the roar that went up and shook the city when the news arrived via the police force at the stadium. Maccabi had won 2-0 with goals in the 44th and 82nd minutes. It was our second title in a row but little did we know that we would have to wait 40 years for the next one.

'After the game we just sat on the pitch and didn't leave. It was the first time in my career that the fans abused us. We lost because simply we didn't believe Be'er Sheva would lose,' said Malmilian to *Shem Hamisehak* magazine.

Nissim Bachar, the manager, sensed that the players couldn't face the stress in Jerusalem and decided that they should stay in a Tel Aviv hotel until Wednesday and the cup final at Ramat Gan Stadium. Jerusalem was on tenterhooks; it was no place to get ready for the big match.

\* \* \*

The social tension in Israel spilled into every walk of life including culture. The state and veterans Sabras (Israeli-born) tried to create a new Israel in complete contrast to the beaten and slain diaspora Jews, their cultures and languages. It was called a melting pot but was more like a pressure cooker, and because the model to Israel was American/British Western secular democracy, the Ashkenazim felt more comfortable with the new model.

With very few radio channels and just one truly god-awful state TV station starting to broadcast in the late 1960s, the mainstream was dominating and oppressive. It was Zionistic, puritan and stifling. Cinema was a main source of entertainment and a new local genre had developed in Israel – burekas films, named after Börek, the Balkan pastry, loved by most Israelis.

The term was probably coined by Boaz Davidson, the director of many successful burekas films as a play-on-words on the spaghetti western genre. 'The Italians have spaghetti – we have burekas,' he said.

It was, and still is, a very popular genre and Dr Avner Shavit, the brilliant film critic for *Walla*, explains, 'The burekas films take place within the context of social tension. The protagonist is a Mizrahi Jew, the antagonist is an Ashkenazi and, at the end, the Mizrahi always has the upper hand. The genre creates a fantasy – the Mizrahi public [half of the Jewish population] gets to see in film what was not accomplished in real life. This film constructs an imaginary social utopia – many of them end in a wedding.'

But what distinguishes burekas comedy as a genre from any other comedy? Dr Shavit says:

> It should feature these tropes: the backdrop is always some kind of social tension. The protagonist is a member of a de-privileged ethnic group and by the end he has the upper hand. He is streetwise and outsmarts the authority. The humour is vulgar and crass and the ending is usually a wedding or a family reunion.

Israeli music was also part of the indoctrination. The Beatles weren't allowed to perform in Israel for fear they would spoil the gentle souls of the youth. Until the 1970s it seemed that Elvis never happened, no guitar had ever been plugged in, there was no anger, angst, power or sex appeal. Israeli music was folkish, serious, boring, lame and didactic. It was called, and still is, without a hint of irony or embarrassment, 'the good old Israel songs'. Just into the 1970s you could hear some Israeli pop and some guitars and only in the 1990s did rock finally arrive in Israel.

It was also discriminatory. You couldn't hear the music that the Mizrahim liked on the radio and you had to buy cassette tapes in the markets where they had been sold in huge numbers. The Mizrahi public had their own musical heroes, although the radio stations refused to play them. They emerged in clubs and were influenced by Greek and Turkish music, distinctive guitar sounds and melodramatic lyrics.

\* \* \*

Beitar would star in real-life burekas films later but first they had to take the big leap forward. The cup final was the opportunity to do so. In 1975 Bloomfield wasn't full for the final but this time the Ramat Gan – two times as big – was packed. Modest estimates talk about 50,000 fans and a feverish atmosphere inside. The opponents were the biggest club in the land and the game wasn't televised because of a sponsorship deal with Goldstar, a local beer, on Maccabi's shirts. And there was the Malmilian effect. Not just Beitar fans came to see the prodigy after his majestic season.

But why was he so popular? He was extremely gifted and a pleasure to watch but there were other stars. Mordechai Spiegler of Maccabi Netanya's title-winning team and 1970 World Cup glory was the biggest star. However, Spiegler was arrogant and sometime unpleasant, while Malmilian was humble and charming. Malmilian was also a Mizrahi superstar who all Israelis could look up to. Not a Black Panther or a feisty politician but a nice guy and fantastic footballer. A perfect Mizrahi for everybody.

Malmilian's big day arrived on 16 June 1976 at the cup final. Yossi Gabay was there as a young fan:

> You couldn't sit, people squeezed in in every row. In the league the fans thought there is no chance so they took it easy. They felt we don't have the tradition and experience to run that marathon to the end. The cup suited Beitar, it's short and spontaneous, great for a club with a passion but disorganised. We knew that in one match they can achieve it.

Danny Neuman opened the scoring on 41 minutes but Viki Peretz of Maccabi equalised three minutes later. Maccabi came close to winning in the dying minutes but a clearance from a Beitar defender on the line sent the teams into extra time and Malmilian's coronation.

It started with a disallowed goal that the player thinks was legal, but without any TV footage we'll never know. In the 101st minute Beitar were awarded a penalty, and Malmilian, the 19-year-old star, took the responsibility. He wrote in his autobiography:

> It was a big moment for me; I felt I'm going to make history and bring the cup to Jerusalem. Usually I don't get nervous before taking a penalty but in this case my legs were shaking. The responsibility was great. I sweated and went to take the kick and suddenly I felt like the goal is moving away from me to a distance of 30 metres.

The ball went out of play. It was such a feeble kick that even if it had been on target the keeper would have saved it. 'I just wanted to get into a tunnel and never go out,' Malmilian said.

During the short break after 15 minutes of play, manager Bachar went up to Uri, put his arm around his shoulders and said, 'Don't worry, you will win it for us.' Sometimes good management is just saying the right words.

Six minutes before the end of the match Beitar were awarded a free kick near the corner flag. Malmilian went to take it. The two teams were waiting for a cross. 'I said to myself, you've already missed a penalty, what can happen. Go for goal,' he said about the moment.

And for goal he went. A fast, curved ball to the near corner of the goal surprised Maccabi's keeper and gave Beitar their first trophy. It took hours for the convoy to reach

Jerusalem as it was stopped on the road by delirious fans. The star of the hour was missing though. Malmilian avoided the trip with the rest of the players, joined a fan and took a side road into the mountains and forests, reached home and went to sleep.

The cup victory changed Beitar. Anybody who went as a neutral or fair-weather fan to Ramat Gan returned as a Beitar fan. Beitar had supporters now in every corner of the country. 'Each peach – Malmilian,' called the hawkers at the Mahane Yehuda market. Tzliley Haoud, the most popular Mizrahi band, recorded a cup song. Yehuda Keisar, a true guitar hero, led it to the catchy hook: 'Yalla ya Beitar – menorah on the shirt and football from Brazil.' Yalla is 'come on' in Arabic, and made it into Hebrew like many other words. The club didn't organise the recording; it was a spontaneous initiative by the band.

But did it contribute to hamahapakh? The political analyst Shalom Yerushalmi thinks so: 'It's the same energy. The same fans who went to the final followed Begin in rallies and brought their energy and belief. It encouraged people.'

The cup final was followed by the Israeli national football team's appearance at the Montreal Olympics. The team had a decent run until being knocked out by Brazil but will be remembered for other reasons.

Alon Ben Dor of Hapoel Be'er Sheva was rushed home during the team's stay in London. His wife Nilly was among the Israelis on board an Air France flight that was hijacked by Palestinian and German terrorists. She and other Israelis on the plane were held hostage in Entebbe, Uganda, until freed by IDF forces in a daring operation. It was a state secret that her father was head of the Israeli nuclear reactor near Dimona, home of the Israeli nuclear arsenal, but talk of the town in Beersheba.

A small piece of history was made on the pitch as well. Rifaat Turk, Hapoel Tel Aviv's midfielder, was the first Arab-Israeli to play in the national team. The 22-year-old from Jaffa, a fisherman by trade, paved the way for Arab-Israelis to join Israeli football. Today it's hard to think of an Israeli team without Arab players, all bar one club.

The new status of Beitar was reflected in the culture. Hagashash Hakhiver, Israel's most popular light entertainment trio, a genuine vox-pop and a national treasure of humour at the time, cemented the club's place in popular culture with their mid-1970s show *Offside Story*. The members came on stage as Shimon Kasach (slang for rough play), a Beitar fan, Yehoyachin Pendelovic, a football referee, and the judge in the case of the state against Kasach, who was accused of attacking Pendelovic during a riot in a game between Hapoel Tel Aviv and Beitar Jerusalem.

Kasach, clad in yellow and black, had a Mizrahi accent, cursed in Arabic and was a short-tempered man. Pendelovic had an eastern European name, accent and was dressed like a typical Mapai employee, while the judge sounded like a dignified Sephardi – a Yishuv veteran. 'I may look like the usher but I'm the judge,' he said as he established his position immediately.

During the description of the match, Kasach told the court that he told the players, 'If you won't win the championship, we will burn the club down.'

The cause of the riot was an 89th-minute offside call against Malmilian, the darling of Kasach. 'I took a knock to the head and saw this parasite throwing cinder blocks at me,' said Pendelovic.

'Gravel, we run out of block in Petah Tikvah,' Kasach corrected him and recalled the glories of past years.

After more tears from Pendelovic, the judge gives his

not guilty verdict: 'Because only a blind and stupid referee can't see the greatness of Malmilian who wasn't even near an offside position.' It turned out that the judge was in on the game and was actually the ringleader of the fans. Then, in a classic burekas movie move, they all sing a triumphant Beitar song together.

Beitar were no longer the vandal army at the gates of Rome anymore, just a loveable naughty boy with some temper issues.

The Gashash trio again used Beitar in a sketch about a popular Saturday live football radio show during the 1990s. A Beitar fan was interviewed and asked about their demands.

'We want to decide who will be the referees. If not, we will burn down the club,' said the fan.

'We want 15 wins a season, minimum! And if not then we will burn down the club. We demand to decide, once and for all, who will be players, the coaches, the result and weather.'

'And if you don't get your demands?'

'We will burn the club down.'

'Why do you think you deserve all of this?'

'We give our soul every Saturday and, in the end, we eat shit.'

'And what else do you demand?'

'Housing for real fans and a representor in the Knesset.'

'Anything else?'

'We demand to have a club. All the other clubs were burnt. We demand a new club.'

Beitar is a valid foreteller of the Israeli society. The club preceded numerous sea changes but in this case Yossi Banay, the writer, saw the future. The entitlement, the self-pity of the fans and finally the burning of the club in 2013.

# 11

# Eli

SACHER PARK (Gan Saker) is the largest public park in the centre of the city, sitting near the government complex. Created in 1963, the vast park, with its rolling lawns, is a hub of physical activity, public celebrations, leisure and, once in a while, a massive snowball fight. It's one of the major meeting places between Jewish and Arab populations and used to host political gatherings. Like many other places, it has a legend attached to its name.

It started when Beitar's youth team were training in the park in 1977 and were one player short. David Davidoff, the coach, noticed a skinny boy sitting nearby watching and asked him to join one of the teams to make up the numbers. The best player in that group was the right-back and captain Motti Dudi, so he placed the new boy as left-winger. There, he would be nullified and wouldn't interrupt the session. After ten minutes and numerous chases down the wing, the right-back asked to be replaced. He had simply had enough. Davidoff thanked his lucky stars and made sure that the new boy joined his team. Eli Ohana went on to leave devastated defenders in his wake for the next 20 years.

More reliable versions of the story are less spectacular, of course, and mention trials for the team. Ohana, born in 1964, having recently celebrated his Bar Mitzvah, was too shy to step up and was playing with a friend close by, but he didn't miss his chance when it arrived. It was no coincidence that he played on the left wing; only an inept coach could play him elsewhere. However, in the next year, Motti, the most promising player in the team until Ohana's arrival, retired. He had seen too much of the back of the winger and had his ears clipped by Davidoff too many times. Another player, the rival left-winger, knew he didn't have a chance and went on to find another hobby. The future king of Jerusalem was destined for greatness from a very young age.

* * *

Sacher Park made the headlines in 1981 when Labour held an election rally there. Likud and Menachem Begin were on the ropes, so it seemed. Begin's premiership started with a dramatic and historical visit of Anwar Sadat, president of Egypt, Israel's fiercest enemy, and a peace treaty between the two old foes. Israel gave back the Sinai Peninsula, although it retained control of the Gaza Strip and for the first time was recognised by the leader of the Arab world.

Despite this momentous achievement, Begin's greatest, the government didn't function and inflation was running high – 133 per cent. Begin looked out of touch and was running low in the polls.

It led to a desperate, vicious and poisonous election campaign that ran wild in the big open squares of Israel. The main issue was the old social tension, and Begin, for most of his premiership a gentleman of the old Beitar's Hadar (code of honour), rediscovered his nasty side. Back in his element, the old and frail man sprung into life and was speaking to tens of thousands every week in the open air, driving them to frenzy. The gifted orator was attacking Mapai, calling them 'millionaires from the kibbutzim', and talking about the ghosts of discrimination, the Mizrahi hurt. All were used to incite internal conflict. It sent shockwaves of hate, excitement and fear into the nation.

Shimon Peres, his rival, was attacked by Likud supporters when he tried to hold his ground. He was spat at, tomatoes were thrown at him and rumours were spread that he had an Arab mother. He was abused mercilessly. At the public gatherings at Sacher Park, Motta Gur, the commander who uttered the words 'Mount Temple is in our hands' in 1967 and who later became chief of staff of the IDF and a Labour politician, was interrupted repeatedly. In his fury he shouted to the Likud supporters, 'We will fuck you up like we've fucked the Arabs.' The subtext was clear. The old stereotypes had been enhanced: Labour was Ashkenazi, entitled and condescending. Likud was Mizrahi, violent and fascistic.

The more violent it became, the more traps Labour fell into and the more intoxicated by his own words Begin became. 'The Likud chavs do hardly any army service. Here are all the soldiers and commanders of the fighting units,' said the presenter of Labour's final event in Tel Aviv. It was an unmitigated disaster. Begin lapped up these racist remarks and used the insults to drive home his point and get all his disappointed supporters back. Together with the impact of the bombing and destruction of Iraq's nuclear reactor a few weeks before the election, it was enough to secure a narrow victory and second term. Hamahapakh was now not just a one-term incident.

Together with the religious and Haredi parties, the Likud established an alliance that would rule Israel for generations and would hold long after the slow and aching decline of an adored leader. Never an emotionally stable person, Begin pained the Israeli casualties in Lebanon after the Israeli invasion in 1982 (which lasted with a heavy price until 2000) and, with the passing of his wife, he sank into depression until he left his office in 1983, saying simply, 'I can't go on.' Still, he had an impact on Israel more than any other leader since Ben-Gurion.

Beitar was now the team of the ruling party and a springboard to public life. Haim Korfu, one of the founding players, became chairman of the club and later a minister in Begin's government. Six others followed the same route into the government with one making the prime minister's office and another becoming the president of Israel. After winning the cup, Beitar finished the next two seasons in third and second, although one home match was moved from YMCA to Katamon due to Sadat's historic visit and the proximity of the old ground to the King David Hotel where the Egyptian delegation stayed. That can only happen to a club from Jerusalem.

Beitar won another state cup in 1979, again with a 2-1 victory against Maccabi Tel Aviv, but once more there was a feeling of a championship lost due to a defeat against the same opponents three matches from the end of the season, when Beitar led the league. The next season was a disastrous one. Malmilian was injured for the most part, and the chairman had no past experience in football and had running battles with the coach and players for the whole season. Beitar finished bottom and were relegated after 12 years in the National League, but they bounced back immediately. The harm was minimal and a new generation of players was fast-tracked during that promotion season. Eli Ohana was one of them.

Ohana's debut wasn't impressive, however. He came on as a sub against Beit Shemesh and kept falling and couldn't keep the ball. 'Falling Eli' was his nickname for a match or two, and although he scored two weeks later against Hapoel Lod, he still didn't show what was expected of him.

His first match in the top league was a big one – Maccabi Tel Aviv at home, Beitar's first back in the top flight. It's one of the most famous fixtures in YMCA history but for an unusual reason. The referee was Abraham Klein, a child who had survived the Holocaust in Romania and emigrated to Israel in 1948. He became one of the best referees in the world, some say the best. In a piece in *The Times* during the 1990 World Cup in Italy, the veteran football writer David Miller said Klein was 'probably the best referee for the past 20 years'. Alan Robinson, the overseas and services secretary of the English Referees' Association from 1968 to 2004, described him as 'the master of the whistle'. Klein had a string of key World Cup finals matches to his name, including Brazil vs England in 1970, Italy vs Argentina in 1978 and the greatest World Cup match ever: Italy vs Brazil in 1982. He was a linesman in the 1982 World Cup Final and had he a bigger FA behind him, he might have been the referee at one of the finals. He wasn't invited to the 1974 World Cup finals in West Germany due to security fears after the massacre of 11 Israeli athletes in the 1972 Olympic Games in Munich, and in 1978 he was barred from taking care of the final by orders of the Argentinian Junta, which didn't like his independence.

After that Brazil vs Italy match, the *Fort Scot Tribune* said he 'showed he had the mysterious and decisive power to move into an explosive situation and calm it down by the simple exertion of cool authority'. In Jerusalem he had moved into an explosive situation and rolled a barrel of gunpowder with sheer arrogance. With the score 1-1 in the second half, Yaron Adiv of Beitar scored his team's second goal and YMCA erupted. Ten Beitar players were celebrating near

Maccabi's goal in a big pile-up when Klein ruled the goal out for offside. Maccabi resumed the game quickly, while none of the Beitar players noticed, other than Yossi Mizrahi, Israel's number one goalkeeper, who tried to call his defence back. One sub rushed from the bench to the pitch and tried to stop Maccabi's attack but nothing helped and Motti Ivanir scored. Beitar's players refused to accept the decision and argued for a long time. 'We should have been suspended until the end of our careers for the things we said there but he [Klein] was in shock and didn't do anything,' said Mizrahi.

Maccabi won 2-1 after a long delay and all hell broke loose in an old-school YMCA riot. Klein and his assistants left the pitch under a barrage of missiles and left the building but not until four hours later. When Klein arrived home in Haifa, he found angry Beitar fans waiting for him there. 'I didn't leave the house for a week after the game,' Klein said. 'It was an offside but I shouldn't have let the game resume when Beitar players weren't ready.'

'The funny thing was,' recalled Ivanir many times, 'that the fans thought the game ended in a 2-2 draw and found out only when they saw the football show on TV that Beitar lost. If they knew that we won I'm not sure we would have got home alive.'

Bizarrely, Ohana was picked by coach Eliyahu Ofer at the start of his career in the league as a defensive midfielder. Ofer and his predecessor, Arie Redler, didn't like the long hair, the flair, the daring, all the things that very soon became Ohana's trademarks. 'Ofer halted my progress for a year and a half,' Ohana told *Mabat Sport* magazine in 1984. 'I played as a defensive midfield and had to chase quality midfielders like Moshe Sinai. Had they let me play in my role, left-winger, you would have heard about me much earlier. Trust me, I wasn't sad when he left us.'

Ofer said at the time, 'The problem is that he is lacking in goalscoring skills. He is very vulnerable and limited in speed.'

When Ohana finally did hit the ground running he was mesmerising.

My old friend Yossi Gabay was part of the team by now as a young right-back. He says:

> Even when I was at the youth team, I couldn't walk in the street without being stopped every few metres. I wasn't a star even but when I went to the cinema with my girlfriend and there was a long queue, people said, come, you don't have to wait. Come have the best table at the café. Everywhere I went I got love and respect and even now people remember me as a Beitar player although I wasn't a star player with 15 goals a season.

Gabay saw Ohana from the very beginning:

> We always knew he would be a star. When you ask a 14-year-old what you want to be, they answer a Beitar player. Eli said, 'I want to play for Beitar, the national team and be a star in Europe,' although very few Israelis played in Europe then. We played against the first team on Thursday so they will get some confidence and we used to hammer them by four goals in the first half. The first coach was yelling at Davidoff, 'What are you doing to my players?!' Suddenly fans came to see the youth team.
>
> When we played against them, we played against some tough guys. There was a centre-half named Itzik Jano, a brutal player. First time

you dribbled past him. Second time he went for your leg. Eli dribbled him once, second time nutmegged him and walked the ball to the net. Jano came to him and said, 'Hey kid, if you get near the box one more time, I'll break your leg.' What does Eli say to him? 'This is the first time today and there will be plenty more.' Couple of minutes later he swivelled him from side to side like telling him who the hell are you to tell me how to play.

Ohana said in 1984:

> I play with force. I'm not afraid of anybody. When I get the ball and I'm one on one with a defender I'm unstoppable. I'm telling myself: I will go past him. I see where he will fall for the dummy and go to the other side. You cannot afford to let me get the ball to my feet. I feel it's like playing in the youth team again. I do what I want on the pitch.

That was Ohana at the age of 20. Still a kind of soldier, with long jet-black hair, nothing like my crew cut in the army. He just had to show himself on Sundays, milk the adoration and give tickets to his commanders. That season he was brilliant, a natural No. 11, the most scintillating position on the pitch. 'A team with a left-wing and ten other players,' said Johan Cruyff once. Beitar were one left-winger, one Malmilian and nine others.

Ohana's football was flowing, effortless and devastating. He scored after long runs, from the box, from outside, outstanding headers and curling shots and simple finishing with immaculate timing. He was always in control. In Israel colours he scored after four minutes of his debut against Ireland. He was fearless, arrogant, charismatic and handsome. Very handsome. He loved the cameras and lights, spoke eloquently and was a new type of Mizrahi. Brash, successful and unapologetic. Israel was in the midst of Ohanamania. He was the only human capable of sporting a mullet haircut and still looking cool. It's even named after him.

With Malmilian he had deep understanding when they played together. They found each other and never competed for the affection of the fans. Malmilian was the one Ohana never rebelled against. Together they made Beitar into a team. Yin and yang. The Western Wall and the Dome of the Rock, hummus and pitta, Paul and John, Bergkamp and Henry – they were different but part of the same organism. Uri was loved, Eli was worshipped and feared. Together they turned Beitar into a more normal football club. The old dark outsider appeal was still there but now with proper football stars. Ask Beitar fans today what made them pick the club and those older than 30 will say Uri and Eli, which are very good reasons. When Ohana was good he was one of the best in the world but you don't have to take my word for it.

Ohana was the Mizrahi story in one person. His parents were born in Morocco and lived in Kiryat Shmona, in the north of Israel after they emigrated in 1955. From the development town they moved to Wadi Salib in Haifa, location of the riots in 1959. From Haifa they moved to a poor neighbourhood in Jerusalem called the asbestos estate – the name says it all. With nine children in a tiny flat, Ohana grew up in poverty within a traditional family. Although a bright kid, he didn't excel in school but he promised his older brother and his father that he would become the best player in Israel.

In the 1983/84 season it all clicked and Beitar looked to be on their way to their first championship. David Schweitzer, who had one of the best football brains in the league, was the manager and the team was forced to play seven matches in exile due to the Bloomfield riot in the previous season. It was a blessing in disguise. YMCA was a tiny pitch with hardly any blades of grass, so with two exceptional players, it harmed the team's performance. So Beitar went back to the scene of the crime and played in Bloomfield on an excellent, larger pitch. It suited them and they gained 19 points from those seven matches and led Maccabi Haifa, the surprise title challengers, by 13 points.

However, the second half of the season was poor for Beitar. They lost to Maccabi Haifa and bled points, but still led the league by two points ahead of their penultimate match, in Jerusalem against Hapoel Tel Aviv. To make history, Beitar needed to win their match and for Haifa to drop points in their away match. The city was preparing for the celebrations and the team was invited to a meeting with Teddy Kollek despite protests from Malmilian, who didn't want to tempt fate. On the eve of the match the team met at Ruvi Rivlin's house, and everything was ready for the greatest day in Beitar's history. Even a scout from Liverpool came to see to Ohana. The balconies in Lincoln Street – the best viewing points in the city – the YMCA tower, the cypress trees around the pitch, were all heaving with fans ready for history to be made.

The first half was goalless and poor. Ohana hit the crossbar but Beitar were crumbling under the pressure while Maccabi Haifa led in their match. Not a lot happened in the second half apart from one good chance for Beitar but one goal would be enough. Just one goal; 0-0 was torture but it could change in a flash.

And change it did. On 72 minutes the ball was passed to Moshe Sinai, Hapoel's main playmaker and another superb player from that time. He ran along the right wing and curled the ball into the far corner. You could hear the doves coo at the YMCA tower as the horror spread. Hapoel's players looked a bit embarrassed and celebrated the fantastic goal modestly.

Two minutes later it happened again. Hapoel's left-back delivered a cross to the right and there was Sinai inside the box at a narrow angle to the goal. He scored with a volley similar to the one produced by Marco van Basten in 1988, to break Beitar's hearts. 'Our players told me I'm mad to score these goals but I'm glad we played the right way,' he said later. The stunned murmur turned to rage when Hapoel scored their third eight minutes later against shell-shocked Beitar players. It ended in a 3-1 disaster.

'We lost the night before with all the events and receptions. We were too gentle on the pitch and then came Moshe,' recalled Malmilian.

'The worst day in my 60 years with Beitar,' said Avraham Levi, the executive manager of the club. In the YouTube clip you can see a whole stand holding their heads in their hands in sheer disbelief. Lincoln Street was littered with glass, cheap champagne and broken dreams after the bottles were smashed by the fans.

Sinai and Hapoel Tel Aviv joined Titus the Roman, Nebuchadnezzar the Second of Babylon and Godefroy de Bouillon the Crusader in the list of destroyers of Jerusalem but were probably much more hated than their predecessors. Sinai, however, said that the players didn't care that much about the match or the title race before it. After this display it became the most bitter rivalry in Israeli football.

Maccabi Haifa won that day and then their next match to celebrate their first title on the road to becoming the great powerhouse of Israeli football with 12 championships between 1984 and 2010 and several fine runs in European competitions. With young Ronnie Rosenthal, later of Liverpool and Spurs, and an Arab forward named Zahi Armeli, Haifa became the team of the north of Israel and much supported in Arab-Israeli society.

The next season ended in another Haifa championship, while Beitar finished third. The two teams met in the cup final and an Ohana goal, following his wonderful brace in the semi-final, was enough to give Beitar their third cup. Their fourth was won in 1986 after a mediocre season in the league. Beitar were known then as a typical cup team, a backhanded compliment.

It felt like a description from a burekas movie. The fervent scally who can charm his way and win the cup but isn't serious enough to sustain a title run. Or a second-rate club capable of performing only for short periods due to its limitations.

It wasn't very far from reality. Beitar was poorly managed by Likud figures and had the huge burden of playing in YMCA. There the players shared the dressing rooms during the week with the tennis players and swimmers, trotted along the Jerusalem stone concert halls in their uniform and played on the worst pitch in the league. With Uri and Eli, YMCA was an obstacle.

The 1986/87 season started with the usual mayhem. Malmilian was negotiating a new contract and played hardball. It was his last contract with the club and an agreement was reached just after he boycotted the pre-season trip to Hungary. In a bizarre but genuine Beitar move, the team's colours were changed for the season. Out went the distinctive yellow and black and in came a pastel sky-blue shirt on the advice of an astrologist. The biggest decision was taken by the new chairman Roni Bar On, a future MP and finance minister. Bar On decided to switch the home matches to Bloomfield Stadium in Jaffa. It was a masterstroke that changed Beitar's fate.

Bloomfield was Israeli football's field of dreams; a place that held memories and a rich history. Just south of Tel Aviv and near the historical Jaffa port (which gave its name to Jaffa oranges), it started as the stadium of local club Shabab el Arab (Arab Youth). Built on a German Templers potato field and a flood plain, it was known as Basa – swamp in Arabic. Every winter it justified its name due to drainage problems.

After the 1948 war it became the property of the Histadrut and Hapoel Tel Aviv, based on Israel's draconian 1950 Absentee Property Law, which gave the Israeli state the ownership of property belonging to Arabs during the war. Shabab el Arab were displaced and metamorphosed as Shabab el Nasra (Youth of Nazareth), an important team in Arab-Israeli football. Beitar Tel Aviv and Herut were up in arms and demanded that those who fought and liberated Jaffa, the Irgun and its team, should share the ground, but to no avail.

Basa had 7,000 seats until 1962 when it was converted into a modern 22,000-seater stadium. A subterranean reservoir was drained and steep cement stands were erected in the tight area. Unlike other Israeli stadiums built in the 1960s, the land restrictions meant that no athletics circuit was designated. Phew.

Bloomfield, named after two philanthropic Canadian brothers, was perfect for Tel Aviv and Israel. The right size and perfectly shaped. The grey stands were close to the grass and the atmosphere at big matches was electric. Looking at its English counterparts from the same time, those Victorian death traps, it was one of the best for its size in any standard.

Bloomfield shrank in size due to installation of seats and new safety procedures until a major redevelopment in 2016. Now it's a soulless, vacuous, ugly and sad 29,400-seater stadium and lagging far behind the modern stadiums in Beersheba and Haifa. However, then it was much loved by fans and players. The derbies there were packed with passion and hate that drove the best teams of Maccabi and Hapoel to titles. YMCA was only about intimidation – of rival players, referees and very often Beitar when underperforming. In Bloomfield with the growing fan base, Beitar could harness the fans in the right way.

The first reason for the move was economics. Bloomfield was bigger and had much better policing. It meant the people actually paid to get inside the stadium, unlike YMCA where people snaked in using many different methods. With the Beitar fanbase growing faster outside the city, there would be enough supporters from all over Israel to come to see the matches and even pay to get in.

Bar On told Ron Amikam of Israeli paper *Maariv*:

> I watched a game in YMCA with 8,000 spectators and asked how many tickets were sold. I was told the number was 1,200. I understood I'm living in a colander. People were passing through the gates with pieces of papers from Herut. I checked the 1986 cup final as a case study and understood that we were very strong in the centre of Israel and the ticket potential of Beitar in Jerusalem is a quarter than in Tel Aviv.

The other reason for moving was a football one and most players were delighted. Yossi Mizrahi said, 'We always were happy to get out of YMCA. We were a technical team and it was hard to play there against teams who played defensively.' Ohana, as usual, called things as they were:

It did us good. With all due respect to YMCA it was a disgusting pitch. The move was the best thing that happened to Beitar that season. We could have not won the title had we had to play in Jerusalem. I don't know how anybody played there. Bloomfield was always our second home.

Hanan Azulay, a no-nonsense defender who lived minutes from YMCA, didn't like the move:

The switch was good for the team but not for me. I had clear signs at YMCA – a cypress tree that one fat fan used to sit on. I knew that when I aim at the fat fan the ball will get to Ohana. I used to know where I am on the pitch relatively to the big tower. In the end the football won.

Under manager Dror Kashtan, a tactician and disciplinarian, and the leadership of Malmilian and Ohana, Beitar became an excellent team who deserved a proper stage. YMCA was a tiny sand/mud pit and barely legal, while Bloomfield had a wonderful, full-sized grass carpet. It was a pleasure to watch and play at. At YMCA, Beitar knew which side to play on rainy days and which parts of the pitch to avoid in the mud, but in the end it cost them dearly. They were no longer the agricultural team of the early 1970s; now they had the quality and could win matches by playing good football.

The season started slowly but on matchdays five and six they beat Beitar Tel Aviv 5-3 and Beitar Netanya 6-0, with four goals by Ohana. Beitar were on top of the league and stayed there for the whole season. It was Malmilian's best season. Over the years some said that he was the one standing between the team and the title: too soft, too many injuries, a luxury player. But he supplied the answer in a majestic season. Ohana was second only to him. Gary Vandermullen, a Jewish player from Southend-on-Sea, and Dido, a Brazilian married to an Israeli woman, supplied an international aura before the time of foreign players in Israeli football.

Beitar ran away with the title and were champions by 15 points, losing only twice, the second time long after securing the championship. They won the league in a match against Maccabi Tel Aviv but the long-awaited celebrations had to be cut short. It was on the eve of Remembrance Day for Israel's fallen, a hallowed secular day in the country. Bar On asked for the celebrations to be put on hold and the fans stopped them at sunset, only to celebrate the championship and Israel's Independence Day together 24 hours later. Malmilian, who was grieving the passing of his beloved grandmother, stayed away.

'We have waited so long for it, after so many near misses. That was the moment that changed Beitar from an almost team to one with a tradition of success,' said Ohana.

It was long overdue. Beitar were the ninth Israeli team to win the league and one can only imagine what would have happened if they had played in a decent stadium in Jerusalem. It turned out to be the most profitable season Beitar had and the best until that point. It was no surprise that they had never won the title in YMCA – that was the price of living in a holy city with a growing religious population.

It was Ohana's last match with Beitar and he left to pursue his dream of playing in Europe, although not with a big club, moving to KV Mechelen of Belgium. His and Beitar's fates took different directions after the transfer, while Malmilian also needed a change of scenery and left in 1989 for Maccabi Tel Aviv after a dramatic cup final against Maccabi Haifa. Beitar won on penalties after a 3-3 draw after extra time. It was their fifth cup and was lifted by Malmilian himself. After 432 appearances in Beitar colours, 140 goals, one championship and five cups, Malmilian had simply had enough of carrying the team, fighting for a salary fitting his status and the pressure cooker of Beitar. Even the fans understood it was time.

'We won and we hugged and I know that I'm leaving and the pain starts. How can I leave this love?' he said, and left. Beitar were without Uri and Eli, with a second-rate politician running the club. Disaster was looming as the city was going through a long period of violence and decline.

# 12

# Holy Light

ON THE Saturday before Easter Sunday, at 2pm, Eastern Christian Jerusalem holds its collective breath. In the Edicule – the shrine that encloses the tomb of Jesus – at the Church of the Holy Sepulchre, a Greek patriarch and an Armenian bishop, together with an Israeli police officer, sit there in the tiny place waiting for the great miracle of the holy fire, also known as the holy light.

Legend has it that a blue light rises from the marble slab inside the Edicule. The light is believed to form a column of fire, from which candles and torches are lit, some spontaneously. This fire is then used to light the candles of the clergy and pilgrims in attendance, again some spontaneously. Handfuls of candles are passed from inside the tomb to the worshippers and soon the whole church is basking in the light of tens of thousands of candles. Every chapel is glowing and outside several torch carriers are trying to plough their way to Jaffa Gate among the packed streets. Then the fire is rushed to Ben-Gurion Airport and from there to Athens, Moscow, Egypt, Georgia, Armenia and the whole of Eastern Christendom, while cars deliver it to the West Bank and Jordan and from there to the Arab world.

It started in the 9th century in Muslim-held Jerusalem when the Christians felt the need to show the strength of their beliefs despite recent losses. The miracle resembles the resurrection of Jesus and his stature as God. It's said that Saladin himself tried in 1187 to put out the holy fire three times, only for it to reappear.

It's a major ceremony for the Eastern Christian churches and nothing short of a minor miracle when it ends up without injuries, burns or fist fights at the holy place. Edward Gibbon wrote scathingly about the alleged phenomenon in *The History of the Decline and Fall of the Roman Empire* (published in 1776):

'This pious fraud, first devised in the ninth century, was devoutly cherished by the Latin crusaders, and is annually repeated by the clergy of the Greek, Armenian and Coptic sects, who impose on the credulous spectators for their own benefit and that of their tyrants.'

It doesn't make it less spectacular or more unimportant. Even in 2020 when due to the COVID-19 pandemic only four patriarchs of the Orthodox, Armenian, Coptic and Assyrian churches attended, a fleet of ten planes waited for the holy fire at the airport near Tel Aviv, to be transported immediately. Yes, today you can ignite it with a simple lighter or candles dipped in phosphorus and some clergymen have confessed that it isn't that spontaneous and miraculous but, still, everybody needs some miracle of light in their lives.

In September 1989 life rolled me to Jerusalem. I lived in a nice central flat in Heleni Hamalka Street (Queen Heleni), named after an Assyrian queen who became a convert to Judaism about the year 30 BC. It was formerly known as Queen Melisende Street, named after the great Crusader Queen and builder of Jerusalem in the 12th century, but like many other streets it was given a Zionistic name after

1948. The flat was situated above a burekas bakery with unfortunate consequences and it overlooked the Russian compound, once a hostel for Russian pilgrims and now a dark bastion of terrifying police and security forces secrecy.

I loved it, at first. It was very different to all major cities in Israel. There was even a proper autumn and the nights were cool and fresh unlike the humid hell of Tel Aviv and Haifa. You could hear church bells toll and the young woman at the Home Office said 'welcome to the Holy City' to me when I updated my address. 'You will understand,' she said when she saw my surprised face. The local market, Mahane Yehuda, was fascinating. Arab women sat there with vegetables and herbs I had never seen before, and the fruits were in many cases 'baladi' (meaning local in Arabic), hand-picked from small orchards, many years before the marking tag of organic. The apricots, for example, were smaller than the supermarket ones but much sweeter. It was essence over appearance. The restaurants were lovely and simple.

The secular women wore sweaters, dressed in a conservative way, had long hair, much longer than in Haifa, while the art school students wore black and stood out for miles. It felt like an international city every time I took a walk. From the Russian Holy Trinity cathedral with its eight towers and domes, just outside my building, to the round Ethiopian one, down to Little Italy with the Florentine hospital, back into a 19th-century east European shtetl in Me'ah Shearim and back to Musrara. I strolled around the charming German colony, had a date at the American Colony Hotel and tea at St Andrew's Church under the saltire (well, that was years later as a Londoner who had to have his tea). Not many cities can rival that.

The place has odd names. Guy Ben Hinom is Hell in Hebrew and Arabic, and the main street in the German colony can be translated as Valley of the Ghosts, not far from the Lepers House. Not to mention Skull Hill. It's a place in Israel with a local accent (musical and rolling, unlike the flat aggressive Hebrew of the rest of the country) and many specific words for the city, almost a dialect, many of them borrowed from Arabic. It's always a privilege to write about such a place.

One day I saw an ad in *Kol Ha-ir*, the superb local paper, looking for new and inexperienced writers. I scribbled two items, posted them and waited. On a Saturday night, waiting for the football show to start, I received a call from Doron Galezer, the editor himself. 'Listen,' he said, 'I can't read a single word with your handwriting. Can you come to the office and type it?'

I wasn't nervous but I knew that one day I would write about that night. There I was, in the very last building on Jaffa Street, just off road number 1 from Tel Aviv, alone with the editor. He gave me my letter, showed me how to use the computer and I started typing with one finger. It took over an hour to type 300 words or so but in the end I felt that it might be significant. And indeed, a few weeks later in the last months of the 1980s, I was invited to work at the paper. I started like the rest of the new writers by doing little bits and pieces. Some sport and music and many colour pieces from around the city. It took me to places in the Old City, the Haredi world, YMCA and the Israel Museum among others.

In a relatively short time I started writing big features and interviews while contributing to the sports pages and sitting in for the sports editor when needed. It was different every week and fascinating as I learned more and more about the city and the people. At last I had found my voice, calling and light and this is why every time I go to Jerusalem, the site of the very first (or last from the other way) building on Jaffa

Street, now some Haredi institution hidden under a huge bridge, brings some meaningful memories to me.

It was a tradition at the paper to recruit new reporters with no previous experience each year. It was a very Jerusalemite thing. A meritocracy of talent in an unpretentious way. Things were simpler, more direct and without the pompous self-importance of Tel Aviv.

At the local paper, Hapoel had a very big majority. 'Inside the city we are more popular. All the Beitar fans are from outside the city,' one of them told me. I took his words with more than a pinch of salt. It didn't look that way at all. I thought Beitar were much bigger inside the city as well. I visited YMCA inside and out, probably the biggest contrast you can think of. The impressive tower and his angel, the stone halls inside, the orientalist charm, the long corridors, the cultural events inside the building all looked wonderful. And the so-called stadium – no more than a clatter of low stands, cypress trees like in a gloomy Van Gogh painting along the side of the pitch and the perimeter wall splattered with glass shards, blood and remains of fabric and fans. I had seen the place on TV many times but to see it in reality was a different thing. I started laughing in sheer disbelief. The pitch was a big bald patch with no more than a handful of blades of green grass. The main stand was dank and the only decent view was from behind one of the goals or from the balconies on Lincoln Street. It was an embarrassment for Jerusalem and Israel and a testimony to the lopsided way of Israeli politics.

April, I soon found out, is the maddest month, when normal life gives way to religious and nationalistic fever. It starts just before the Hebrew month of Nisan when some Jewish believers can't attend the graves of loved ones during the blessed month. So the day before Nisan the whole of the west of the city is gridlocked when massive numbers of family members make their way to the huge necropolis on the mountain overlooking road number 1. It means that the road to and from Tel Aviv is also affected, as almost a month's load of visitors make their way to the cemetery in one day.

Nisan means that Passover is coming soon. It's the most frantic time of year for worshippers as they clean their homes desperately of any leavened food. Everything is washed, boiled, scorched, vacuumed and burnt to death in fear of any grain of wheat. In the Haredi courts, gigantic tanks of water are boiled and the holy flocks bring their utensils, pots and pans to be dipped and deeply cleaned for the holy week of Passover. It also means that you can't find any leavened food in the shops or the bakeries for more than a week.

It's also the holy week of Easter with the ceremonies and rituals. The washing of the feet of the poor by the heads of churches, Palm Friday, the holy light ritual on Saturday, and Easter Sunday. It all comes thick and fast, one event after another. You can feel the syndrome lurking for its newest victims as Via Dolorosa is surging with passion.

Soon after comes Israel Remembrance Day for the Holocaust and a week later is the Remembrance Day for the fallen of the army and from terror attacks. Independence days start with Jerusalem in its centre. The more fragmented Israel becomes, the more oppressive the rituals are and the more the leaders talk about Jerusalem. The air during that month is so thick, even more than usual.

But it also means that the city becomes an international one. It's full of tourists and if you struggle with Passover laws and crave baked goods you can go east and buy a supply of pitta, ka'ak (Lebanese-style bagel covered in sesame seeds) with za'atar or sit down for hummus. Not that I travelled deeper than the Old City into Arab Jerusalem. The city and Israel were reeling from the intifada, the Palestinian uprising that shattered the illusion that the Israeli occupation can go on forever while eating watermelons together in the summer.

The intifada, which started in December 1987, wasn't in most cases armed, although some terror attacks happened in Jerusalem and on the way to the city. A bus from Tel Aviv was derailed into the abyss in the most shocking event. It was a long and draining struggle that Israel couldn't suppress despite enormous losses to the Palestinians. For all the talk about a united city, it felt broken. Jerusalem was divided and frightened again.

Teddy Kollek and his advisors thought that Jerusalem would be spared but it wasn't. Nir Hasson writes in his book *Urshalim*: 'The intifada became the fault line between the two populations. In Jerusalem it was manifested in mass protests, throwing stones at policemen, strikes, burning cars and knife attacks. The immediate result was that Jews stopped coming to the Old City and to East Jerusalem.'

In October 1990, 17 Palestinian protestors were killed by police fire during riots and stone-throwing from Temple Mount plateau at the tens of thousands of worshippers down at the Wailing Wall. Al Aqsa was established as a symbol of Palestinian resistance and the separation of the two sides of the city was clear. Sometimes it's a matter of a few metres. There are no signs on walls but you just know where the invisible border is.

\* \* \*

Eli Ohana, the exiled 'king' of Jerusalem, found himself in Mechelen, a provincial town in Belgium, without friends, family or adoring fans. The first months were lonely and hard. Ohana had to work on his fitness after playing in the slow Israeli league, get to know the town, the demands, a new home and life. 'Aad de Mos, the Dutch manager, used to say to me that through the Cup Winners' Cup I will get famous, it's the only way,' Ohana told me in an interview for *Shem Hamisehak* magazine. 'He said it from the first moment. Mechelen was well known in Belgium but they wanted to make a name for themselves in Europe.'

In the first round of the 1987/88 European Cup Winners' Cup, Mechelen beat Dinamo Bucharest 1-0 and 2-0 over two legs. Ohana played well in the league, was becoming more and more popular and felt at home. In the second round they drew Scottish side St Mirren, who weren't a household name but still a tough British opponent. 'The first game at home ended in a boring 0-0 draw. In the second leg I scored two goals, my first in Europe and it was fantastic. We made it into the last 16 and now we were taken seriously,' Ohana said.

Ohana by then was the star of the team, although playing with Erwin Koeman, part of the Netherlands' victorious 1988 European Championship team, and a string of local national team players such as the famous goalkeeper Michel Preud'homme and Lei Clijsters (father of tennis player Kim). 'L'etoile de Malines' was born.

Dinamo Minsk were the next opponents, in the middle of the winter. In Mechelen, Ohana and his colleagues won 1-0 and headed to what's today's Belarusian capital. He said:

> We brought all the food and drink from Belgium. We were there for two days in which it kept snowing. The pitch was frozen and we didn't know if we would play the game. Snow ploughs and soldiers worked around the clock to get the

surface ready. We played with a red ball just so we could see it on the snow. We played with special boots, gloves and tights in minus eight degrees.

On YouTube you can see – you have to look hard though – Ohana running alone from his own half with the red ball on the snow and ice. You can hardly see the ball on the white pitch but it's there by Ohana's feet and then in the back of the net after a cool finish. The game ended in 1-1 draw, which was enough to send Mechelen to the semi-final and Ohana to stardom.

The next challenge was the biggest one so far: Atalanta of Italy's Serie A. Ohana said:

> By now they were calling me Mr Europe. In the first game against Atalanta I was outstanding. It was my best game in the whole campaign, I scored the first goal and did whatever I wanted on the pitch. Simple as that. We won 2-1 and the Italian press joined the festival. Without being arrogant I took it naturally. That was the reason I moved to Belgium. I could have made more money in Israel but I had a purpose. To make it in Europe. I knew I was good enough to do it.

In the second leg, Atalanta led 1-0 but Mechelen won 2-1 again and made it to the final against the holders – the mighty Ajax of Amsterdam. The great Marco van Basten, scorer of the winner in the previous year's final, had left for AC Milan. But it was still a formidable team with Danny Blind, Jan Wouters, Peter Larsson, Aron Winter, Arnold Muhren, John van 't Schip, Rob and Richard Witschge, alongside a young Dennis Bergkamp.

In front of 40,000 fans in Strasbourg, few gave Mechelen a chance but when Blind was sent off in the 16th minute, the match turned on its head. Eight minutes into the second half, Ohana faced Frank Verlaat on the left wing. One Cruyff turn and one dummy later the Israeli had enough space to cross the ball towards the head of Piet den Boer, who scored from close range. Jonny Bosman of Ajax was denied by a superb save by Preud'homme in the dying minutes, and that was that. Mechelen and Ohana were the Cup Winners' Cup champions, while Eli was the first and only Israeli to play and win in a European final. 'There is nothing more beautiful than winning a European Cup. A piece of history. It will never happen again,' he said.

How good was Ohana that year? He was young Van Basten good, Emilio Butragueño good, on the level of Paolo Maldini, Roberto Baggio, Robert Prosinečki, Pep Guardiola, Ryan Giggs, Patric Kluivert, Alessandro Del Piero and the Brazilian Ronaldo when they broke through. They and Gianluigi Buffon, Iker Casillas, Wayne Rooney, Cristiano Ronaldo and Arjen Robben all won the Bravo Award, which was an annual prize handed out by the Italian magazine *Guerin Sportivo* to the most outstanding young European footballer.

In 1988 Ohana was the most outstanding young European footballer and won his well-deserved Bravo. And there are more: Cesc Fàbregas, Karim Benzema, Sergio Busquets, Thomas Müller, Eden Hazard and Paul Pogba won it, until 2015 when it was last awarded. And don't forget the 2007 winner, one Lionel Messi. For Ohana, an unknown player from the hinterlands of Israeli football in the 1980s, to win such an award tells you about the rarity of that season.

Ohana had star qualities like no other player before in Israel. It wasn't just football but also his attitude and charisma. From an early age he spoke eloquently about his ambition in life: 'I want to be the education minister,' he said while in his 20s. Mizrahi footballers weren't expected to dream about such positions, but he did.

For one glorious moment it was all there in Sydney in a crucial World Cup qualifier in 1989. After two gruelling battles between Israel and Australia they had a chance to beat their most hated rivals, and when a loose ball fell to Ohana he produced in typical style. He ran towards the goal, left one defender behind, had the keeper tumbling on the ground, moved around him, had one defender scrambling helplessly and then slotted the ball home. 'I was always in control; I knew what I want to do. I had a look later at the goal on the big screen and thought to myself, wow, this is some goal. This is what separates good players and the very good ones,' he said. False modesty was never his thing.

With two fingers raised to Australia, Israel advanced to the play-off, where they lost to a star-studded Colombia team, but Ohana's goal is probably the most loved in the national team's history, even more then the single goal scored at the World Cup finals in 1970. Ohana's European career didn't follow on from his sensational debut season though. He fell out with Aad de Mos, a transfer to Atalanta fell through and the limitation on the number of foreign players in the pre-Bosman days didn't help him. He played for Braga in Portugal in 1990/91 and had offers there and from Mechelen that summer as his career and life reached a fork in the road.

\* \* \*

Without Ohana and Malmilian and under the leadership of Likud personnel, Beitar plunged to new depths. Their second title in 1987 was supposed to fortify their status as a key club but despite the cup win in 1989 the cycle came to an end. Israeli football was changing and it was the dawn of private ownership. Maccabi Haifa, under the ownership of Yaakov Shahar, were first out of the blocks to operate in the new world. In a short time they became a professional club, with their own complex at the foot of Mount Carmel and a business model of getting the best Israelis (and some young foreign players) and selling them to Europe via the Pini Zahavi agency. Yossi Benayoun (sold to Racing Santander in Spain), Eyal Berkovic (Southampton), Yakubu Ayegbeni (Portsmouth) and Haim Revivo (Celta Vigo) are just some of the names.

Beitar, in comparison, looked like a small club with a big fanbase stuck in the days of political football, like it was a muddy YMCA. Like the old biblical tale about Pharaoh's dream in which seven skinny cows eat seven fat cows, a warning about a famine that young Joseph deciphered for Pharaoh, Beitar went through circles of boom and bust, fat cows and skinny ones. Beitar ran mainly on donations, sugar daddies and tax avoidance, without real structure.

They were losing key players, not just Ohana and Malmilian, and, in 1988, languished in 11th out of 14 teams. A year later they were ninth, although they also won the cup, but in 1990 they ended tenth and things looked desperate. Ehud Olmert, now a minister and the patron of the club, was eager to find an owner, one who was respectable, trustworthy, rich, with experience in football and loved by fans. The man who ticked all these boxes, so they thought, was Robert Maxwell, who was having a frantic shopping spree in Israel at that time. 'Buy me Maxwell' was a popular car bumper sticker. The English publisher bought a big newspaper, a major book publishing company, invested in industry and was donating to causes close to his heart.

Maxwell's people did one thing right: they looked into the numbers and realised that the whole business was unsustainable. In the meantime Hapoel Jerusalem fans also demanded that Maxwell should pay some attention to them. Maxwell, besotted by fantasies of Jerusalem United FC, came up with the gruesome idea of uniting the two foes into one club after one season.

I was working then at the local paper and can recall that all fans hated the idea. Both clubs needed money and modernisation, but Maxwell and his people didn't understand the city, fandom or football in general. It felt like a whim based on the name Jerusalem for the businessman who found his Jewish identity in the later stages of his life. It happened to Guma Aguiar and others. The city does it without even blinking.

'It is a business challenge for me but my Jewish love for Jerusalem is beyond any rational reasoning,' he told *Maariv*, the newspaper he bought. It's a sentence that every Beitar owner should know but it was lost in the Maxwell festival.

In June he signed a contract with Beitar and Hapoel Jerusalem. Both clubs were to keep their identity for a season, get money from Maxwell, and in one year's time would form the basis of a united team. 'I can't see Beitar and Hapoel merge,' Ruvi Rivlin said. 'It doesn't make any sense unless there is no other option.'

'It is a dream of any Israeli player,' said Sami Malka of Beitar. Hagay Efrat of Hapoel said, 'I can't see what he has found here in business terms but it will only do good for the sport in the city.'

Maxwell, the owner of Oxford United and later Derby County, was toying with the idea of merging Oxford and Reading into one Thames Valley Royals club back in 1983. This football-Frankenstein horror was stopped by the two clubs' fans and later the Football Association's regulations. In Israel the idea fizzled out and died naturally when Maxwell gave up his half-baked plan.

It was hard to find the exact size of Beitar's debts, the Israeli FA refused to rubber-stamp the deal and the whole saga sank without trace during one tedious summer. 'Instead of giving us offers we couldn't refuse he gave us offers we couldn't accept,' concluded Rivlin. Beitar wasted the whole summer on this golden goose chase and had to cut the budget just to start the league. The sad, pitiful season ended in a relegation sealed by a defeat to Hapoel Tel Aviv of all clubs. The Tel Aviv reds were just recovering from their own downfall after the collapse of the Histadrut. It was a different epoch.

That wasn't the worst part. In May 1991 YMCA hosted its last derby and one of the last of Beitar's 262 matches there. With four matches until the end of a dreadful season, Beitar needed three points but lost to Hapoel by one goal. In the collective memory it was the goal that sent Beitar down, although it wasn't confirmed yet. Little did everybody know that it was the last league victory for Hapoel over Beitar. Still, for many it felt like the golden days of Hapoel domination and Beitar suffering. They couldn't have been more wrong.

On 5 November, the corpse of Robert Maxwell was found floating off the Canary Islands and was recovered from the Atlantic Ocean. He had fallen from his yacht and drowned; well that's the main story but there's no shortage of other suggestions. He died riddled with debt and corruption after he used his company's pension funds to cover his losses. He received a lavish funeral at Mount Olive, watching over the Old City, and was mourned by Israeli heads of state. This was one bullet that Beitar dodged but more, many more, were to follow.

\* \* \*

During my time there, I heard the editors of *Kol Ha'ir* talking about 'Jerusalem's Sorrow' over a lunch of rice, meatballs and beans or when discussing new features. 'Jerusalem's Sorrow' is a seminal reportage by Doron Rosenblum written in May 1988 for the *Hadashot* newspaper, a national publication by definition but local to Tel Aviv by nature. The full name is 'Ask for the State of Jerusalem's Sorrow', a play on Psalm 124 and 'Ask for the wellbeing of Jerusalem', but it's remembered and quoted still after 33 years as 'Jerusalem's Sorrow'. It's a long, wordy and virtuosic feature about a weekend in the city and tells the story of the decline of the old Ashkenazi secular Jerusalem.

The sorrow is the mental state of 5,000 'pie eaters', cinematheque subscribers, Hebrew University staff who understand the difficulty of the situation and wait for an apocalypse according to the writer. Rosenblum could have just written 'Hapoel Jerusalem fans' but that would have been too direct. He wrote:

> Tel Aviv is indulgence. Tel Aviv is a note from the parents that releases you from the stagnation of Zionism, from the suffocation of theocracy, from the armed sense of community, from what we truly are. In Jerusalem there are no discounts. Jerusalem's sorrow is the sorrow of the thing we are.

Some of Rosenblum's observations haven't aged well, and some are as sharp as the day they were written. 'There is a lot of fear here, fear of non-kosher, and of course fear of bombs, fear of Arabs, fear of Ashkenazim, fear of the media and in general – fear,' he observed correctly and sadly.

The main reason the brilliant piece made the rounds in the media was the key premise: 'Jerusalem is foretelling every cultural process social and political that reach Israel later.' The rise of the Likud, Mizrahi power, Haredi and religious political sway, political violence – they all reached Jerusalem before the rest of the country. And I may add, Beitar Jerusalem is also a valid prophetic agent. It's even more concentrated, more emotional and more direct. It screams in your face the future of the city, the Israeli right and in many cases Israel as a whole.

Meron Benvenisti, deputy mayor of Jerusalem under Teddy Kollek from 1971 to 1978, is quoted as saying:

> The conflict with the Arabs is tangible here, personal even, without catharsis, in a great tension that has no chance of disintegrating. People can't live in this cognitive dissonance so they get addicted to the sorrow. You Tel Avivians can't comprehend that this tragedy is real, this sorrow has reasons, it's authentic, because down in their heart they know that the situation is hard.

Rosenblum concluded that the problem of Jerusalem would be solved:

> Only if there wouldn't be Jerusalem. The conflict defines Jerusalem and Jerusalem defines the conflict and the future of Jerusalem is already here. Jerusalem won't get the catharsis because the messianic expectation for the apocalypse, or for a solution that won't come – is from the essence of Jerusalem.

I share some of his views but my take is different. Rosenblum loathes Jerusalem, it appears, while I care for it. I feel pain when I see what has happened to the city, how ugly, megalomanic, racist and vicious it has turned and how irresponsible its leaders are. One deputy mayor called for the bringing down of the walls of the Old City. There are plans for a cable car and a train to the Kotel, both ideas of sheer madness and oppression. For a city with peace and whole in its Hebrew name the place is hopelessly short of both.

After about a year in Jerusalem I felt that I needed a change. I understood that I couldn't stand the constant demand for directness and simplicity. Jerusalemites like it humble and plain, so much so that it becomes their own way of condescending. They have so many words for the quality of being real, unpretentious, original and genuine that it can actually lock creativity. That false modesty, with more than a hint of superiority because we live here, because we believe, because God is on our side. Because they're THE real people.

The conflict was there. I loved the fact that the city has so many stories to tell but I couldn't stand that everything was distilled into a narrative of the national conflict. Beitar was the best example but even food, archaeological finds, language – they were all reduced to Israel vs the Arabs. And there was the conflict itself. You don't forget the sirens after an attack, you can't erase the calls of 'death to the Arabs' in the streets after the funerals, even after 30 years. In Jerusalem you hear 'you people don't understand it' almost every day. And it is the Holy City. Every Friday afternoon just before the start of the Shabbat a siren is heard. It was too depressing for me. I moved to Tel Aviv, which is everything Jerusalem isn't until you get it out of your system and enjoy the beauty and many layers of Jerusalem again, but this time in small doses.

It was the right move but I stayed at the local paper, which was the right call too. I enjoyed working there, learned a lot and didn't mind going to Jerusalem when needed. It was like being in a relationship but not living together. I worked for two more years at the newspaper and then another one with a sports magazine and had very meaningful relationships with local women from Jerusalem, and important memories. I still miss some elements of my time there but short visits are enough.

* * *

In the summer of 1991 Eli Ohana had to make up his mind. He had an offer from Mechelen that he rejected without hesitation. He could have stayed in Portugal but he felt it was time to come back to Israel. Hapoel Tel Aviv made a very generous bid, the best he received, but he had one thing in his mind: 'Hapoel offered me 50 per cent more than Beitar and it was all agreed but something in my heart wouldn't let me do that. Something didn't let me go to Hapoel Tel Aviv and I knew that I would come back to Beitar,' he said years later to Channel 5.

Ohana retuned to Beitar, a second division team, and led them back up to the top league. In the history of Beitar, Ohana is the greatest, but not for the 142 goals, glory, four titles and cups. In the darkest hour he came with the miracle of light. He was the resurrection and led Beitar to their greatest decade from their lowest ebb.

# 13

# Hamizrahi

'REMEMBER THE Sabbath and keep it holy' is the fourth commandment and one of the most important pillars of Judaism. There are 39 prohibited activities on the Shabbat, which starts on Friday's sunset. Among the rules are that you can't work, drive, or light a fire, and the punishment for such acts on the holy day is death by stoning. Thankfully, that's still illegal in Israel.

In Jerusalem it means that some parts of the city are closed on the seventh day. The city is very quiet when traffic and activities are turned down. The secular neighbourhoods are open and today there are more open restaurants and shops than ever. In some mixed areas it's an ongoing battle between the Haredi and the secular and conservative people, and usually there's only one winner. In time, mixed areas will become Haredi.

The Haredi and religious parties had disproportionate power in Israel even when they were a small minority, due to coalition politics. It led to severe restrictions on life during Shabbat with long-terms effects. Shops were closed on Saturdays until the 1990s. With no public transport on weekends, Israel is suffocating with private cars on the roads and the national airline isn't allowed to fly on the day.

Football was historically played on Saturdays and in many places was the only entertainment of the day, but it came with a price.

For Beitar and Hapoel Jerusalem the meaning was the lack of a proper stadium. Hapoel played for years at Katamon, which was a decent ground and much better than YMCA. It started as a pitch for British clubs and between 1955 and 1980 was the home of Hapoel Jerusalem in the heart of its fanbase. In a myopic move it was sold to cover the club's debts, a move that started the downfall of the club. To add insult to injury, Uri Malmilian bought a flat overlooking the pitch in the new buildings that replaced the stadium.

My third piece for *Kol Ha'ir* in 1989 was a short history of the stadium that was never built in the Holy City. It had been talked about since the 1970s and the plan was to build a national sports area overlooking Shu'afat in the north of the city, a place called Ramat Shlomo. It was stopped after a protest by the Haredi party in Menachem Begin's coalition, demonstrations and sabotage of the heavy machinery at the site. Today it's a big Haredi area. Two other sites in Arab Jerusalem were checked and rejected. The result was the spending of millions and further delays to the frustrations of the fans. When push came to shove, Beitar, for all the connections, political benefits and personal gains of the Likud and its men, was insignificant in the eyes of the decision-makers in city hall and government in comparison to real politics.

Plans came and went. It wasn't always just the Shabbat; sometimes it was good old-fashioned NIMBY (not in my back yard) behaviour by residents of Katamon, who refused to have a new and much bigger stadium in their posh back yard and joined the Haredim in the fight against the development. Everything is political in Jerusalem, from having pizza with toppings or going to a swimming pool where women are dressed immodestly, or having one decent football ground. You have to fight for each one.

From 1984 the focus was moved to the south of the city to Malha, a former Palestinian village that the Irgun conquered in 1948. Kollek promised to unveil the stadium in time for the 1985 season and the plans were approved in 1987, but due to the political deadlock between Likud and Labour in those years, nobody dared to confront the Haredi parties. In January 1989 the high court forced the Home Office, under the Mizrahi Haredi party Shas, to accept the plan. In a magnificent Arab villa on the end of Jaffa Street, near the offices of *Ko Ha'ir* and the British First World War Cenotaph, work by the local firm of architects began in earnest.

Yossi Ben Naim and Pascual Broid were the architects of the new stadium. It was the first sports project of many by the office of Goldschmit, Arditi and Ben Naim, including the outstanding Turner Stadium in Beersheba. The local firm from Jaffa Street designed a modern stadium covered in Jerusalem stone and with a wooden roof to keep the noise in. Alas, the sight lines were far from perfect. The first match in the new stadium was Hapoel Jerusalem vs Hapoel Tel Aviv, which ended in a 3-0 defeat for the locals. Moshe Sinai of the 1984 debacle had the honour of scoring the first goal in the stadium. The mood at the newspaper was gloomy. Hapoel fans, in their typical mood, sensed that their team were destined for relegation and, although it was a huge improvement on YMCA, the stadium was a bit of a disappointment. It was rectified after major works in 1999 during which the pitch was raised by two metres.

Ehud Olmert, who as the first mayor after Teddy Kollek was in office from 1993 to 2003, says:

Every time there were new plans at different places. Once at Ramat Shlomo, another on the way east at Maale Edomim. Every time there were problems with the land and objections of communities. People inside the city are all in favour of a stadium or a cemetery but only if it is on the other side of town. They are never against the project but just wanted it far from them but what can you do and, in the end, it has to be near someone. I also think that Teddy Kollek didn't really like football. I followed Beitar in the second league too, when they played in Acre and Tiberius I went there with my kids. Teddy never went to games. Somehow he gave in but the stadium came out poorly and I had to invest millions in raising the pitch.

Hapoel were relegated that season and disappeared from view, yo-yoing for a while between the leagues and making a cameo appearance in the cup final of 1998. Their defeat to Maccabi Haifa was the swansong of the team. The derby matches became few and far between while the team declined. Hapoel were relegated in 2000 and had to wait for 21 years until their return to the top league, after many troubles and almost becoming extinct.

Eli Ohana joined Beitar for the seventh round of matches due to a dispute with the Israeli FA over his appearances in the national side. He scored 17 goals in 24 matches and assisted nine more. With him, Beitar led the league but had to fight to the last match for promotion. It wasn't the easy season most fans had predicted. Michael Kadosh, the manager, had to endure the frustration of the fans throughout. 'For weeks I couldn't leave the bench to give orders to the players,' he said. 'The second I had my head out, a barrage of vegetables followed. I had to get out of the stadium in a police car every week. They had to build a little shed with a roof to protect me, the Kadosh Shed.'

Still, it was mission accomplished with the crowd celebrating for the first time at Teddy. Moshe Dadash, a local businessman, was at the helm again and persuaded film producer Yoram Globus to finance Ohana's return and build a strong team for the new season. Dror Kashtan, who led the team to their first title, was reappointed and a young promising striker named Ronen Harazi was signed on loan from Hapoel Ramat Gan, thanks to Kashtan's strong recommendation. For a change, Beitar had two excellent foreign players in Russian midfielder Vladimir Grechnyov and Ukrainian central defender Serhiy Tretyak, who balanced the attacking powers of the team with solid defence.

Hapoel Ramat Gan, from greater Tel Aviv, became national champions following promotion in 1964, the only team to achieve that feat until Beitar's 1992/93 success. With Ohana (14 goals) and Harazi (15 and player of the season) Beitar led the league for most of the season and hit the right notes in the third and final round of fixtures, which were split into three sections. They won six and drew two of their 11 matches, scoring 20 goals in that time. Beitar were champions by nine points from Maccabi Tel Aviv, and had bounced back from their dismal relegation of two seasons previously. Something big was in the making.

This championship was different. It wasn't a cup run or the first title in Tel Aviv. Little David was on the way to become a Goliath, not there yet with Maccabi Haifa and Maccabi Tel Aviv but with Teddy the glass ceiling of YMCA was shattered and the club could grow. Inside the city the battle was over. In the past the kids used to play Hapoel vs

Beitar in the school yard. Now there weren't enough Hapoel fans in the classes for a five-a-side. Beitar lost its stigma and it was socially acceptable to be a fan now; it wasn't just for Likudnikim and Mizrahi. Others could sit in the Teddy stands and enjoy the team, unlike the YMCA days. Now the tag of 'the team of the country' sounded almost right. Beitar had followings all over Israel and from all classes and origins and claimed to represent the people. The real people. Somehow, they didn't lose their underdog charm but they were beginning to grow. They would enjoy this bizarre image for a few more years but the process of radicalisation had begun.

Teddy changed everything. It gave the club space to develop, with a supportive home where fans could come together. The eastern stand, Hamizrahi in Hebrew, was the equivalent of an English kop. With the sun in the eyes of the fans it was the cheaper stand of the only two Teddy had (today it's complete with four stands). The young, more active fans bunched up there and formed the most boisterous and notorious stand in Israeli football. Later with the development of online forums it became the home of La Familia.

Alon Hadar, my colleague at *Kol Ha'ir* and *Shem Hamisehak* and a Beitar fan says:

> It was a very emotional place. I found there warmth and emotion that I never knew before and when it's gone, it felt like a farewell from a partner. I do miss it badly, a genuine warmth, real one, not Tel Aviv sentimentally but authentic unpretentious emotion. There was lots of help and respect there and together with great football if was wonderful; even after painful losses I came

out feeling that I was part of something deep. I used to go there as a fan and a reporter a lot. I saw it as a psychological venue. Before LF [La Familia] took over it was a perfect place to let your demons free. If you had racist demons, the racist demon got out. If you had a mad one, barbaric one or just football-mad one – it was a territory where they thrived and got out. It was a pleasant place because otherwise I wouldn't have been there so much.

Many groups lived there in harmony, lefties and Haredim, and they were all Beitar fans. On this fertile ground LF spread like the corona. The silence of the club suited them. The club shut their eyes and it spread like cancer.

The seeds were there when Cyrille Makanaky, a star of Cameroon's team in the 1990 World Cup in Italy, signed for Maccabi Tel Aviv in 1993. Maccabi were a pet hate at the time: violent, rich, entitled and successful. One match in Teddy during those years ended up in a small riot after Maccabi's victory by a penalty. They blamed *Kol Ha'ir* for it after the whole sports section was dedicated to : 'Why everybody hates Maccabi Tel Aviv'. This is something I'm still very proud of. However, the abuse Makanaky received on other occasions was despicable.

In the first match between the two, huge sections of the crowd made offensive monkey noises whenever he touched the ball. There were several black players at the time in the league, and they suffered from racism (although nothing like England in the 1970s), but this was different. A whole new scale of vileness. Israel, not just the football fans, was aghast, and those Beitar fans enjoyed the pearl clutching even more. This pattern would be repeated ad nauseam and would eventually poison the club.

*Kol Ha'ir* provided a fascinating glimpse into the mind of a racist, two racists actually. Brothers Yehuda and Efi Morad took the credit for starting the trend. Yehuda said:

> It started at Teddy and invaded other grounds and I hope all places won't stop it. We work like donkeys all week and want to let loose on Saturday and nobody will tell us if to curse, how to curse or what noises to make. You don't have a clue what joy it is. Come and stand next to me on Saturday and you will only laugh. We chant only when Makanaky gets the ball. When he is not with the ball, we don't do it.

Efi added, 'He's like a monkey on the tree. Oo-oo-oo.' Yehuda continued:

> The idea came from his state of beingness. He looks like such a monkey. So, we found something that maybe will drive him mad. Seriously, if a cameraman sits and looks how he plays, they will see that because of us he touches the ball one time and wants to get rid of it because he's afraid. The oo-oo-oo is affecting him hard.
>
> Only when we see a little negro or Arab-negro do we do these noises. This noise will not stop, it will be the symbol of Beitar from now on. Every person that moves and looks black we will do it to him. It is our right to do this noise to a player that looks like a monkey. What does a monkey do? He eats bananas. This is his scoop. So, I took

212

a bunch of bananas to the games, stood on the fence and played with the bananas to him and it ate his heart. He's a great player so if I drove him mad because of a banana then I'm great now.

But although the Beitar players had asked for the abuse to stop, Yehuda said, 'The players should worry about scoring goals. What happens up in the stands is up to us. They should make sure that the net moves. They only say it for the media. A journalist told me that.'

Soon those fans had other more burning issues on their minds.

Labour had been in the rare position of power under Prime Minister Yitzhak Rabin since 1992, and on 13 September 1993 Israel was reeling from the biggest political shock in its history. After long negotiations in Oslo, the Norwegian capital, Israel and the Palestinian Liberation Organisation (PLO) with its leader Yasser Arafat reached an agreement for the base of a future peace treaty between Israel and Palestine. The papers were signed on the lawn of the White House with the blessing of US President Bill Clinton before the astonished nations and the world.

It was the DOP – Declaration of Principles – that needed to be transformed into an action plan. This is how *Encyclopaedia Britannica* described it:

> The Oslo Accords, in fact a compromised series of agreements, the second of which, the Cairo Agreement on the Gaza Strip and Jericho, was signed in May 1994. This pact enacted the provisions set forth in the original declaration, which had endorsed a five-year interim self-rule for a Palestinian authority to be executed in two

stages: first in Gaza and the city of Jericho and then, after an election, throughout the remaining areas under Israeli military rule.

Talks on final status were to begin after three years, with a two-year deadline for an agreement to be reached. Issues such as borders, the return of refugees, the status of Jerusalem, and Jewish settlements in the occupied territories were reserved for final status talks. The PLO recognised Israel's right to exist, renounced terrorism, and agreed to change the portions of its charter that called for Israel's destruction. Israel recognised the PLO as the sole representative of the Palestinian people.

The Israeli right and the religious nationalistic forces declared war on the accords. The threat of giving most parts of the West Bank to a Palestinian authority, including parts of Jerusalem (and the Gaza Strip), was unacceptable in their eyes. They vehemently opposed the process and Rabin was the target. He was called a traitor, rabbis declared him as death-worthy and the leader of the opposition, a young Benjamin Netanyahu, led a vicious campaign against him, verging on incitement. Zion Square in Jerusalem was again the location of a violent demonstration with Israelis baying for the blood of an elected leader. A young man named Itamar Ben Gvir managed to pick up the hood ornament from Rabin's car in October 1996 during a public event. 'If we got to the car, we will get to the man,' said Ben Gvir. Remember that name.

And get him they did. On 4 November 1995, after a peace rally in Tel Aviv's main square, two minutes' walk from my home, a religious Jewish student shot PM Rabin dead.

The assassin just waited for him and shot him in the back, in an astonishing blunder of the Shabak, Israel's general internal security force. The finger of the murderer pulled the trigger but the inspiration came from others. Carmi Gillon, head of the Shabak at the time, said later that the background to the murder was the incitement of rabbis and their rulings and right-wing politicians and radical right-wing organisations' refusal to obey the law. The murder shocked the nation to the core and increased tensions in the broken society.

In May 1996 Netanyahu won the election by a margin of less than one per cent of the votes from Labour PM Shimon Peres. The 47-year-old politician didn't try to heal the nation; his first tenure was remembered for raising the internal rift and hate even higher. Teddy was a natural place for him. He took the stage at a home match, exchanging headers, quite skilfully, on the pitch at half-time and milking the adoration of his fans. The linkage between Herut/Likud and Beitar was subtly switched to Bibi (Netanyahu's nickname) and the club. The age of Bibism – the cult of Netanyahu – had started.

One of the main reasons for Netanyahu's victory was the wave of terror on Israeli streets. Hamas, the Islamic organisation, opposed the Oslo Accords and the Fatah (Arafat's nationalistic movement) leadership and wreaked havoc on Israel using suicide bombers. The first major atrocity after the Oslo declaration was carried out by an Israeli settler though. In February 1994, 29 Palestinians were murdered in Hebron's Tomb of the Patriarchs by Baruch Goldstein. The Israeli ultra-nationalist racist party Kach, of which Goldstein was a member, was declared a terrorist movement and was outlawed. Eighteen Hamas attacks followed between 1994 and 1997, bringing fear to the streets of Israel with Jerusalem badly hit.

It was a horrible time. One day in 1996 I left my flat in Tel Aviv and heard an unmistakable sound. The two-part explosion still rings in my mind. I turned back immediately and called my parents in Beersheba to tell them I was okay. Soon the phone network fell. It was an explosion at a shopping mall full of kids celebrating the festival of Purim. Thirteen people were murdered and 125 more were injured. A year later I was working in Jerusalem, interviewing the wonderful Michael Robinson, the former Liverpool player who became a TV personality in Spain. We were both having a great time over the phone until the big windows began to tremble violently and sirens were piercing Jerusalem's sky. I paused for a second, and continued. What else could I do? What else could we do? The front page of the Tel Aviv local paper came with the chilling echoes of 1948 by local poet Eli Mohar: 'Here lay our dead, at the bar in Dizengoff Square'. The conflict reached Tel Aviv too.

In the summer of 1996 my old friend from *Kol Ha'ir*, Uri Sharedsky, and I founded *Shem Hamisehak* (translated as Name of the Game), a glossy sports magazine in Jerusalem. Uri was the editor of the sports section at *Kol Ha'ir* and became the editor of the new magazine. I was his deputy. Yossi Gabay was the manager, running everything from selling ads, subscriptions and the money. It was run on a shoestring but we produced something we were proud of and we had some of the best writers in the world. It was never a big seller but, looking back, and please forgive me for this analogy, it was a wee bit like The Velvet Underground's first album. Everybody who read it wanted to be a sports writer, or at least to read the best writers.

During the first year I drove to Jerusalem about five times a week but I enjoyed coming back to the city. Our offices were in a big, long space in Givaat Shaul among garages, factories, a large bus depot and small workshops near the site of Deir Yassin, now a psychiatric hospital. The place was boiling in the summer, freezing in the winter and felt like the transit camps of the 1950s. It was hard work but we felt like pioneers building something new from scratch. It also opened a whole new world of football accreditations for us.

Lunch was a key issue. At the start of the month we usually went to Lina, a celebrated hummus place in the shadow of the Holy Church of the Sepulchre near a Via Dolorosa stop. The hummus was lemony and delicious, accompanied by perfect balls of falafel and crunchy pickles. Later in the month we ended up at a local branch of Morduch for kube soup, which was always a good idea. Towards the deadline we just had time to go down the stairs to the local snack bar and have the most Israeli thing possible: a chicken schnitzel in a pitta, with hummus or tahini and pickles. The guys running the place were two funny Beitar fans, enjoying the run for the title of their beloved team but saying 'well done' when Be'er Sheva snatched a victory at Teddy.

It was a crucial time to be in the capital and to follow Beitar because it was the period when things changed. The time when racism and bigotry started infecting the club. It was hard to see at first because the success masked it but all the key ingredients for future troubles were there. With the eastern stand, more fans could attend matches and they forged supporters' organisations. It wasn't the sardine cans of YMCA; you could move now and pick your stand-mates. The atmosphere was electric. Beitar were doing well with an exciting team, and politics was all the rage again. The revolt against Rabin and the Oslo Accords gave the Israeli right a spark after a decline. Netanyahu was a charismatic leader who used Beitar fans to attack the left and there was another crucial factor: Arab-Israeli football was becoming more and more prominent.

After the 1948 war and until 1966, the Palestinians living in the new State of Israel were under military rule. They could vote and be elected but everything was under the watchful eye of the internal security service. They needed permits for everyday activities such as movement and work, while the state took over the property of former Arab citizens. Unlike their relatives living in the West Bank and Gaza Strip (East Jerusalem Arabs have different status) they're full citizens of Israel by law but suffered from systemic discrimination.

Since the 1950s, Arab teams had played in the lower Israeli leagues and made their way up. Rifaat Turk of Hapoel Tel Aviv was the first Arab to play in the national team in the mid-1970s and numerous players followed him, but only in 1996 did an Arab club, Hapoel Tayibe, from the centre of Israel, make it to the top tier. It was a disastrous season for them as they were relegated and the main memory is an emotional speech of the chairman Rafik Haj Yihya in front of TV cameras a season earlier after a troublesome match in which he gave a V-sign, which in those days was associated with the PLO.

The slim, tall man shouted, while tearing off his buttoned shirt to show he wasn't carrying a knife:

> Yes! I did a V gesture! Is it forbidden? I won and this is my right! Are we beaten people? People of losers? We are people with the right to win and to gesture! Do we have guns? Do we have knives? No, we don't, I don't carry knives. I have a ball and a good team. Are we grade F people?

It was a Shylock from *The Merchant of Venice* moment. Arab-Israeli football demanded recognition for the first time but Tayibe weren't ready to carry that burden. The club was poor, badly managed, had a Polish coach who didn't know the league and the strength of his team, and the fans were too demanding and, in many cases, violent. To make things worse, the team weren't allowed to play in Tayibe and were searching for a home ground throughout the season.

They did start reasonably with three wins in their first seven matches but soon they were found out. Their eighth match was at home to Beitar, the first time that Beitar had played an Arab-Israeli club in the top league. During the British Mandate it was a regular feature but now it was small history. The match was in the 16,000-seater stadium in Haifa due to demand after a media circus. Politicians from both sides attended the match, scuffles broke out between the fans and there was no shortage of provocation. Tayibe fans shockingly waved a German flag, Beitar used voting papers of an ethnic cleansing supporting party and a bizarre placard saying 'Welcome to Hell', accompanied by a skull and 'Enough with Violence' in small writing. I doubt whether they really meant the last part.

Huge roars of 'death to the Arabs' and 'death to the Jews' signalled the start of the hostility. Even more menacingly, it was followed by praise of the Hebron murderer Baruch Goldstein. Racism was now televised on national TV. The football contest was over in the first half as a hat-trick from István Sallói, the Hungarian star of Beitar, demonstrated the quality gap between the two teams. Beitar won easily, 3-0, and Tayibe lost their way, losing most matches, changing coaches and giving up the fight for survival.

I followed them for a month in March 1997 for *Shem Hamisehak* and saw first-hand their decline. Four matches, one goal scored, 14 conceded. It wasn't pretty. I witnessed clashes between Tayibe fans and the club management. I saw the police force brutally hit their supporters and I heard racist chants against the Arabs when things heated up. I also saw matches without a single racist occurrence and many fans who cared just about their own team. And there was the match against Beitar at Teddy. It happened less than 24 hours after a terror attack in Tel Aviv where three women were murdered. The atmosphere was as dire as it gets.

I stood for the whole match at pitch level, near the Tayibe bench, below the western stand (I even successfully returned the ball to a Beitar player). To the right of me was the VIP stand, occupied by ministers, MPs, mayors, journalists, celebrities, guests, army generals, policemen who joined the singing, and Beitar officials. To the left, Tayibe's bench wasn't even full with the number of subs allowed. The first row of the western stand was active. They teased the players, mocked them and in some cases crossed the line. They called the Arab players terrorists, the Jewish ones traitors, and then moved to sexual deviations.

I felt for the Tayibe people, Arab and Jewish, as Beitar, then the best team in the league, kept scoring. They looked miserable and lonely, a clutter of players just waiting for the season to end, and having to endure the worst 90 minutes of their careers. Rifaat Turk, their coach, stood bravely on the touchline, not cowering in the shade, absorbing the verbal filth thrown at him. In the middle of it I heard somebody calling me: 'Shaul, Shaul, my brother, what are you doing here?' I wasn't sure at first that I was hearing right but I turned around and it was the two fans from the schnitzel place below the paper offices. The nice guys were sitting on the fence taunting the worst team in the league. They were having the time of their lives; it wasn't a routine win for them.

On the other side the eastern stand was in full-blown racist mode. There were thousands of them, I wrote in my piece. They kept chanting 'death to the Arabs' and 'terrorists', sang songs against the prophet Muhammad, shouted 'go to Gaza', 'come on Bibi!', 'build in Har Homa [a big disputed settlement]' and finally 'we want a goal from Eli [Ohana]'. It didn't happen, but Beitar won 5-0 on their way to a convincing title, but no Ohana goal.

The season ended in a real tragedy. Tayibe player Wahib Gbara suffered a cardiac arrest and died on the pitch during a league match against Bnei Yehuda. In the rematch, Tayibe won for the only time in the second round of the league, only their fourth victory in a troublesome season. Their last moment of pride before relegation and finally folding. The Israeli FA held a minute's silence in all the grounds in respect to Gbara; some of the Beitar fans chose to desecrate it despite Ohana's pleas to stop.

Still, it was a breakthrough moment. For a while Tayibe became a team for all Arab-Israelis, not just from its region, but all over Israel, a pattern that would happen again with Bnei Sakhnin. Their successors learned to walk the line differently. They played the diplomatic game when they needed to and upped the ante when possible. Tayibe didn't have the experience or a good enough team to carry the unrealistic expectations. Twenty-five years later, the presence of an Arab club in the top league isn't an issue anymore and poor Tayibe have a little part in it.

The impact on Beitar was far beyond the two matches against Tayibe. Winning 3-0 and 5-0 was fun but chanting 'death to the Arabs' was fulfilling for those who shouted it. It became a *raison d'être* for a big chunk of the crowd. Far from being the majority of the fans, it was enough to taint the club and attract other racists. 'Death to the Arabs' became the norm, with more and more Arab players in the top league teams and the national one. The Israeli FA tried eventually to eradicate it but without success. Beitar's hardcore enjoyed the reaction, just like the Morad brothers. The targets changed, from black players to Arab and even foreign Muslims. The provocation had to become more and more offensive. It reached the unavoidable conclusion in 2007 when La Familia went for the big one: the Rabin memory. 'It is a hard core and a shitty core,' said Ohana angrily once, but the damage was done.

It was still easy to ignore as the Beitar team was at its best. They won their third title in 1997 in a convincing manner, with a majestic season from Ohana. The 33-year-old scored 14 goals, including his best goal in Beitar colours, against Hapoel Petah Tikvah, the runners-up. It was the best of times, their best football, a full stadium and when not political, great support from the fans. Teddy felt like a castle with Bibi in power, and the peace process dying slowly.

But it was the root of the worst of times. In a period when Israeli football lost its political ties, Beitar became hooked on the stuff. The racism, nationalism and Bibism would all reach a new high during the next season.

# 14

# Goliath

THE KINGDOM of Israel under kings David and Solomon ruled for 80 years, but the Bible tells us that due to the sins of the kings it was split into two: Judah and Israel. Another more prosaic explanation is a revolt against high taxes, but in any case, the kingdoms fought each other and left a living narrative and a metaphor. The friction is always there between Judah and Israel, the cradle of the nation and the coastal plain, Jerusalem and Tel Aviv, Jews and Israelis.

Ever since the Six-Day War and the occupation of the West Bank and the holy places, or the return and liberation of the holy places, the divide just grows. The messianic zeal is the motor behind the Israeli right, the king-makers of local politics. 'How much does it hurt us that so many of our people don't believe and don't observe the orders of the Torah?' said Eli Sadan, the head of Beni Eli, the most prestigious educational institute of the religious Zionism, in a lesson in 2019. 'As far as we feel and understand it is a stab in the back of the nation.'

Rabbi Giora Redler of the same institute said this to his students, 'The Holocaust is not the killing of the Jews. Humanism, secular culture – this is the Holocaust. The real

Holocaust is to be pluralistic. Hitler was right on every word he said. Absolutely right.'

Knesset member and former minister Bezalel Smotrich is the leader of the Religious Zionist Party. His views reflect many among Religious Zionists: 'You are here by mistake because Ben-Gurion didn't finish the work and didn't kick you out in 1948,' he shouted at Arab-Israeli Knesset members. 'The original sin is that 54 years since the liberation of Jerusalem and Temple Mount there is a mosque there and not our temple. By the way, we are not going to pray in Al Aqsa, it is away from the holy place. God's will, we will build the temple on Dome of the Rock,' he said about the most sensitive of issues.

Many in Israel feel and understand that the seculars are 'the donkey of the Messiah', a beast of burden like the one that will carry the Messiah into Jerusalem; in other words, democratic Israel is just a phase before Israel and will become a country run by the laws of the Torah, financed by the secular working people. When asked about it, religious leaders tend to answer in two ways: yes, but it's a great honour to be the Messiah's donkey; or, you infidels don't understand a thing.

Jerusalem and Tel Aviv grew apart from the early days of Zionism. The new city by the Mediterranean soon established itself as the hub of finance, culture and a creative force, while Jerusalem was slow to change and still an historic city, place of values and devotion. Both places define themselves as the opposite of the other so much that it has become a cliché. Tel Aviv is everything that Jerusalem isn't, for example. I've read it so many times and probably used it myself.

It stretches to every walk of life. The budding pre-Israeli art scene left Jerusalem and the influential Bezalel Art Academy in the 1920s to get away from Judaica and tradition in favour of modern influences and abstraction in Tel Aviv. Hebrew theatre also grew first in Tel Aviv, and in football, Hapoel and Maccabi Tel Aviv marginalised the Jerusalem clubs during the British Mandate. Even during wars, the tension didn't ease. In 1948, a 23-year-old soldier wrote in his diary: 'From reading the papers it seems that there is still life in Tel Aviv after all. Theatres and cinemas are still performing while in Jerusalem they are on guard for months in the front.'

The understated tone became a nasty public debate throughout Benjamin Netanyahu's days with the accusation that the people of Tel Aviv avoided military service. It was easily checked and disproved. The numbers of the fallen from Tel Aviv were always higher than the city proportion in the population but the accusation was still alive. Today they call it the State of Tel Aviv, meaning left-wing Ashkenazi, or privileged. While the centre of Israel does get the lion's share of budget, benefits and indeed privileges, it's worth remembering that the most pampered sector in Israel is the settlers in the West Bank.

When the Bibi–Beitar alliance was forged in 1996 the old Judah vs Israel trope resurfaced. The priggish Tel Aviv local paper *Ha'ir* (at which I worked for a year previously) had long-running battles with Beitar and Jerusalem. The abject racism was the main reason for the attacks but you could sense that there's more to it.

Amos Noy, a left-wing Hapoel Jerusalem fan, wrote in *Shem Hamisehak* in February 1997 about it:

It is pretty obvious why it happens right now when Beitar are about to win the title in the first season after Rabin's murder, the victory of the right in the elections and the forming of the coalition of others – Haredi, Mizrahi and Russian immigrants. When you take the toys from a spoiled brat which someone had made him believe that they will have forever, he beats you up, cries, throws a tantrum, and scratches. Only when he understands that there is no choice, he convinces himself that he doesn't feel like playing with them in any case.

Hagai Levi, now an acclaimed TV writer and director perhaps best known for US drama *In Treatment*, wrote:

Take this championship, proclaim a sovereignty, close the streets, sign a treaty between nationalistic Haredi, American Kahanist with manic look in their eyes, vegetable hawkers with pumping veins, Hummus philosophers, devoted fans and ordinary nutters that roam your streets. Take that title and just leave us alone.

Ali Waked, an Arab-Israeli from Jaffa, wrote about the game against Tayibe at Teddy:

On the way back I thought that Beitar deserved the title. I also thought that Jerusalem is maybe the holy city but is for sure the city of darkness. A city in which there are people that even the most disgusting beasts would refuse to accept among them. Beitar fans were born to racist parents and will raise racist children. They deserve it, those fans – to live in a city where there is no moment of calm and security.

Erel Segal, a well-known Beitar fan who later became a mouthpiece to PM Netanyahu, answered them on the very same pages:

> *Ha'ir* writers prove time after time that a hypocrite stays a hypocrite. Your attacks are rooted in a historic hate to what Beitar represents for so many in Israel: the menorah that will never burn out. They attack Ohana and mean Netanyahu but nothing will change the facts: the Likud has won the elections, Netanyahu is the PM, and Beitar in a coordinated move are on their way to the championship.

In the 1997/98 season it all climaxed: Beitar Jerusalem and Hapoel Tel Aviv competed for the first and only time, neck and neck in the league. Both sides stuck to their familiar narratives. After that season they became identities and an eternal source of hate.

It was another stressful summer for Beitar. The inland revenue was after their share again. Ronen Harazi was sold but Dror Kashtan was at the helm and the team was good enough to fight for another title. With nine draws in 30 matches and a decent opponent in the shape of Hapoel Tel Aviv, it was a battle to the wire. Eli Ohana scored two goals at the start of the season and became Beitar's top scorer with 142 league goals, but on matchday seven against Hapoel Petah Tikvah, he tripped on the ball and suffered a cruciate ligament rupture. He tried to return to the game, scored a penalty at Ibrox against Rangers, but it was the end of a glorious career.

Towards the end of the season Hapoel Tel Aviv led the league and Beitar were in trouble in an away match in Be'er

Sheva. In the first minute Beitar scored an own goal then first-choice goalkeeper Itzik Kornfein was injured and rushed to the local Soroka hospital. His replacement was the club's third choice, in his first appearance. Things turned from bad to worse when key midfielder Yossi Abuksis was dismissed after 20 minutes for fouling a young Yossi Benayoun. In the 45th minute Hapoel Be'er Sheva scored a second goal against ten-men Beitar, who were facing defeat.

The second half retains a special place in the annals of Beitar's history. A defeat would have handed a major boost to Hapoel Tel Aviv at the top of the table, but after an emotional team talk by the usually calm Kashtan, the ten men gave it a go. 'Kashtan told us, "We are going to win the game,"' recalled István Pisont to the Walla! News website. 'He said, "We will press at the centre, and go on a break. I want everybody to fly to attack and then score. We are not trying to get back into the game but we are winning it. After the first goal, many will follow."'

Kornfein recalls:

> I got injured in the first minute. Before the game I was sidelined with backache and I didn't want to play but because it was such an important game Kashtan insisted and I was playing after being injected with painkillers. In the first minute I dived like thousands of times before and my back tightened. They scored and I was moved to hospital. Two goals down, a man short with a keeper in his first game, it was all against us and this is why the game is so well remembered. It was about self-belief. The moment we scored the first goal, just as I got back to the stadium, it was clear that we would win. Without a doubt.

It took two minutes for Beitar level the scores, and Be'er Sheva crumbled again in a disastrous season to lose 5-2. It meant that Beitar and Hapoel Tel Aviv were still in touching distance of the title, while Be'er Sheva were still deeply mired in the relegation scrap.

Five matches before the end of the season the two challengers met at a packed Bloomfield in a key match. Beitar won 1-0 with a superb performance thanks to a goal from Pisont. 'Don't be afraid Beitar, don't be afraid, as you are a cub of Lions, and if a lion roars, who is not to fear?' sang the Beitar fans – a version of a folk song in defiance.

With one match to go in the season Beitar led by one point, away against Hapoel Beit She'an, a tiny team from a small town near the Jordan River south of the Sea of Galilee. Located on important trade roads, the place has been inhabited for 6,000 years and has seen better days. Summers are punishing but the region at the foot of Mount Gilboa is flourishing thanks to beautiful springs and brooks all around.

The Romans built the city of Scythopolis there, which became a major location until its destruction in the 8th century in an earthquake. Built on the Syro-African Depression, the place is prone to quakes. The Arab town of Bisan was taken over by Israeli forces in May 1948 after the Palestinian citizens fled and were expelled from it. It became a development town, populated by olim, many of them working on excavating the wonders of Scythopolis, now a gorgeous preserved Roman city with fantastic amphitheatre, baths and mosaics, even more so on the background of the poor and run-down town. Others found work at the nearby kibbutzim.

The most famous citizen of Beit She'an is David Levy, a prominent Likud minister from 1977 to 1999. Levy, born in Morocco, was ridiculed during Begin's reign. He was pompous and conceited but a lot of the ridicule had racial undertones. It became known as David Levy jokes, which made fun of his alleged stupidity but actually was intended to outcast him as a primitive Mizrahi. A typical one was: 'David Levy walks with his family in Beit She'an and one of his kids falls into a puddle. "Should we wash him or make a new one?" he asks his wife.'

The team actually was a kind of a national sweetheart – battling against the odds, a novelty from a relatively faraway town and the hero of a documentary about the struggles of the club. The film ended in a surprising survival after a shocking 3-2 away victory against the mighty Maccabi Haifa on the last day of the 1995 season. The fans were locals and kibbutznikim from around the town and the team was the usual Israeli mix of local boys, Arab-Israelis, some stars past their prime and foreign players.

Beit She'an had their own worries before the match, needing points to secure another season in the top league, but they weren't allowed to host the match in the 3,000-seater stadium near the Roman site due to high demand. The match was switched to the Kiryat Eliezer stadium in Haifa, near the port and beneath Mount Carmel and the spectacular golden dome of the Bahai Gardens. The site of the great escape in 1995, the pivotal moment in the club's history. It was another date with fate.

With a one-point lead, Beitar went to Haifa for the possible coronation of their second championship in a row. However, Beit She'an started well and scored in the third minute. Meanwhile, at Bloomfield, Hapoel Tel Aviv were playing against Hapoel Petah Tikvah and hoping for an upset in the north. In the 37th minute it looked like it might happen when Beitar defender Smulick Levy cleared the ball with his hand from the goal line. It was a red card and a penalty. Eitan Tayeb, Beit Sh'ean's best player and a free-scoring centre-half, took the kick. He had a perfect record of five penalties out of five during that season.

'Two goals down with ten men,' says Kornfein. 'I wasn't sure that we could do it again.'

Tayeb tried to place it and skied the ball. It was still only 1-0. Just before half-time Sallói scored for Beitar and normality resumed. Beitar fans, 90 per cent of the capacity crowd, could breathe again. At Bloomfield it was still 0-0.

The start of the second half was delayed so the match was running eight minutes behind the match in Jaffa. In the 63rd minute things took another turn. As Abuksis scored with an accurate free kick to gave Beitar the lead, news came from Jerusalem that Hapoel Jerusalem had beaten Hapoel Be'er Sheva at Teddy, which meant that Beit She'an were safe for another season. The players received the update and the air fizzed out of the game immediately. Both teams were content and just waited for the final whistle. Only a handful of people noticed when the underdogs made a substitution and a player called Almog Hazan came on in the 68th minute. 'I wasn't happy with this sort of game and told Yossi that we need one more goal to make things sure,' says Kornfein. 'One-nil is not enough.'

Meanwhile, in Bloomfield the deadlock was broken when Hapoel Tel Aviv scored 14 minutes from the end, which meant that Beitar had to win to maintain their slim lead in the league. Then, in the 86th minute, Almog Hazan received the ball 17 metres from goal at the right-hand corner of the penalty box. 'I knew it was in the second he hit it,' says Kornfein. It was a goal heard around Israel. An unstoppable arrow from the right into the top-left corner. The silence in Haifa, the roar in Jaffa.

Hazan, unknown even to most Beit She'an fans, ran in joy but no one came to celebrate with him in his greatest moment. 'Beitar players asked me why I have scored. One player of our team came to me and said, "It's a pity, the game is settled, everything is fine. Why score?"' Hazan said in a One website documentary. 'I told him that I respect my profession. I think that lots of things were agreed before I was subbed on. Among the players, they discussed that it would end in favour of Beitar.'

Yoram Aharoni was the fitness coach of Beit She'an and was on the bench during the match. 'Almog was a fast player but not very gifted,' he says. 'He couldn't even bounce the ball on his feet more than five times. He hit the ball with his little feet and just caught it right. It was a one in a thousand shot. A Beitar fan came and asked who he was. What the hell is he thinking? They won't get relegated so why score?'

While in Bloomfield Hapoel fans celebrated their team's victory and the news from Haifa, Beitar attacked in a frantic fashion during the final minutes. Nobody tried to stop them. Beit She'an players just stood there; only four or five bothered to get back and defend their goal. But the keeper Meir Cohen had other ideas and denied Beitar again and again.

Avi Cohen, the former Liverpool player, Maccabi Tel Aviv's greatest symbol and altogether a wonderful and decent human being, was the pundit on TV duties. He grew up hating Hapoel Tel Aviv but was a man of truth and spoke his mind: 'It's a fixed game,' he said off the air to the broadcaster. 'Beitar will win it.' On air he was milder: 'Beitar doesn't take it but Beit She'an give it. It's clear; it's obvious,' he said.

In the middle of the siege on Meir Cohen's goal, Meir Melika, one of the subs with a good career at Maccabi Tel Aviv and the provider of Hazan's goal, broke and passed the ball to Croat Sergen Culakovic, who was free with only

Kornfein to beat. He tried to lob it over the keeper to the disbelief of Avi Cohen. 'It is a disrespect; he didn't even try to score,' Avi said angrily.

'I came on and just tried to play like a sucker. Just wanted to do my job,' said Melika.

Melika, Hazan and Meir Cohen were almost the only players who maintained the club's honour. While in Bloomfield some fans opened their champagne bottles, Beitar kept on pushing. Four minutes were added and two and a half of them had passed when Beit She'an gifted Beitar a corner. 'Last corner, I joined the attack,' says Kornfein. You can see Beitar players standing freely in the box, while their opponents are spread around keeping social distancing. Tayeb is doing his shoelaces, the second time in four minutes, when play is resumed. It's an act that will shape his life.

'Then I found myself alone with the ball,' says Kornfein. 'Let's say that it was a miracle that I didn't kill a bird or send it to Mount Carmel because it came to my right leg, which I use only for walking up the stairs. I kicked feebly and the keeper saved it. And then ...'

And then, Jamil Hader, an Arab-Israeli player, didn't clear the ball but passed it to Pisont, who scored from close range. With just over 60 seconds remaining it was 3-2 to Beitar, the same result as the match against Maccabi Haifa, in the same place. One match made Beit She'an loveable, the other brought the opposite reaction.

During the pandemonium the fans rushed on to the pitch and started celebrating the Mahapakh. It took some time to clear the pitch, then the referee whistled to resume play, while 10,000 were hugging the touchline. One second later the referee called it a day, one minute short of the added time allotted. And that was that. Beitar won. The fans exulted on the pitch while at Bloomfield people walked shell-shocked with empty bottles in their hands. 'Tears of joy,' says Moshe Ziat, a well-known fan. It was an anti-establishment act, a Mizrahi identity and act of the periphery. For a Beitar fan nothing is better than scoring on 94 minutes and see Hapoel fans crying at Bloomfield. Pure happiness.'

\* \* \*

'It was obvious that Beitar will score, like a sun in the middle of the sky during the day,' said a drained Avi Cohen.

'It's a good thing they didn't film our bus,' said an anonymous Beit She'an player to One's film. 'It was full with Beitar flags and scarves. There was a big party because Beitar won the league and not Hapoel.'

It was the burekas movie turned into football. The two loveable Mizrahi rascals outwit the lame powerful Ashkenazi and win the prize. So it seemed for a while but, unlike a classic burekas, this one didn't have a happy ending with a reconciliation and a wedding. This one was more like a social kitchen sink drama movie. The rich get richer while the poor get poorer.

It wasn't just the collaboration of most of Beit She'an players, local, foreign and Arab. It was the violence and intimidation of Beitar fans. 'We will burn your father's shop,' they shouted to Meir Cohen. 'Two experienced players told me that they are sure that if it was a draw, they wouldn't make it out alive,' says Aharoni. The game ended a minute short just because of the pressure of Beitar fans. 'I felt that they done it again, the right is using violence to cheat, like during Rabin's assassination,' said Ari Shamay, a well-known Hapoel fan.

Hapoel filed a complaint but the FA moved on. Beitar officials were gloating and a week later they won the title again. Ruvi Rivlin, now an MP, mocked his peers in the Knesset: 'Beitar Jerusalem are the champions. Bibi won the elections, put it well into your heads. Thank you.' Netanyahu and mayor Olmert greeted the fans at city square. The link between the prime minister and Beitar was growing stronger.

'No problem at all. No asterisk or anything. Champions,' says Kornfein.

Eli Cohen, who won the league with Beitar in 1997, was the manager of Hapoel Tel Aviv in 1998. 'I saw the end of the game on TV at Bloomfield,' he says. 'My assistant called me and said, "Come and watch how they throw the game away." And there we stood watching Tayeb tying his shoelaces.'

It wasn't the happiest of times in the magazine office, now in Tel Aviv for commercial reasons. Hapoel Be'er Sheva were relegated after 27 years in the top flight, for the first time in my life as a fan. Hapoel Jerusalem, the team of the editor, lost in the cup final (and Beitar won the title again). Even Yossi Gabay wasn't beside himself despite Beitar winning the league back to back for the first time in their history. He says:

> I remember watching the game and at one point calling my wife: 'Hey, come and see how they fixed a game. See the opponent give the game away.' I felt that I must share it with someone because it was unbelievable. Avi Cohen told the truth and I didn't have a doubt, it was fixed but not for money. As a fan I was disgusted. I didn't like it. I didn't like the reactions from Beitar people. Had Hapoel Tel Aviv done the same I would have gone mad. I don't recall if it came later or then but I would have felt better with a replay.

We felt for Assaf Gefen, a gifted writer, a former kibbutznik from Messilot in Beit She'an Valley and a fan, who wrote:

> In contrast to Beitar fans that keep on lying to themselves about the rotten way they gained the title, and some people from Beit She'an film who are supposed to represent my team, I acknowledge the hard fact that since that game we are a stinking team … those eight minutes against Beitar was one test too many for me. The only thing I asked for from my team, the last shred of trust, was severed by the players at that game.

Avishai Ben Haim, a TV journalist and one of Netanyahu's most loyal outriders in the media, had a different take:

> The whole battle for the league that year was a fight between first-class Israel and second-class Israel – clear, the clearest. There was a solidarity that our Moroccan brothers from Beit She'an gave us the game because they wanted Beitar to be the champions. It is sweet and charming. Beit She'an decided and said the elites help each other all the time. In lands, the huge things, the big money, media and everything. We can help each other in football.

It sounds romantic but he's wrong on every level. Beitar were and are the hegemony in a pauper's clothing, the team of the ruling party and power. They didn't show solidarity with little Beit She'an, they sacrificed them like a worthless pawn. It wasn't sweet, nor charming. It was a sad day for Israeli football. Most fans were appalled. In a survey we held at the magazine 90 per cent said it was the defining moment of the season and an awful one. In the media the match was described as shameful and to this day is known as the 'Shoelaces Game'. The date, 2 May, is a day of rage and joy in both camps more than 20 years later.

Beit She'an claimed their reactions were so strong just because Hapoel had many fans in the media. That's the handy default reaction of the Likud, Bibi, Beitar. The anger, however, was because for us Israeli football lovers the match destroyed our suspense of disbelief. We want to believe that the football is maybe not good enough but is still honest. When you live in Israel you have enough of politics every day. Football is one way of escape. Beitar and Beit She'an abused the trust of football fans and turned it into a political manipulation.

Beit She'an paid the full price. Sponsors and fans from the kibbutzim felt betrayed and cut their relationship with the club abruptly. Money was too tight to keep a decent team. The next time Hapoel Tel Aviv played Beit She'an at Bloomfield the match was ugly. Hapoel fans waved shoe laces and chanted 'work, bread', mocking the old working-class chant for basic justice in Israel. Hapoel won 1-0 but it wasn't over yet for Hapoel fans.

One of the local papers had a column titled 'Until They Get Relegated'. Eitan Tayeb was a marked man. One Hapoel fan recorded a whole CD of well-known songs with new lyrics under the title *Friends Sing for Tayeb*. It wasn't that friendly:

*We will strangle Tayeb*
*Will hang him by the rope*
*Will put him on the cross.*

Tayeb's career was over. With the mark of Cain, or shoelaces, he couldn't find a club after Beit She'an were relegated. His last hope, Beitar Jerusalem, rejected him. 'We didn't dare take him on,' said Avram Levi, the powerful club executive. 'We didn't want to get public harm. We had enough slurs thrown at us and them.'

Tayeb, the pawn who was a king for eight minutes, retired from football at the age of 30. He doesn't cut a well-balanced figure today.

Hapoel Beit She'an kept sinking down the leagues until they folded in 2006. In 2009 the club was re-formed and have been yo-yoing between the lower leagues since then. It's hard to see them making it back to the top league ever again. In May 1999, after their first relegation, Assaf Gefen wrote:

> The team made it to the top flight without knowing how to behave there. That's the reason why they caused mayhem and stole the show. They also did a terrible thing and before disappearing, managed to uncover the illness and weakness of their fleshy surroundings. And not for their own good, even ushered a new era of poor norms of Israeli football.

Beitar, on the other hand, were having a great time. According to Kornfein:

> It was a crazy time. Everywhere we played they showered us with love and I, who came from small clubs, wasn't used to it. We actually represented what they wanted to be. The team that didn't have the big money, that somehow scraped some money to sign players, and salaries are always late. We

look everybody at eye level and when we won the
joy was natural and real. Other teams lost it. We
were the team of the people.

Kornfein is a wise and honest person who knows Israeli
football inside out but Beitar was the establishment. Bibi
and Olmert. Half the government at Teddy weren't batting
an eyelid when they heard the racist calls. Companies were
queuing for sponsorship despite the fans' ignominious
behaviour. The biggest stars play for the club for big money.
They weren't the little heroic slingshot hero David anymore.

It's not just Beitar. The Likud and Netanyahu also
claimed to be the underdogs, the poor old Mizrahi that the
labour forefathers used and abused, even in 2021, after the
best part of 44 years in power. These are the words of Nathan
Eshel, a close confidant of and advisor to Netanyahu: 'This
public of non-Ashkenazi, what turns them on? Why do they
hate the media? They hate everything. The hate is what
unites us, our camp.'

There are problems in Israeli society that go back to the
1950s but it's clear that when this is the policy of the PM in
the eternal election campaign, the aim is to escalate and not
to solve them. It was good as an election tactic for a while,
but it's a disastrous way to run a country and a football club.

It's worth looking into the old narratives in detail.
Professor Amir Goldstein says:

> There are two strong narratives in Israel regarding
> the Mizrahi immigration. One is criticism of the
> state and one is of victimhood. It was done to
> them, they hurt them, they made them into a lower
> class, being racist to them and put them aside. It
> is based on facts and sometimes accurate but it

is extreme and doesn't represent the complexity. It is also based on victimhood that it takes the humanity out of the Mizrahim because they are not active in this narrative. Everything is done to them. They have no influence.

There is the opposite defending narrative of the veterans. It was a new state, doubling the population in short time, it was a meeting point between east and west and they should say thank you. This one isn't humanistic either. In my research I treat the Mizrahim as active people that took decisions and have a voice of their own. There are lies and myths but reality was complex. In Kiryat Shmona where I live, 25 per cent of the olim came from Romania and Hungary and some of the Mizrahim asked to get there. Maybe we need to be more charitable, maybe things were rushed and forced but we have to understand the people who received the olim. We need to understand the subjective experience of the olim and what happened to cause major rifts in the society.

As an expert on Begin he sees the similarity between Begin, Netanyahu and Beitar, all of them claiming to be the underdog despite being in power:

Begin created a hybrid as a prime minister. He wasn't fully the hegemony and on the other side not a fringe and still an alternative. He was the prime minister but his speeches are half statesman-like and half inciting. Being the underdog is part of the right DNA but in Israel Begin and later

Netanyahu made it into a political system despite being in power.

Beitar were Goliath now. Very popular, well connected, successful and with a home. Rival fans were terrified they would monopolise Israeli football. Twenty-three years later they're not the team of the people anymore. They have competition inside Jerusalem and they're not even the team of all Beitar fans. How the mighty have fallen.

# 15

# Al Aqsa

*'The angel of the Lord also said to her, "You are now pregnant and you will give birth to a son. You shall name him Ishmael, for the Lord has heard of your misery. He will be a wild donkey of a man; his hand will be against everyone and everyone's hand against him and he will live in hostility toward all his brothers."'*

Genesis 16:11 NIV

*'Glory to him who made his servant travel by night from the sacred place of worship to the furthest place of worship.'*

The Koran 17.1

JERUSALEM IS a city where everything has a meaning and consequences. When a massive stone fell from the Western Wall in the summer of 2018 it made the headlines in Israel and some parts of the USA. The holy place is actually just a supporting wall to the huge platform that's Temple Mount on which the Jewish temples once stood. It was built by King Herod, the great builder of the city, who turned a narrow hill into a flat plaza on top of it. The wall is made of thousands of hand-carved giant stones, placed one upon the other without cement. The weight of the beautiful chiselled rocks kept them together for more than 2,000 years and the proximity to the Foundation Stone made the architectural structure a holy place after the sacking of Jerusalem by the Romans.

When the stone fell from the wall to the ground, narrowly missing one woman, it led to thinking of what it all meant. Of course, it wasn't just any other day and any other place. It happened the night after Tisha B'Av, the day of mourning for the destruction of Jerusalem by the Babylonians and the Romans, and it fell in a secluded area reserved for the Jewish Reform movement and group of liberal women. These worshippers are under constant attack from more traditional believers and the Kotel rabbis.

Engineers suspect it fell because of water trickling down the wall or the growth of the roots of golden drop, the plant that thrives between the gaps in the stones, but these are just logical explanations. Legend has it that evil King Jeroboam, the first king of the separated kingdom of Israel, cast a spell and placed a cursed stone among the holy stones of the wall to halt the redemption of the Israelites. 'We are minutes before the redemption, the stone that fell was put there by an evil king,' said Lea Azriel, to Channel 12. 'The king of all kings is about to reveal himself and the temple will come down from heaven!'

Some said it was because of the Gay Pride parade or due to the wrong kind of prayers by the reformed Jews and women. Most, however, thought it was rather a good sign. 'Look how Putin and Trump love Bibi and want his success and how they love Israel,' said Azriel. 'The two strongest people in the world love the people of Israel. It is unheard of! It means that Bibi is the last one, and after him is only the king, the Messiah. Put it in your head. God is about to reveal himself!'

Palestinians told a Channel 12 reporter that the stone fell because of works to demolish the Al Aqsa Mosque carried out by the Zionists. A default allegation in this part of the world over 140 years. One can dismiss such a baseless claim but not its potential to light the fuse.

Three months later the wise men of Jerusalem had to decipher another celestial message. A coin-marked snake, non-poisonous and native to the region, slithered among the stones, probably trying to catch a swift or rodent. American evangelists had a field day. Satan is angry, they said; others were sure it was just another harbinger of the Messiah. The olive-skinned snake was collected and normality resumed for a while. The wait for the Messiah or the wrath of God is still ongoing, while Bibi and Trump are now out of office.

Above the Western Wall stands the most recognised symbol of Jerusalem, probably the most photographed place in the city and undoubtably the most photogenic. No matter how many times you've seen photos of it, when you stand next to the Dome of the Rock, the beauty of it will astound you. Built in AD 691 by Abd al-Malik, it's a piece of spectacular religious art. The 45-metre-high structure replaced a Roman temple that stood at the site of Solomon's temple.

Unique, colourful and harmonious, the dome, which is approximately 20 metres in diameter and is mounted on an elevated drum, rises above a circle of 16 piers and columns. Surrounding this circle is an octagonal arcade of 24 piers and columns. The interior and exterior of the structure are decorated with marble, mosaics and metal plaques featuring Arabic script and vegetal patterns intermixed with images of items such as jewels and crowns.

The combination of the golden dome with the blue, turquoise, green and yellow ceramics, plus the off-white Jerusalem stone of the surroundings and the olive trees, creates an almost dynamic yet tranquil monument that protects the famous rock – the start of it all. There inside lies the rock that made Jerusalem. It's a very big rock with a natural cave beneath it. Walking near it feels like walking on an active volcano ready to erupt. You can feel the energy bubbling, its effect on people; you can almost hear the mountain groan and shake. One wrong step, act or move and an irreversible process might begin yet again.

The structure isn't a mosque but has become an important site over the years. Nearby is Al-Aqsa Mosque, the third holiest to Islam, although some refer to all Haram al-Sharif as Al Aqsa today. The Islamic history of al-Quds (The holy – Jerusalem) began in AD 639 when the Arab invaders conquered the city from the Byzants. It was Abd al-Malik, the fifth Umayyad caliph (the second of the four major caliphates established after the death of Muhammad) from Damascus who changed the fortune of the city.

Tom Holland is a historian and expert on Islam:

> The early followers of Muhammad believed they were descendants of Abraham from Ishmael and they felt they had the right to the Holy Land, to Palestine, and that is why Palestine is their first target. Jerusalem is obviously very important in this promised land. The centre of the caliphate is Syria and Palestine. Abd al-Malic is to Islam what St Paul and Constantine is to Christianity rolled into one. He is the first great figure who

transformed Islam into justification to his own imperial rule of the Arabs. He also cast himself as the interpreter of the Islamic message. He built the Dome of the Rock and proclaimed in the most public way possible that Jewish and Christian dispensations had been superseded.

The inscriptions around the dome are anti-Jesus and that he is not the son of God. The aim seems to have been to put the Church of the Holy Sepulchre in the second division. Because the focus has begun to move to Mecca much more there is a slight problem of what you do with Jerusalem. And so after decades and centuries that followed you get the stories about Muhammad's night ride from Al Aqsa and why Jerusalem is so important.

Israeli scholar Milka Levi-Rubin thinks the dome was built to restore Jerusalem as the most important holy city, not in competition with Mecca but against Constantinople and the newly built Hagia Sofia Church. According to her the builders saw themselves in line with kings David and Solomon and the building as the new temple. Soon, however, it became an Islamic symbol and today the most potent Palestinian icon. The most sensitive place in the region.

After the Six-Day War, most rabbinical authorities declared Temple Mount a forbidden place for Jews due to its holiness. Today there are ever-growing numbers of rabbis and politicians who call for Jews to pray there. Some are openly calling for the building of a new temple on the site, with all the ramifications. It will lead to clashes sooner or later.

\* \* \*

On 24 September 2000 I left Israel and moved to England, where I live to this day. I felt that I needed to change my life and it was the right decision, although not without the price of immigration. In my worst dreams I could see the horror that was about to engulf Israel that same week.

Jerusalem is a city where everything has a meaning and consequences but every so often people choose to ignore them. Four days after I moved, Ariel Sharon, then the leader of Likud and the opposition and a frightening figure for the Palestinian public, visited Temple Mount. The touchpaper had been lit, the volcano had erupted.

It started as another riot and a reaction on the plaza but it didn't cease for years. The second intifada was far more deadly and devastating than the first. It brought an end to the peace process, which never recovered from the murder of PM Rabin. Even before that dark day in 1995, the Oslo Accord was in trouble. Israel kept building settlements on the West Bank and the Palestinians kept attacking Israeli civilians. When Ehud Barak defeated Netanyahu in 1999, he tried to revive the process. A summit to solve it all was summoned at Camp David with Arafat and President Clinton, but when it failed in July, you could sense that disaster was looming. The question of Jerusalem was and still is a major obstacle for peace. 'We have no partners for peace,' said Barak. The Palestinians felt the same.

Sharon delivered the spark and within a matter of days violent demonstrations escalated to armed clashes. The IDF with all its force had to deal with suicide bombers from all Palestinian factions, not just Hamas, who left death and destruction in their wake. The casualties on the Palestinian side were higher but this time they managed to inflict pain unlike any previous round. Over 1,000 Israelis and more than 4,000 Palestinians died in the horrendous bloodletting.

The peace process, hope, trust and the Israelis remaining never recovered.

Death was a daily occurrence. The buses I used in Haifa, the cafés I visited in Jerusalem went up in flames. An army base in Beersheba visible from my parents' balcony was attacked. Whole families were wiped out in a single blast in the cities. Kids on a night out were massacred in Tel Aviv beside the coast, almost whole classes of a school. A terrorist entered a kibbutz where my niece was living and went on a killing spree. She survived, unlike others. The kibbutz, Mezer, has a united Jewish-Arab football team with the nearby Arab village of Meiser, and the grief was felt in both places.

As always Jerusalem was targeted and badly hit. Bus after bus, café after pizza restaurant, Saturday night and Sunday morning. The city was drowning in blood. It was the hardest time, says Yossi Gabay:

> Not a week passed without an attack. Neighbours, friends from school, friends of my wife, dozens of dead and you were subjected to it all the time. One Saturday night after another one, I watched TV in bed and started crying, real sobbing. Maybe the only time I cried like that as an adult. I told myself, what kind of future do we have here. What will be the future of my children? I used to see films about Sarajevo and think how can they live like that and now it has happened to us. Living in a war zone.

'I used to take bus number 18 to school and I remember the fear in my mother's eyes every morning,' says Itsek Alfasi, a doctor of social psychology (and founder of Beitar Nordia, a splinter club of Beitar). 'We felt under siege. Home-work-home-work. That's all. The city was dead, empty, lifeless. Horrible days.'

Ehud Olmert, mayor of Jerusalem during that time, says:

> A part of normality was to keep having football games in Jerusalem. It was a huge risk because it was targeted but the security forces prevented all the conspired attacks. I used to collect bodies from the streets. People at cafés, kids and parents on their way to school, civilians at shops. It was difficult but we didn't surrender. I will not forget the day when I arrived as mayor at the King David Hotel in the middle of the day and it was darkened. No light at the lobby. I asked the manager what's the story and he said that he has only three guests.

Israel managed to crush the intifada eventually and it subsided around 2004. You can still see and feel the scars in Jerusalem. It also left a legacy that drastically changed the city in the shape of the separation wall. The barrier, part wall and part fence, was meant to separate Israel from the West Bank and to protect it from further attacks. However, at some places it goes further east than the green line (the former border), grabbing more land for Israel, about 10 per cent of the West Bank territory. It slithers into East Jerusalem, the Judea Desert and Bethlehem in the shape of a cement wall around eight or nine metres high, cutting through villages, neighbourhoods, families and schools. Some parts of Arab Jerusalem are now islands on the wrong side of the wall. Locked between Israeli-controlled East Jerusalem and the Palestinian Authority, they're neither here nor there, just enclaves of human misery and neglect. Arab Jerusalem is now almost cut off from the West Bank and getting closer to Israel.

Barak was deposed in 2001 and replaced by Sharon. Israel took a sharp right turn despite withdrawal from the Gaza Strip in 2005, and Netanyahu returned to power in 2009 until 2021, the longest-serving PM in Israel's history.

* * *

Football continued during that time and, as Olmert says, it was seen as an important way to cling to a sliver of normal life. Israeli teams had to play outside the country in European competitions but it did help morale. It was also the time of the rise of Arab-Israeli football. It wasn't a one-off like Tayibe; in the new millennium, Arab-Israeli football is well represented at club level and at a personal one. The national team and all Israeli football clubs have Arab-Israeli players, bar one.

At the first home match of the new 30,000-seater stadium in Haifa in the summer of 2014, the place was full of emotional Maccabi Haifa fans draped in green flags and banners. One corner of the stadium was populated with the travelling fans of Bnei Sakhnin, a team from a nearby Arab town in the north of Israel.

Sakhnin fans had one huge banner of their own: a drawing of a barefoot ten-year-old child in ragged clothes, with his hand, clasped behind his back. The drawing was of Handala, the creation of Palestinian caricaturist Naji El Ali, which symbolises the resistance of Palestinian refugees who lost their homes in the 1948 war. The writing in Arabic on the banner said, 'Sakhnin el Arab' – (Arab Sakhnin).

'He [El Ali] was assassinated by the Israelis because of a drawing. A drawing!' says Mahmud Galia, a journalist from

Sakhnin. According to creditable Israeli sources, the artist was actually murdered in London by a Palestinian hit squad after he insulted Yasser Arafat. Mossad, however, was well aware of the plot but did nothing to stop it.

Ihud Bnei Sakhnin in Hebrew or Ittihad Abna Sakhnin in Arabic (Sons of Sakhnin United) began as a local club of a small town but over the years they became one that represents the minority in Israel. Sakhnin has become kul al Arab – an all-Arab team in the top league. The club gathers fans now from all over Israel's Arab communities. While most Arab-Israeli institutes are careful not to overstate their Palestinian identity, Sakhnin sometimes can't resist it.

Relationships between the Arab citizens of Israel and the state can run into problems. In the 2015 general election, PM Benjamin Netanyahu based his campaign on fear and hatred regarding the Palestinians and the Arab world. 'Arab voters are coming out in droves to the polls. Left-wing organisations are bussing them out,' was his shocking rallying call on polling day. It was effective, as the fear from the Labour government backed by the Arab party that drove many Israelis to vote for Netanyahu at the last moment.

It leaves the Arab sector between a rock and a hard place. They're citizens of Israel but part of the Palestinian people and the greater Arab world. Some of them see themselves as Israelis, others as Arab-Israelis and most as Palestinians, although 73 years of living in Israel has had an effect. For part of the Jewish society they're a potential enemy, while for Palestinians outside Israel they're Israelified Arabs. This is also the place where Arab-Israeli football finds itself.

Israeli sociologist Dr Tamir Sorek looked into the subject in his book *Arab Soccer in a Jewish State – the Integrative Enclave*. He researched the subject around the turn of the century and his findings are illuminating:

There's a power struggle around the club of Sakhnin, and while the board wants to keep the definition of an Israeli team there is a significant group of fans who want to bring elements which were not seen until 2008. There is an inclination to emphasise Palestinians' foundations and identity. In the unwritten code in Israel, it is seen as defiance when they call themselves Palestinians. For them the success of the team allows them to imagine integration in the Israeli society from a position of power. Emphasising the Arabness is not disconnected from the desire to be valued as citizens.

They want to integrate, and in Israel the opportunities are limited. The public sphere emphasises the Jewishness. There is ethnic discrimination. And suddenly there is a meritocracy where a man is judged by his achievements. Football receives lots of coverage so they try to take it as far as they can. It has interesting implications. Arab fans tend to vote more for Zionist parties. My explanation is that involvement in football gives them the feeling that not all routes are blocked for them.

Under Netanyahu, Israel did its best to let the Arab citizens of the state feel unwanted and to abase them. The PM used them as a prop to send fear to his supporters and then in 2018 the Knesset passed 'Basic Law: Israel as the Nation-State of the Jewish People'. According to Amir Fuchs of the Israel Democracy Institute:

It is an unwanted development. It doesn't kill the democracy but the whole aim is to disrupt the balance of Jewish and democratic and make Israel less democratic. It says that you have to calculate the right for equality with the fact it is the state nation of the Jewish people and if you cut the euphemism, it says that there are cases in which you can discriminate against Arabs citizens even though they are citizens of this state.

\* \* \*

The town of Sakhnin sits in Galilee, a region of natural beauty and historical importance. In this hilly corner, Jesus walked in ancient times, Saladin beat the Crusaders in the battle of the Horns of Hattin, and the Israeli army fought and won major battles. However, there's almost a feeling that one site to the south of Sakhnin casts a shadow over the land: Har Megiddo (Mount Megiddo) – Armageddon. It's a time of despair, and you don't have to look for long to find people who think that the Third World War will start from here, or more likely from Temple Mount in Jerusalem.

In the meantime, Bnei Sakhnin is becoming an important symbol of the complicated life in Israel. The forming of the club in 1992 was almost prophetic. In the 2015 general election (and in 2019 first elections, 2019 second ones, and 2020) a united Arab party ran for the Knesset for the first time. Communists, Islamists, secular Arabs and a token Jew shared one political front. Bnei Sakhnin led the way on the football front.

In 1992, Maccabi and Hapoel Sakhnin rose above years of rivalry and formed one united team. Instead of petty local politics and conflicts along the lines of the town's clans, Bnei Sakhnin took a different route. It was no coincidence it happened in Sakhnin. 'There is something proud about Sakhnin. Day of the Land started here, it's the first town

to embrace the Arabs of the West Bank and Gaza Strip,'
says Galia.

'We have given many martyrs,' Nidal, a political activist,
is quoted in Sorek's book, 'whether it was in October
2000, in 1976 or 1948. Our entire history is a history of
people who love their land, who always identify with the
Palestinian people.'

In 1976 a protest rose after the government announced its
intention to confiscate lands from Sakhnin and neighbouring
villages. A general strike and demonstrations were called
and, in violent clashes with the border police, six people were
killed, three of them from Sakhnin. That day, 30 March,
was declared Day of the Land, an annual day of memorial
and protest by the Arab minority in Israel. 'By blood, by
spirit, we will redeem you, oh Galilee' has been the rallying
call ever since.

Sakhnin's place in the centre of the narrative of struggle
was cemented in October 2000 when 13 Arab demonstrators
inside Israel were killed by the police during the early days of
the second intifada. Two of the victims were from Sakhnin.
Even in the bloody history of the conflict the events of October
2000 had a long-standing impact. Arab-Israelis took them as
proof of how fragile their human rights were, while mainstream
Israelis saw this as treason by the country's citizens. Both views
added to Sakhnin's status as the Village of Martyrs.

The new club stepped up the leagues steadily and after 11
years made it to the top Israeli league, only the second Arab
team to do so after Hapoel Tayibe. They avoided relegation,
but it wasn't pretty. Under manager Eyal Lachman, Sakhnin
played tough, aggressive and sometimes brutal football.
Even by English standards it was harsh, and when the team
played against Newcastle United in 2005 the tackles were
followed by winces, gasps of astonishment and then rage by

the Newcastle fans at St James' Park. Still, Sakhnin became part of the league.

An even greater achievement was reaching the cup final that season, the first Arab team to do so in Israel's history. In a packed national stadium near Tel Aviv, they beat Hapoel Haifa 4-1 on an emotional night. 'Unforgettable night. My father is still celebrating in his grave,' says Galia.

Fans from all over the country made the pilgrimage to Sakhnin that night and the Israeli media celebrated with them. 'Sakhteyn [for health in Arabic; used by Hebrew speakers to say well done] Sakhnin' was the headline in one tabloid. 'An achievement which will open doors' and 'This is how one creates coexistence'.

*Yedioth Ahronoth*, the biggest paper at the time, went with 'Mabrouk [congratulations in Arabic, a word also used in Hebrew] a historic achievement for the Arabs of Israel.' Zuheir Bahalul, a well-known Arab journalist and a former member of the Knesset, famous for his pompous Hebrew, wrote:

> No more the same simplistic, supercilious and arrogant view of him [the Arab]. Perhaps from today onwards the attitude will be more respectful, more human and decent. There is hope. A new chapter in the cultural conflict between Arab and Jewish citizens of the state was written yesterday. A chapter of reconciliation. A sport has succeeded where others, for so many years have failed. The educational system in Israel never learned to inculcate the values of coexistence ... Behold! Sport overcame the historic obstacle, disposed of the stereotypes, the sowed pride and the new hope in the Arab population.

Limor Livnat, the minister of education, culture and sport, said, 'Championship for a team from the Arab sector – a certificate of honour for Israeli society.'

The website of Beitar Jerusalem's ultras was shut down for 24 hours as a mark of mourning.

The reactions were genuine. Israeli football for all its faults was far more open than most public spheres for Arab-Israelis. The best Arab players found their way to the top clubs and to the national team. At some matches Israel opened with five non-Jewish players and during a 2006 World Cup qualifier against Ireland, Abas Sawan, Sakhnin's cup-winning captain and probably their finest player ever, scored a wonderful last-minute equaliser. Among the celebrating fans was Galia:

> I was always against Israel's national team but with that game I was happy. Not for the team but for Sawan. We are an inseparable part of this country and we do have influence. Some fans put on me a scarf of Israel and I went home with it. I woke up the next morning, saw it, and thought, 'Oh dear, what have I done?'

Sorek explains in his book, 'Soccer provides many Arab men with a secure sphere of competitive masculinity and identification with flags and emblems and at the same time it avoids both Palestinian and Israeli national narratives ... The soccer sphere is constructed to serve as an enclave of integration.'

For many years that was the model. Arab national symbols were kept away from the football stadiums; the chairmen of the teams spoke frequently about coexistence and the fans chanted, cursed and sang in Hebrew, even in

*Jerusalem from the air, 1931. YMCA building and pitch, and King David Hotel Looking south-west*

*Temple Mount, known to Muslims as el-Harem al-Sharif with its golden Dome of the Rock Islamic shrine and lead-domed al-Aqsa mosque above the Western Wall*

*Beitar Jerusalem owner, Russian-Israeli billionaire Arkadi Gaidamak in 2006 before it all came apart*

*Beitar Forever Pure, 26 January 2013*

*Chechen football players Dzhabrail Kadaev (L) and Zaur Sadaev, presented to the media, 30 January 2013*

*Members of 'La Familia' confront supporters of the purchase of the club by a member of Abu Dhabi's royal family during the club's training session in Jerusalem on 11 December 2020*

*Eli Ohana, Beitar's greatest player in action for Israel, 1997*

*President Ruvi Rivlin, chairman Itzik Kornfein and Eli Ohana; Beitar royalty*

*An unhappy fan throws money at Moshe Hogeg, owner of Israeli Beitar Jerusalem football club, during the club's training session in Jerusalem on 11 December 2020, after a member of Abu Dhabi's royal family bought half of Beitar*

Holyland Old Firm: Beitar
Jerusalem v Bnei Sakhnin

*The separation wall in South Jerusalem. The wall cut Arab East Jerusalem from the West Bank and turned Jerusalem into a mixed city. Pic: Shaul Adar*

*The entrance to Me'ah Shearim, the Haredi autonomy. Pic: Shaul Adar*

Black Panthers, the Mizrahi protest movement billboard in Musrara.
Pic: Shaul Adar

Beitar Nordia players celebrating under the flag of Ze'ev Jabotinski having a pint
of beer in the disputed ground at Har Homa. Pic: Gilad Imas

games between two Arab teams. In the Arab press there were much more nationalistic tones but the football enclave was flourishing. The state and the FA were happy to show the world that Israel is a fair society and the Arab-Israelis enjoyed success and recognition. There's an element of sport wash and Hasbara in it, but it's an oasis that made life in Israel better.

Beitar vs Sakhnin has become over the years the Israeli *clasico*, the Terra Santa's 'Old Firm'. The match has evolved to be one of the focal points of the season. It usually comes a short time before or after a terror atrocity, a military offensive or election (just normal probability) to add more heat to the encounter.

The match in November 2014 was one of the most policed ever in Israel. Around 900 policemen and stewards tried to control fewer than 5,000 fans (800 of them from Beitar) and 22 players, to no avail. The match in Sakhnin came to pass after a military conflict in Gaza early that year and only days after a terror attack on a Jerusalem synagogue during which five Israelis were murdered. Tension in Jerusalem had been brewing for months.

At the Doha Stadium, a gallery of Arab politicians took their places, while some right-wing extremists stood among the Beitar fans. Never before had a top-flight match had so many Palestinian flags on display (an act illegal until 1992), while Beitar fans brought Israeli flags and one of Golani – the fearsome infantry brigade of the Israeli Defence Army.

'By spirit, by blood, we'll redeem Al Aqsa,' called out the local fans. There were chants about Palestine and the shouts of 'Allahu Akbar' (God is great). Beitar fans answered in the usual way of nationalistic and anti-Muslim chants. 'Temple Mount is in our hands' was one of them.

The annual matches are the much-needed adrenalin rush for two mediocre, at best, football teams. 'This is why we are in this league,' said a local fan. 'During the game we can express our identity.' For at least 180 minutes a year that crystallises the essence of Ittihad Abna Sakhnin.

The match ended in a 1-0 win for Sakhnin and five added minutes due to fouls, flying umbrellas and other objects, and players pleading for some restraint from the fans. Three Beitar players should have been sent off but the referee decided to ignore their fouls. Later the Israeli media complimented him for using his common sense, hence preventing a riot. Beitar fans took their rage out on the public toilets and the buses instead.

One Beitar player later told the press: 'We said to each other, "We can't believe we lost that game." It was like a war for this country, more than sport and we should have won it.' Another player said, 'It drove me mad to see the media after the game. Did you forget you are the Israeli media? What we went through should be the headlines and not some broken sinks. Five thousand people singing "by blood we'll redeem Al Aqsa" and you let them get away with it? If they could, they would have made their way to the pitch and killed us all.'

I went to a match in Sakhnin in 2014 against Hapoel Be'er Sheva with about 1,500 travelling fans who had made the long journey and expected to win easily. The visitors and Sakhnin's vocal fans sat behind the two goals and ignored each other. Be'er Sheva fans sung their version of 'Bad Moon Rising', while the locals chanted some generic support for their team. It was almost 100 per cent in Hebrew. Among the Sakhnin fans was a group of Bedouins from the south, usually a supporter base of Be'er Sheva but much less so since the rise of Sakhnin.

Uri Aviram, a famous Jewish fan of Sakhnin for over 20 years, told me:

> I took my kids and we were warmly welcome, like no other, with coffee and barbecue and I liked it and I said to myself, 'I want to be here.' Then the talk was still about coexistence. I found here wonderful people, warm and caring but flattering. They are not 'pet Arabs' like the ones the Israeli left is looking for.
>
> The whole league missed the chance to have such a team as a calling card for Israeli football. Sakhnin could have represented the country in a great way with players of all religions. We've missed it. Now it is a political team. Too political. I wish it was the team of old.

Mahmud Galia was sitting next to me in the small press box. 'Can I smoke?' he asked me during the match. 'You can do whatever you want, it's your home,' I said. 'No, you are my guest so now it is your home, just like you did to us with the country,' he joked.

Galia thinks that the waving of Palestinian flags started at the matches against Beitar and took on from there: 'People saw that they can express their opinion in the football grounds. It is a stage where you can protest against everyday life, the killing of shahids, the situation in Jerusalem and to do it in front of TV and press. It's the only time that the national media are here.'

Sakhnin started the match without a single Jewish player but midway through the first half their goalkeeper Muhammad Kandil was injured and replaced by Ran Kadosch, formerly of Barnet in England and one of only two Jewish players in the squad. On his Facebook page you can see a picture of Kadosch celebrating a Sakhnin goal with a Jewish prayer, while his team-mates bow for the Muslim prayer and another player makes the sign of the cross. Three religions, one team and one game we all love. Each man shall live by his own belief. 'Bnei Sakhnin' is the writing on the wall.

Sakhnin won the match 2-0 against a much stronger force and in the streets around the Doha, Be'er Sheva fans shook hands with Sakhnin supporters and said, 'Mabrouk.' The previous season, when Be'er Sheva won 3-0 at the same venue, the scenes after the match were similar. Some local fans tried to provide a reaction ('this is Palestine') but were ignored. Sometimes, even in Israel, football can be, however fragile it is, just football.

'We tried to get into the league but we were rejected,' says Galia. 'For us it was more than a football league, it was an acceptance league but we were rejected. It's like in politics, like those offensive words by Netanyahu. We are citizens of this country, not refugees! But thanks to him the unity of the Arab society will continue after the election.'

The story of Arab-Israeli football is also the story of football. Put two goals, one ball and sets of kit in a city, town, factory or a village, and people will form teams, clubs, leagues. They would like to play each other and be recognised for their achievements. It's a basic human expression. Just ask the people behind Bnei MMBA, who risked a lot to play in Israel.

Bnei MMBA is a club that was formed in 2015. It's based in the Golan, at the north-eastern tip of Israel on the Syrian border. The wonderfully named club represents the four Druze villages in the Golan Heights (Mas'ade, Majdel Shams, Buca'ta and Ein Qiniyye, hence the acronym), combined population 20,000, living under Israeli rule since 1967.

The narrow roads of the Golan are flanked by minefields and the twisted remains of tanks and dozens of memorials for the dead, testimony for two wars on this basalt land. You have as much chance of seeing a wild boar, jackal, vulture or even wolf as another car there. It snows in the Golan every winter and the wind in the valleys bend the trees at 90 degrees. It's wild and harsh but nothing compared to the troubles they had to go through to form the club.

Based in the Golan, 220 kilometres from Tel Aviv, and with some parts of Majdal Shams touching the border fence, MMBA had to overcome 50 years of local hostile resistance to take part in Israeli football. They had their own minefields to negotiate.

The Druze, an esoteric ethno-religious group, branched out from Islam in the 11th century and since then have lived as a close religion. 'The Druze suffered from Islamic persecutions because they were considered infidels and this is the reason they live on mountain tops,' says Salim Brik from Israel's Open University.

The Druze are mainly based in the Middle East, with 700,000 living in Syria, 350,000 in Lebanon, 135,000 in Israel and a large diaspora in the USA, Canada and Colombia. 'The Druze are not allowed to form their own army; they have to be loyal to the country they live in and that is the obligation of loyalty. They aren't allowed to form their own state according to their religion,' says Brick.

This rule has complicated the lives of the Golan Druze since the Six-Day War. While the big Druze community inside Israel proper is loyal to Israel and many of its sons serve in the Israeli armed forces, the Golan Druze, under Israeli occupation since the war in 1967, remained loyal to Syria.

When Israel conquered the Golan, a mountainous plateau above the Sea of Galilee and northern Israel, most of the Syrian population fled or were deported. Only the four Druze villages near the slopes of Mount Hermon were left to stay, in a typically grandiose and deluded Israeli plan to form a Druze buffer zone.

The plan fell apart and Israel found itself with a Druze population loyal to Syria. Along with cultural reasons, there were also practical considerations behind this. For many years Israel and Syria negotiated a peace agreement in which the Golan would switch hands and go back to Syrian control. In such a case, it was better for the Druze to show loyalty to their future masters.

When Israel annexed the Golan in 1981, demonstrations broke out in the villages, people refused to take Israeli IDs and those who did accept an Israeli passport were boycotted and isolated. However, the Druze population became more embedded in Israeli life, and most of them work with Israelis, speak fluent Hebrew, meet on a daily basis at work and benefit from the booming tourist industry in the beautiful Golan. There was one symbol that the old generation held on to despite the eroding hostility to Israel: football.

Many Druze players from the Golan joined Israeli clubs but the idea of a local team in the Israeli leagues was taboo. The villagers had to make do with an internal tournament of the four villages, which was far from satisfactory. In 2013 a group of locals dipped their toes in the water and formed a youth team that joined the Israeli league but their first match in Majdal Shams was cut short when protestors told the kids, 'This is Syrian land and the IFA doesn't have any rights there.'

Nadib Ayub, the manager of the team, said at the time, 'It is a disaster for us and especially for the children. It was supposed to be a historic game for us; to host our first game at home. Nothing prepared us for such a scenario. I'm very sorry.'

Two years later in the autumn of 2015, Bnei MMBA was formed and this time managed to put down roots in the volcanic fertile soil of the Golan. It was long overdue as the team started in the fifth tier. It was a sign of the times; the last barrier had been breached.

One of the founders of Bnei MMBA is Wejdi Elkish, a player-coach and the face of the club in the media. He is a PE teacher from Buk'ata, in his mid-30s, a former player of Hapoel Ironi Kiryat Shmona, the best team of the region, and a 'footballer from birth' according to his friends. When we met in Mas'ade, he told me:

> I dreamt about it for many years. I saw that there are many players from the villages and if we gathered them, we can build a good team. It's not a secret that some people objected to the idea and they did manage to kill the initiative in the past but the war gave us a push. The time did the job. What is allowed now was forbidden before.

The war in Syria was felt in the Golan. The tourists fill the restaurants in Mas'ade high street beneath the snow-capped Hermon but the risk of local clashes or regional war is never far away. Until then, you can see the border from Majdal Shams houses and you can hear the war in Mas'ade. The main concern is for their Druze brothers on the other side, and those in the nearby Syrian town of Hader. 'Everyone in the Golan has a relative in Syria,' says Brik, 'and they care about them. The most important rule in the Druze faith is to look out for your brothers.'

The Druze of the Syrian Golan live under the threat of Islamic terror from one side and the barbaric and oppressive Assad regime on the other. While Israel has played a more and more active role in the war in the last year and helps the rebels, there's one clear fact says Brik, 'There is an existential threat to all Druze in the Middle East, apart from, paradoxically, in Israel including the Golan.'

With Syria disintegrating, the chance of a return of the Golan to Assad's hands gone, and a safe and comfortable life in Israel, the old emotional ties to the motherland became weak. The young generation growing up as Israelis at last had a chance to accomplish their football dream.

Elkish is the friendly face of MMBA. 'Just like there are Israelis of Moroccan decent, or Yemeni origin, I am a Druze of Syrian decent but I live in Israel in a respectable way and I love my life here,' he says. To convince the hardliners, they needed one of them on his side.

Another founder is Samikh Samara. He grows mangos near the Sea of Galilee for a living and he's the political force behind MMBA. He named his kids Fidel and Havana and attended Fidel Castro's funeral. 'I am a revolutionary,' he declares. Unlike the loveable Wajdi, he is an outspoken person with a taste for provocation and a past in Israeli jail for smuggling arms across the border:

People change. Rabin of 1987 [Israel's hawkish defence minister] is not the Rabin of 1992 [assassinated prime minister and peacemaker], Samikh of 2001 is not Samikh of 2018. I was 20 years old, I smuggled arms, did time, learned in jail, and changed. I live in Israel and work with Jews every day. Ninety per cent of them accept me and understand me. Yes, I was in jail but I did not murder anybody. I did not do anything unforgivable.

People used to ask me why do I want a team in the Israeli league and I answered, 'You tell me why not?' Golan Druze contractors work with the Ministry of Defence, teachers teach at Israeli schools, lawyers act in Israeli courts but to play football with an Israeli team was forbidden.

So what has changed?

The war made it clear that you need to take care of your people. The Golan Druze, despite the linkage to Syria, wants to live in a place that gives them safety. And where is it? The state of Israel, brother. A person can't belong to a place where his son is murdered. Where his family is kidnapped and where he doesn't have food or a roof over his head.

I am a leader and with my charisma and rhetoric ability I've managed to persuade many people who said, 'Well, if Samikh Samara the politician joins the club, the one who did time for crimes against the state, then there is something good going on.'

We know that our destiny is not in our hands. There is an occupation since 1967 and the uncertainty is the most constant factor in our lives. We didn't choose to live in Israel and we won't decide if to go back to Syria. In the meantime I'm living my life here like any other citizen. The occupation started in 1967 and I don't see it ending soon. Until then I can't go on without football.

And there's the heart of the matter. Put some people together and they'll form a team that will represent them and their cause. It's as basic as the urge to play. Years without a football team to follow, to care for, to be proud of or to make your life a misery is a high price to pay for a conflict in which Elkish, Samara and their friends are just pawns.

MMBA have four academy teams with some Israeli players alongside the Druze. On a clear winter's day in 2018 the youth team played on the pristine synthetic pitch in Kiryat Shmona against a team from the Arab town of Tamra. Not far from the local stadium, scarred by shrapnel after the 2006 war with Lebanon, Israeli football displayed its unique character. Two teams, one Arab, the other Druze, played in the Israeli league, shouted commands in Arabic and Hebrew, cursed in Arabic that every Israeli understood and celebrated goals in Hebrew. In the stands four fans watched from Buk'ata. Three girls in all-black trendy western clothes and one boy in traditional baggy trousers and big white religious skull cup.

This is why, for all its malaise, Israeli football is an important social institution that contributes to the quality of life in the much troubled land. It gave a sense of normality to life in abnormal Jerusalem. It gave a voice to the Mizrahi population before they achieved it politicaly. It gave Israeli-Arabs a sense of pride and a presence in Israeli life and, more often than not, it's a fine example of life together.

This is why Beitar's ultras' attitude is so singular. The presence of Sakhnin and Arab players gave the racist core someone to hate at arm's length. Soon it became a cause célèbre. All Israeli football fans suffered during the terror periods but only a section of Beitar fans, not all of them, made it their calling to be 'pure'. It attracted more and more radicals and pushed the moderate ones away from the club.

It's a triple whammy. They've tarnished the Beitar image, they've prevented their club signing 20 per cent of Israeli footballers and many Muslim ones from around the world and, crucially, they've ruined the aspect of normality. Football can serve you as an escapism from the daily politics and war in Israel; the conflict is omnipresent. You can go to a Be'er Sheva or Maccabi Haifa match and forget about it. That wasn't the case at Beitar matches.

I attended one match between Beitar and Sakhnin in 2015, in Petah Tikvah due to another Beitar punishment. I sat in the VIP box and saw how a proud father taught his little girl to sing 'here she comes, the racist team of the country' and 'may your village burn'. They both laughed and had a great time.

He stopped just before the national anthem, a practice that only Beitar carries out. Sakhnin fans started booing and chanting during the anthem, then the father turned around in rage, looked at me and shouted, 'Listen to them, who the fuck do they think they are, the dogs? The fucking media won't say a word about these fuckers but will keep on saying that Beitar fans are racists. Fuck them!'

And there it was. The racism, the making of the match against Sakhnin bigger than the rest, the blindness. The joy of sticking two fingers up to the pearl clutchers and well-heeled. Beitar won 1-0, the fans sang the whole song sheet and felt they saved the country, but they brought the club to its knees.

# 16

# Curses

JERUSALEM HAS been cursed by sanctity but also by grim spells. Places, people, football clubs, they all had to deal with it. A former Russian hospital now hosting the Municipal Parking Department in a charming edifice is rumoured to be haunted and nobody dares walk there by night. Every single commercial building with too many empty spaces and not enough revenue, like two ugly buildings near the market, is said to be under a spell and a rabbi is sent to deliver a blessing to ward off the jinx.

On 86 Jaffa Street, by the exit from the market, there's a decorated stone house, now part of the Israeli health authority. It was destined to be the home of a young Christian Arab couple in 1881, wrote author Haim Be'er, but sadly the groom died the morning of his wedding day. The celebration turned into grief and the groom was sat in his suit on a chair in the middle of the reception hall. The bride in her white dress and jewellery, her faced veiled, sat by the side of her destined husband with all the guests still in their best clothes attending the event.

At the time when the wedding should have started, the mother of the bride danced with candles in her hands, calling loudly, 'Is it a command that I should dance?'

'Yes, a command!' answered the guests and so she danced. When she finished her morbid dance she tore her clothes, let out a blood-curdling yell and ripped the veil from her daughter's face. That was the cue to start the funeral. The next day the builders left the house, which stood empty under the curse for years until the Ottoman authorities built a hospital there. More than 140 years later the people of Jerusalem still tell the story.

\* \* \*

After winning the 1998 title Beitar Jerusalem fell from grace. It happened when the tax authority finally had enough of Beitar's shenanigans and demanded its due. Players were also fed up with delays in payment and asked for their salaries, so Beitar needed to find money and fast. Backed by mayor Ehud Olmert they had all their hopes in a deal with a Jewish-American businessman, Ron Lauder, son of Estée of the perfume dynasty, and then a supporter of Netanyahu. He was about to buy the club but, like Robert Maxwell before him, the debts and more so, the opacity of the subject, made him think again. It was another story of cold feet.

The 1998 title cost the club a lot, both in terms of image and money. Beitar had to pay bonuses to the players but, unlike other Israeli clubs, they failed in the Champions League. Maccabi Haifa, Maccabi Tel Aviv, Hapoel Tel Aviv and Hapoel Be'er Sheva all had good European runs but Beitar never made it to the group stages in any European competition.

Beitar were eventually sold in 1999 to Kobi Ben Gur, an Israeli businessman who turned out to be a one-season nightmare. This was at a time when the year 2000 was just around the corner and the Christian messianic fever was above normal levels. After a season of internal fighting at management level, public squabbling with manager Eli Ohana and gathering more debts, the club was sold in April 2000 to local billionaire Gad Ze'evi. The kibbutz-born business mogul had a portfolio of ownership in 50 companies, including the national telecommunications operator.

Ze'evi was big money and aspirations were high. 'We have sound foundations – the fans. We will be like Maccabi Tel Aviv basketball club, the European Cup is the target and the Israeli league the vehicle,' said Momi Peretz, the new chairman of the club, sending shivers down the spine of football lovers. The basketball club had won every title bar one from 1970 until 2007, enjoying privileges and state support, like the teams of the Communist party or the secret police in the old Eastern bloc. With the Likud behind the team, it was a scary thought.

A team fit for the new boss was assembled. Eli Guttman, an up-and-coming manager, was signed, having delivered a historic title to Hapoel Haifa. He brought with him stars in a *galàcticos*-like project. A date was chosen to unveil the new team, just before Tisha B'Av, to the astonishment of the Jerusalemites.

Tisha B'Av, the ninth day of the Hebrew month of Av during the height of the summer, is a bleak day in the Hebrew calendar. Tradition has it that the two temples were destroyed on that day among other catastrophes such as the expulsion of Jews from Spain and England and the fall of the town of Beitar, the last stronghold of Jewish rebellion during the time of Hadrian the Roman emperor. It's a day of fasting and prayers and the nine days before are a period when the believers don't celebrate, have any joyous activity or sign contracts.

Rabbis demanded the event be cancelled, and Rabbi Kaduri, a well-known kabbalist, issued a warning: 'If you go on with the ceremony during the time of penitence a seven-year curse will befall the club.' You didn't want to mess with Rabbi Kaduri in Jerusalem. He had political power and many are sure he had magical powers as well. A photographer for *Kol Ha'ir* was once sent to take photos of him. The rabbi refused but the photographer took some frames anyhow. Back in the darkroom he found out that the whole film was black.

Beitar didn't have to wait for seven years. The big show at Teddy was all bells and whistles, rock performance and fireworks but it cost the club much more than the money it made. The rapper who performed, a famous Beitar fan, even sued the club when he didn't receive payment. He joined a very long line.

Results at the start were good but the style was dire. It was defence first for Guttman, keeping the right positions and winning 1-0. Guttman had a great football brain, understood tactics and prepared his team meticulously. His emotional intelligence, however, was appalling and his football at Beitar was beyond drab despite having one of the league's star players, Croat Đovani Roso, at his disposal. Beitar fans who grew up on Ohana and Malmilian couldn't stomach the boring displays even when the team was first or second in the league.

Goalkeeper Itzik Kornfein told *Shem Hamisehak*:

> I think the first cracks started to appear following the pressure on Guttman. The criticism of the 1-0s influenced him and he added another striker to the line-ups. Players said to themselves, 'if he adds another striker the positions of the pitch can get looser.' Without the tactical framework, our guiding light, everything got out of control.

We started losing, fans didn't come to games or
did and swore at us and that had a huge negative
impact on the players.

Step after step the façade eroded. First the relationships
with players and then results. By February it was a mutiny
by players and fans and Guttman left because of ill health.
Beitar finished fifth and ended the season with a record
defeat, 7-0 to Maccabi Tel Aviv.

Ze'evi wasn't doing any better. Like many before and
after him, Beitar lured him, like a moth to a menorah. He
spent more time on the club than the rest of his businesses
put together but didn't do anything to clear the historic debts.
They didn't go anywhere. His empire, built on leverage,
came undone bit by bit. Money that was initially splashed
out became scarce. Ze'evi and his people rented lavish offices,
created jobs that weren't needed, gave away cars to employees
and in one bizarre case moved the goalposts, physically not a
metaphor, from the Jerusalem base to Lod, where the team
had a practice session, on the demand of Guttman. It would
have been cheaper to buy new ones (or just to use what they
had there; a goal is a goal). It was typical of the coach, trying
to look the perfectionist but missing the point altogether. To
make things worse, the club was run by people who didn't
understand football, finance or Jerusalem. 'We used to run
the club with three people, now 32 are doing it,' said Avram
Levi to *Haaretz*.

It came to a farcical end when Michal Ze'evi, daughter
of Gad, became a club director and came up with the bright
idea of bringing actual live lions to Teddy. 'Beitar is slam
dunking a goal!' she exclaimed during a TV report on the
club, mixing her football and basketball. Beitar became a
laughing stock, while the Ze'evi empire crashed. Ze'evi is

now remembered for the profligacy, incompetence and near disaster he brought the club. He's one of the top contenders for the oddest Beitar owner list – a piece that keeps on being published with regular updates.

'Ze'evi got Beitar after five years of a reckless and ostentatious management when they were sick and empty of assets,' concluded *Shem Hamisehak*. 'The opportunity to rehabilitate the club was wasted by him in negligence, misunderstanding and poor choice of people. The fans are maybe happy because of his misfortune now that his empire is crashing down but it won't bring their team back.'

Beitar was facing extinction. Ze'evi left behind a club without money to start the new season and mountains of debts. Time was running out and the new season was about to start when a new saviour rose. District judge Vardy Zailer gave Beitar more time for negotiations beyond the deadline of the trustee, explaining in court in unforgettable words: 'It is forbidden to hurt the holy flock that sits here in front of me and represent the team fans.'

The judge was right to give Beitar an extension; the negotiations did come to fruition and a group of wealthy fans bought the club and saved it – but his words, the fact the league had to wait for three weeks for Beitar and that the club got away with it without any punishment, showed that the little underdog was now part of the hegemony. Clumsy, incompetent and terrible with money but a hegemony for all purposes.

For four unglamorous years Beitar was run by this group. Some of them were the people who owned *Shem Hamisehak* during the first years in which they never interfered with the editorial work and what we wrote about Beitar, some of it highly critical. The football wasn't good, the style of Meir

273

Penigel, the most prominent of the group, was undiplomatic to say the least but they saved the club and acted for the love of Beitar, so should be remembered as such.

All this turmoil made the club weak and susceptible to infection. Its immune system couldn't fight germs, bugs, viruses and tumours efficiently anymore. The fans have always had a much bigger influence at Beitar than those of any other club. They're in touch with the owners, chairmen and players, present at training sessions and even put pressure on agents. After chasing Guttman out they felt even stronger. Beitar survived the threat but were miles behind the leading Israeli teams. Hapoel Tel Aviv made it to the quarter-finals of the UEFA Cup, Maccabi Haifa beat Manchester United in the Champions League and Maccabi Tel Aviv also got to the Champions League group stage. Meanwhile, Beitar was riddled with racism.

\* \* \*

I miss the food of Jerusalem. I mean the good food. Most of the restaurants serve tawdry chow, good enough to keep you going on a budget and according to kosher laws. There's no shortage of awful tourist traps and it's hard to find good international food in the city. However, when it's good it's wonderful. It's unpretentious and grounded with rich history. It isn't trendy (not on purpose), doesn't change every season and it tells you a lot about the city. On the Israeli side it's influenced by the kosher laws, so at most places there's no pork or meat and dairy together. These are the key legal points among endless regulations. Because of the Shabbat laws there are slow-cooked dishes that you can keep in the stove, influenced by many meals from all around the Jewish diaspora. When it's done right it's lovely honest cookery from the many countries of origin. The Old City is a packed wonderland of outstanding food of the levant cuisine, a must for every foodie. Native Yotam Ottelenghi, Paul Hollywood (check out the Jerusalem edition of his brilliant *City Bakes* programme) and the irreplaceable Anthony Bourdain among others came to film the magic Jerusalemite food, with good reason.

The food of Jerusalem, like football, is another dimension of passion, conflict, narrative and identity. It's part of the city's uniqueness, character and pleasure too. There are many foods named after Jerusalem. One is the Jerusalem artichoke, which isn't an artichoke nor from Jerusalem but a lovely tuber. Italian settlers in the United States called the plant girasole, the Italian word for sunflower, its botanic relative. Over time, the name girasole was corrupted to Jerusalem.

However, other foods do deserve the adjective.

'The most local dishes of Jerusalem are kube soup, Kugel Yerushalmi and Me'orav Yerushalmi,' says Alon Hadar, my colleague at *Kol Ha'ir* and *Shem Hamisehak*. He still writes mainly about food and he cooks in New York. He was born metres from Mahane Yehuda to a Kurdish family and wrote a lot about what Israeli cuisine is, if there is one and its relationship with Palestinian cuisine. It's a minefield. In any case, we both agree that kube soup is the jewel of Jerusalem's food crown.

When I started writing at *Kol Ha'ir*, Shalom Yerushalmi took me under his wing and showed me the ropes. It was very generous of him as he was already an established star of the political press. His column, 'Political Text', was much better than the national paper dross and he was well connected in the Knesset and government. When I met him again in 2019, I thanked him for his welcome and another important thing: he had introduced me to the wonderful and wired world of kube soup, the Kurdish staple dish.

It was one evening before we both went to a Hapoel Jerusalem basketball game. He was a fan and I had to write about it. He quoted a line from Amos Oz's book *My Michael* about the cold nights of Jerusalem and drove to Morduch on Agripas Street by the market. 'Listen, when in Jerusalem you have to try this one thing,' he said and ordered two red kube soups. A deep beetroot-red plate with yellow burgul dumplings and a small forest of herbs arrived. It was strange at first; sour, aggressive, the dumpling was a bit dry but it felt right for the time and place. I've had it hundreds of times since, tried it in other places and checked out the yellow version, heard about a secret kube goddess up in the mountains who cooks on demand, but I stayed loyal to Morduch for sentimental reasons.

Over the years I've found out that kube is Jerusalem's Guinness. It doesn't travel well. Once you get west of the Castel you should try looking for something else. Tel Aviv flirted with it but it was all wrong, all vegan gluten-free kube made by a fictional Iraqi grandmother with a made-up Arab name. Near to a falafel boutique 'with a concept' – I kid you not.

Me'orav Yerushalmi (Jerusalem mixed grill) is also as Jerusalem as you can get. It was invented in one of the cheap eateries on Agripas Street called Macam (radar in Hebrew, named after a daring raid of the IDF who airlifted an Egyptian radar in 1969) by members of the Piro family, stars of the 1969 Bloomfield riot (it's just wonderful how everything is connected in this place!). The secret of the dish was a cheap supply of fresh chicken offal, which used to be thrown away by the local slaughterhouse. It consists of chicken hearts, spleens and livers cooked on a flat grill, seasoned with onion, garlic, black pepper, cumin, turmeric, olive oil and coriander. It's not fine dining but a late-night yellowy oily grab served in a spongy pitta. It was trendy for some time in the 1980s and is still served on Agripas Street but it's only a niche food today.

Kugel Yerushalmi is served by the Haredis for locals and visitors hungry for Jewish food, a trend boosted after the success of the TV Haredi hit *Shtisel*. It's a slow-baked noodle dish for Shabbat and a local twist on the Ashkenazi one. The Sephardi of Jerusalem didn't like the sweetness of the eastern European version and added salt and black pepper to make a classic dish.

There are two dishes that are very popular around the world and Israel but I can't recall having lunch in Jerusalem without seeing somebody having it at a table beside me. The first is the humble white rice with beans, with or without meatballs. It's a spicy, red, tangy, ubiquitous cornerstone of every basic food joint. The other one is the national obsession that's hummus. In theory it's a very simple dip. It's popular because it's cheap, healthy and fills you up nicely with pitta – the Israeli national bread, but there's more to it.

In *Jerusalem's Sorrow*, Doron Rosenblum describes Jerusalem as a city full to the brim with hummus joints. In the 1980s a comic strip in *Kol Ha'ir* by the great, late Dudu Geva and Koby Niv followed the adventures of Ahalan and Sahalan, two hummus-mad guys. Today it's a national fixation, with constant articles about where to find the best one in Israel and the most boring, tedious debates by hummus wankers, sorry aficionados. Israelis abroad whine about the lack of it, although it's very easy to make at home. It's presented as Israeli food, to the anger of the Arab world.

In recent years I've come to the conclusion that it's a myth, an over-rated dish, and often a supermarket product served decoratively with all the trimmings of olive oil, ful (cooked broad beans), harissa (hot sauce) and whole chickpeas just to cover the taste. 'Ha ha ha, I see you haven't lived here for long – it's obvious! Everybody knows it,' one of the hummus journalists who wrote a generic 'Best Hummus in Israel, piece laughed at me. 'Don't quote me but it is just nice cheap filling food.'

Still, I had to check it myself. Pinati, a famous establishment on King George Street, served a bland and boring hummus. On the walls there were pictures of Beitar players and a drawing of Ahalan and Sahalan devouring hummus by Geva. The place was full of tourists from outside the city. They all ordered hummus, while most locals munched their rice with beans.

I wanted to try Akrimawi, an Arab place with extra-sour hummus, if only for the best location: at the end of Nevi'im Street watching the magnificent Damascus Gate, but it will have to wait for next time, after the pandemic. Not far away, inside the Muslim quarter is the much talked about Arafat. I went there and was given an ugly plastic plate of hummus with ful. It looked like vomit at first sight, none of the frilly nonsense of other places. I tore a piece of pitta, scooped some hummus, tasted it and had to stop. It was crème de la hummus. Like a summer puff of essence of hummus, the best one I've ever had. Not just the best hummus, also one of the best dishes I've ever come across.

They also serve makluba at noon, a magnificent rice and lamb dish, and around it you can find small holes in the walls that sell sumptuous kebabs, and sweet shops with baklawa and knafeh dripping with honey and syrup. Arab women sell fruit and vegetables in little corners and the smell from the tahini factory can make you dizzy. The bakeries sell ka'ak, and the smell of za'atar, the aromatic herby green mixture dominates the air. How I miss it during lockdowns and travel restrictions.

Food is just another sphere where Israelis and Palestinians fight their narratives. Falafel captures the whole issue of the conflict of food beautifully. According to Muein Halabi, an Israeli Druze chef, falafel is one of the few dishes that's truly local. It was invented in Egypt but there it's made with broad beans. When the Egyptian army moved north to attack the Turks, the army ran out of broad beans when it was in Palestine and used chickpeas instead for the first time.

It was popular street food before Israel was formed, but in the 1950s the new Israelis were the first to make a meal out of it (pun intended). They improved the slim, not-fit-for-purpose pitta into a perfect bready pocket, added salad, sauerkraut, pickles, tahini and more. It was immortalised in a song in 1957, claiming it's the national dish. There you have it: the Israelis took an Arab food, tweaked it and then called it an Israeli food. Just like hummus and other dishes.

Arab food in Israel is changing for the better. For years it was run-of-the-mill hummus, chips, salad and kebabs, which became a racist slur in football grounds. There was stereotyping of Arab-Israelis as a waiter in a cheap restaurant. In the last 20 years, more and more Arab-Israeli chefs have opened their own places where they can cook superb traditional food, such as the wonderful Magdalena at the north of the Sea of Galilee. Recently Arab food became all the rage. Long lines of people were meandering along the streets of Jaffa, followed by a tsunami of knafeh, a sweet, addictive pastry dessert all over Israel. Arais, meat cooked in a pitta, became a hit, and tahini is undoubtably the queen of the kitchen, either on its own, with aubergine or like a grown-up ketchup, on everything.

With Israel being Israel, nothing is that simple. When Julia Zhaer, owner of Al Arz, the delicious tahini from

Nazareth, announced in 2020 that she would support a helpline for Arab youths from the LGBT community, all hell broke loose. Politicians, imams and shop owners were enraged and a boycott was announced. The much bigger Jewish market reacted with increased sales of Al Arz tahini. The subject exposed rifts at the Arab Joint Party between secular and Islamists, a tension that would bring their cooperation to an end.

It led to a bitter dispute. Cultural appropriation is something that nobody cares about in Israel. For most people it's just another 'woke' idiocy. Israelis are enjoying their sushi, practising their yoga and have dreadlocks without bothering about it too much. But when the Arab-Israeli chef claimed angrily that their Israeli colleagues used cultural appropriation, it was hard to ignore. Israeli chefs say correctly that that's the food they also grew up on in their Mizrahi homes. It could easily be solved; the Arab chefs just wanted recognition.

Dr Nof Atamna-Ismaeel is an Arab-Israeli microbiologist who won the Israeli version of *MasterChef* and became a chef and a food consultant. She told Alon Hadar for *Yedioth Ahronoth*:

> In the last few years there is an aggressive campaign to brand the Israeli cuisine around the world and it comes with the price of cultural appropriation and erasing the Arab cuisine. In the name of Hasbara they wipe out the rights of a people for their food. I'm glad for the inspiration we give for the chosen people. I don't have a problem when they sell arais in Tel Aviv like the Japanese do not care if you open a sushi place there. But it is outrageous to promote it around the world as a flag dish of the new Israeli cuisine.

At home I have two packets of za'atar: one Israeli and one from Jordan. On the Israeli one it says 'a Mizrahi Ethnic Spice', while the other one is under the name of Palestinian Thyme. On a closer look I saw that the main ingredient of the Israeli one is parsley, which has got nothing to do with real za'atar. The point is that Israel is becoming more Mizrahi-Arab culturally, in food, music, language and tradition, but instead of bridging gaps, new ones appear, often due to Israeli insensitivity.

The biggest change in the food scene is the market. Now Mahane Yehuda is like the famous Barcelona Mercado de La Boqueria, and is a tourist attraction. Out with most of the stalls, in with little spots of kanfeh, pasta, hamburgers, and even fish and chips, along with some of the old places. People buy their fruit and veg at the big supermarkets now and not at the market. But it's not all bad. It's alive and some of the places are lovely, but it's very different.

\* \* \*

Like the market, Beitar changed and became a flashy club. Still Beitar but different. After a relatively quiet, dull four years Beitar became the stage upon which Arcady Gaydamak, a Russian-born billionaire and father of Alexandre Gaydamak of the Portsmouth FC debacle, played out his act. The angular-faced martial arts expert who made his money by arms dealing in war-torn Angola burst into the Israeli nation during the summer of 2005.

First he bought the Hapoel Jerusalem basketball team and gave a donation to Beitar. Fifteen minutes later he had 50 per cent of the club, and 48 hours after that he became the new sole owner. It looked like a match made in heaven. Both thrive on the underdog image, enjoy annoying the bigwigs and like to place themselves as true lovers of Israel and Jerusalem. 'Mayor of Jerusalem is a representative of universal moral,' he said.

Gaydamak became an overnight sensation. He gave millions to charity, hosted lavish parties and bought huge companies on a whim. His managing style at Beitar was as capricious. He fired managers on a regular basis and when Beitar made a slow start to the season, heads were rolling: chairman, spokesman, marketing director, they were all out.

But he put money into Beitar like never before. Beitar's budget dwarfed the budgets of their competitors and, even now, nobody has come close to it since. For a league this size, it was an Abramovich-like impact.

The best Israeli players joined the club, Luis Fernandez and Osvaldo Ardiles spent some time as managers, and in 2007 and 2008 Beitar were champions again. Teddy was full of glory hunters who were happy to jump on the Gaydamak bandwagon that seemed to enjoy the adulation.

Michael Zandberg, the best Israeli player of that period, says:

> Beitar offered me much more than any other club. They offered me three times more than Maccabi Haifa – I mean Maccabi Haifa, not just any other club. I had to think about it, but it wasn't just the money. It felt like an adventure. I like to change clubs and it was exciting. I gave Haifa an option because I wasn't sure Gaydamak would be there for the whole time but they couldn't compete with Beitar's offer and I moved.

Shlomi Barzel, the sports editor at *Haaretz* at the time, and a former Beitar fan says:

I knew it wouldn't last for long. We had a reporter who covered the club and I noticed that he is becoming too friendly in his writing. One day he came up and said that he received an offer to become their spokesperson.

He was a good guy and good journalist so we wanted him to stay. He earned something like 7,000 shekels and we thought we will give him 8,500 and keep him. He said, 'Leave it, there is no point. They want to give me 30,000 and car costs.' Four times! It wasn't just in football. It was unsustainable.

Backed by Gaydamak, Beitar looked ready for domination but Assaf Gefen foresaw it all. At the start of Gaydamak's reign he wrote in *Shem Hamisehak*:

> Calm down everybody, it is hard to see how Beitar will become the football version of Maccabi Tel Aviv basketball. Or even something normal. The casting of Gaydamak among oddballs will provide an endless comic situation the likes of which we haven't seen yet … These are not the materials for a love story or sporting success. These are promises for a new round, better and glorious than anything we have seen before for arse jokes and falling on your head. It will be fun.

Beitar fans felt the need to defend their image as brave Robin Hoods, poor outsiders, the little plucky fighters despite the fact their budget was relatively on the same scale as Manchester City.

According to Erel Segal:

Beitar has turned into a very rich club that is run differently but I can't say if they are different in essence. Maybe they will become the team of the Russian immigrants and not first-class Israel since Gaydamak is not first-class Israel. He is not part of the elites, and he is a reject persona. Beitar is a rich team that have a new angle of discrimination. It is not that a huge company had bought it but a persecuted man and hunted by the police.'

Segal gave the game away. For him Beitar and Bibi are always the teams of second-class Israel. It's not about facts but image, identity and political gain.

It would be foolish to dismiss two successive championships and two cups (one double in 2008). Teddy was full, many young fans of all backgrounds came to matches and enjoyed the victories but in the history of Beitar and Israeli football they're considered the least loved and convincing of Beitar's titles. Looking back at the coverage, the overall sensation is sour. The fans were looking for someone to blame – directors, coaches or players – for their frustration and David Frenkiel, the man behind Beitar's first website, wrote: 'I do hope that Gaydamak will invite all the scapegoats for the title celebration. They have all earned their place under the fireworks. Hating them gave the fans much more joy than all the football that Gaydamak's money bought.'

'It felt a bit artificial; you can't compare it to the championships of the 90s,' says Itsek Alfasi. 'I hardly celebrated.'

The cup win of 1976 was historic and had a lasting social significance. The first championship with Uri and Eli established Beitar's football identity. Those of 1993 and

1997 were won with good football, buzzing Teddy and great storylines. But 1998 is the most political one. All of them were crucial to the growth of the club and left memories and heritage.

The latest two are a paragraph or so in the history book. Both were won with 67 points from 33 matches, after hoovering up stars from other rivals. It was far from convincing, and it was followed by another dismal outing in the Champions League, losing 6-2 to Polish side Wisła Kraków over two legs in 2008.

Despite having all the money, the club didn't improve, not in structure, and didn't deal with its chronic problems. 'Gaydamak grovelling before Beitar's hardcore would have been forgivable had he rooted the anti-Muslim racism that's unique to Beitar ... as long as the apartheid is continuing, the fans run Beitar, the same crowd that got Gaydamak into it,' wrote Hemi Uzan, editor of popular website Walla Sport and a fan.

Itzik Kornfein, the goalkeeper who became the chairman of Beitar in 2007, says:

> Arcady was like winning the lottery. They took the prize money and wasted it without any thinking about the future, just for the momentary pleasure. They have wasted the money and kicked out the man. Yes, they won two titles and two cups but the money went to the wrong places. If they at least would have invested 30 per cent of it to build a home to Beitar, youth academy, infrastructure, but nothing. Nothing of Arcady's heritage has survived. Nothing of his money has stayed at Beitar and it is sad.

In 2008 came the crash. Amongst a global crisis, a succession of poor investments, court cases and police investigations, Gaydamak lost most of his money. To add insult to injury, he stood for the mayoral elections in November 2008. He received 7,988 votes, a humiliating 3.55 per cent, and a valuable reality check. Anybody with a little sense could have warned him. Most Beitar fans don't live in Jerusalem and there was no reason to vote for him. He was generous, donated money to many worthy causes but was chaotic and disorganised. 'If I could, I would have banned the fans from Teddy,' he said after the fiasco. The tap was closed shut. He still owned the team but didn't support it anymore. The mood had changed, like a wedding with a dead groom.

'I don't think it was worth it,' a senior figure at the club told me in 2011. 'Hardly anybody that was bought during Gaydamak years is here now.' It was like an old Bedouin proverb: what the wind brings, the wind takes. 'Winning championships is nice,' said Frenkiel, 'but I miss the old Beitar, the wild, special team.'

'The price is heavy,' said Uzan. 'Beitar has lost a big proportion of its fanbase. Many fans stopped coming to games when the glory hunters filled the stadium, and now they are gone as well.'

Some felt vindication when Beitar won the championships, thinking that the seven-year curse of Rabbi Kaduri was over. Others, with the benefit of hindsight, knew that it wasn't. Gaydamak was just a dramatic pause in the tragedy that's Beitar Jerusalem. He was about to hit the club such a devastating blow, that it hasn't recovered from it yet. Enter the Chechens.

# Forever Pure

*'The days will come upon you when your
enemies will build an embankment against
you and encircle you and hem you in on every
side. They will dash you to the ground, you
and the children within your walls. They will
not leave one stone on another.'*

Luke 19:43-44 NIV

*'A country is not only what it does
but what it tolerates.'*

Kurt Tucholsky

WHEN CAN you say that an organisation is a racist one? Is Beitar Jerusalem a racist club? While there's a vast group of fans that are openly racist, the club tries, now and sporadically in the past, to fight them. 'Here they come, the racist team of the country,' they used to sing for many years. But they're a minority among Beitar fans. Were the English clubs racist entities during the 1980s when fans threw bananas at black players? Are they racist now because some fans abuse players online?

Beitar isn't a racist club but an organisation deeply infected with racism. Numerous owners and chairmen tried to fight the racists and paid a personal price for it, as we'll soon see. If Beitar could get rid of racism and racists they would do it but it's getting harder and harder. It could have been done in the past more easily but now it looks like a herculean task.

Most fans would love to have a normal club but they don't call the shots. When Aviram Bruchian, Beitar's captain in 2009 and nephew of Uri Malmilian, said that he would be happy to play alongside an Arab player, he was summoned to an urgent meeting with La Familia. The next day he released the following message:

> I am sorry for the pain that I've caused the fans and I do understand that I've hurt them. It is important for me that they will know that I'm with them in all circumstances. I'm not the one who takes such decisions but if the fans don't want an Arab player, there will be no Arab player in Beitar.

When these kind of fans decide on club policy you have a serious problem. You just need to listen to their songs:

> *Witnesses are the stars in the sky*
> *For racism that is like a dream*
> *The whole world will testify*
> *There will be no Arabs in the team!*
> *I don't care how many and how they will get killed*
> *Eliminating Arabs makes me thrilled*
> *Boy, girl or old*
> *Will bury every Arab deep in the ground*

It didn't happen overnight. Beitar was formed as a club of a right-wing liberal movement and during the British Mandate years there was an alliance between the rejected of Beitar and Arab clubs. They never took a decision to become the home of choice for the rabid Arab-haters. That would be too simple. It's a story of radicalisation by neglect, of opening the club up for political abuse, of turning a blind eye by the party and state. Yes, there's no shortage of racist football clubs around the world where a person of the wrong colour, ethnicity or nationality can't play, but there are no places as important as Jerusalem.

David Frenkiel, a software developer, was behind Beitar's first website. He used to write about Beitar in *Shem Hamisehak* and says:

> The anti-Arab wave started after the terror attacks in the second half of the '90s. The reaction from the media and the left led to a childish reaction. The more the fans got attacked the more the provocations grow. I'm not sure all those who chanted were racists but that's the way in the stand. You shout exactly the same chants as the guy next to you. People blamed the normative crowd for not standing up against the racists with a ridiculous claim. Who wants to confront those people? So after a while it became the flag that the fans were waving.

The growing presence of Arab clubs and players in the league made it easy to foul the air with such chants. It didn't go unanswered; provocation met provocation. 'Death to the Arabs' was replied to with 'death to the Jews'. And then Hapoel Tel Aviv fans joined in. Originally their image was anti the Maccabi Tel Aviv basketball club, the prudish, sanctimonious, smug, clean-faced club of aggressive Israeli nationalism.

During their glory years in European competitions, Hapoel Tel Aviv fans always carried a big red banner saying: 'We represent Hapoel, not Israel'.

They similarly went for the jugular with Holocaust songs against Maccabi and got the reaction they were craving. For Beitar they had a treat:

> *Put Jerusalem in Jordan*
> *Give it to the Palestinians*
> *In the 1967's lines*
> *Split it in two*
> *Give it to the Palestinians*
> *There is no need for Teddy*
> *Nor for Beitar*
> *Not the Kotel and the Knesset*
> *Everything in this city is redundant*

Still, the media and rival fans didn't create the racist problem, they just added some fuel. Beitar's fan demographics are similar to many other teams but the problem developed among them for various reasons. The obvious one is a bit of tautology: when you have Arab players in your team it ceases to be an issue anymore. All major clubs had Arab-Israeli players since the rise in their numbers and so avoided the problem.

Bnei Yehuda had the same 'no Arabs' disease but Eli Ohana stood his ground as a manager and relieved the club of this drawback. Beitar had many negotiations over the years with Arab-Israeli players but never managed to sign the deal. They must regret it now.

And there was the encouragement from higher echelons. 'I remember sitting in Teddy and telling [mayor] Ehud Olmert that what is happening on the East stand is not good and by shutting our mouths we give them legitimation,' said Ruvi Rivlin, former chairman of the club, minister and the president of Israel between 2014 and 2021, in the *Forever Pure* film. 'You are the leaders of a community, of the government, say something. But they ignored it so they won't make their supporters angry.'

'We have made a mistake when we didn't stop it at the time, we thought it was just nonsense that will disappear. We were wrong,' he said on a different occasion.

In the late 1990s half the government sat in the VIP stand at Teddy masquerading as fans and ignored the chants. When Netanyahu greeted the jubilant fans after the infamous 1998 title in the city square, he didn't mind the 'death to the Arabs' calls. He never did when it was addressed to PM Rabin, leaders of the left or to Arab citizens. He could only hear adulation.

And there was worse. Itamar Ben Gvir, the young man who took the hood ornament from Rabin's car, played at the club as a kid and grew to be an admirer of Baruch Goldstein, the Cave of the Patriarch murderer. He was a follower of Rabbi Meir Kahana, the leader of the Jewish supremacy party and member of the Knesset between 1984 and 1988. Ben Gvir became a frequent visitor to Teddy, and not just for the football.

Kahana was the most extreme of the extreme right. He had proposals such as separated beaches for Jews and non-Jews, and a ban on any non-Jewish person taking a political role of power or being able to vote for the Knesset. He also said that non-Jews shouldn't be allowed to live in Jerusalem. He called for prohibition on marriage between Jews and gentiles and a ban on sex between Jews and non-Jews. The punishment for that crime, he suggested, should be 50 years' imprisonment. It wasn't dissimilar to the Nuremberg race laws of Nazi Germany. 'Israel should be a Jewish state and not a democracy,' he said out loud.

Almost all parties of the Knesset decided to boycott him, a move supported by the Likud PM Yitzhak Shamir. In 2021 Netanyahu turned heaven and earth and made sure Kahana's disciples would be elected. 'We wish we were a terrorist organisation,' said one of the leading Kahanists in an event hosted by Knesset member Ben Gvir. 'I wish for every bomb on a bus we will put a Jewish bomb. For every Jewish victim they should have sevenfold.' Israel would pay a heavy price for having these people inside the Knesset.

The yellow-and-black fist flag of Kahana was on display at Beitar matches, although the movement was made illegal after the massacre in Hebron. Leaders of the neo-Kahanists went on pilgrimages to Teddy and Sakhnin during the loaded matches between the two teams. Nobody protested against it. Beitar didn't try to step away from their abusers. Teddy over the years became the place for Likud politicians to show themselves. Miri Regev, former minister for education and sport and Netanyahu's wrecking ball, was filmed with La Familia members who sang 'may your village burn'. She looked happy and glorious and didn't mind that Israeli civilians called for the burning of others because she didn't want to cross her voters. She even posted that clip on her Facebook wall. She also had a photo taken with a man wearing a shirt displaying the face of Kahana and the logo 'Kahana was right'. During a debate in a Knesset committee, Regev said, 'La Familia is not a terror organisation. I don't recognise they have a charter of racism, incitement and violence.'

Although the connections to the Likud aren't as clear as they used to be, the party didn't hesitate to use the club as a prop. Once after a defeat to Hapoel Be'er Sheva when some of the refereeing decisions were controversial, the official Likud Twitter account came out with a bizarre post: 'It won't help you.' Well, it did help Be'er Sheva and it was another clumsy attempt to portray Beitar and the Likud as persecuted. Before an election the Likud put banners around Teddy of Netanyahu with the pun 'The Mizrahi with Netanyahu'.

Ben Gvir and his ilk made Teddy one of their places of choice for photo opportunities. Netanyahu rode the wave and spread fake news about Sakhnin fans following a national tragedy, claiming that the Arab supporters didn't respect the minute of silence in 2018. A move right out of Donald Trump's playbook. It was a lie but it didn't stop Ben Gvir, by then a lawyer, calling for the shutting down of the Sakhnin stadium. No wonder La Familia felt they had their backs covered by the government.

During the first decade of the 21st century, a process had been going on in the stands. More and more fans had had enough of the violence and bigotry. Some fans didn't feel safe and were rejected, although they were Beitar from birth. Gabriel Haydu, a features reporter for Sport 5 TV, says:

> I remember a game against Maccabi Tel Aviv in the late '90s and I sat in Hamizrahi with a goatee in honour of the Alice in Chains singer. I look Ashkenazi and leftie but I was in black and yellow and I sang and supported Beitar and they could see that I was a Beitar fan. It didn't stop them pestering me. I understood it was a Mizrahi–Ashkenazi thing and it bothered them

to see me there. At half-time I went home, the
first time it happened to me.

Other fans were disgusted by the songs about Rabin's murder,
the mocking of his widow and praise for the murderer.
Attacks on Palestinians in the nearby shopping mall and the
open racism made it harder to make the separation between
one group of fans and the whole of Beitar. There's only so
much you can ignore before finding it hard to go to matches
anymore. 'It is only a handful of fans,' was Beitar's reaction
all the way from the violence of the 1950s.

As the moderate fans left, the radicals took their place
and the process escalated. Technology also made a crucial
difference. Towards the turn of the century fans could chat,
group and organise in online forums (and later via Facebook).
In November 2002 *Shem Hamisehak* ran a big story on the
new generation of supporters. It started with an article about
young fans of Hapoel Be'er Sheva, then a struggling team,
who took it upon themselves to change the supporter culture
around the club. They bunched up away from the old violent
fans and started backing the team through thick and thin. It
made a huge difference and slowly but surely the big crowd
became a force behind the team. Between 2016 and 2018
Hapoel Be'er Sheva won three titles in a row in front of
capacity crowds in a modern stadium. The team was backed
and financed by Alona Barkat, a businesswoman who bought
the club in 2007, but the first step was taken by the fans. At
Beitar the same means were used to destroy the club.

The Beitar fans did form groups, but their aim was
different. The main group called themselves Gov Harayot
– The Lion's Den. They published a charter for the group
including a clause to ban signing an Arab player. It was later
mellowed to 'a right-wing identity will be kept' but it fooled

nobody. Nahum Shabo, one of the leaders, was quoted as saying, 'We don't want an Arab player at Beitar. The day it will happen my head will spin around. I don't think that an Arab player can do well like at Bnei Yehuda. Ask anybody at Teddy and they will agree.'

Gov Harayot didn't last long and La Familia took its place. La Familia were organised, passionate and had the Mizrahi at their command. It was a power not easily dismissed and Gaydamak, always eager for support, opened Teddy to them. He supported the group with flags, transportation, budget and a storage room at Teddy, and in return enjoyed their vocal support. When they put their mind to it, they did support the team vocally and made Teddy a fearsome place to visit but it came at a heavy price. Like the inspiration for the name, they were an organisation you shouldn't do business with. For Gaydamak, like almost all of his deals, the La Familia one was doomed and costly.

In 2008 came the crash, financial and political. Gaydamak lost his money and face following his humiliating return at the polls at the local elections and Beitar were left stranded. Beitar hadn't become the monster they hoped to be. The dreams of European glory looked doomed in the blink of an eye of the angry owner stepping away. After all the investment, Beitar won two more championships but the club was in a worse condition than before. By now the fans had too much power.

In 2010 the supporters had to endure the ultimate humiliation. Hapoel Tel Aviv came to Teddy on the last day of the season with a chance to complete the double. A goal by Eran Zahavi in added time meant that Hapoel won the title on Jerusalem's soil. The manager of Hapoel was the hated Eli Guttman and the captain was Walid Badir, one of the best Arab-Israeli players ever. The revenge on the

'Shoelaces Game' had been served and La Familia swore to kick out any player who took part in the disaster. They felt they ran the show.

In 2011 I interviewed Itzik Kornfein for *The Blizzard*. I met the general manager at Bayit Vagan, Beitar's mishmash of portacabins, training pitches and a wooden stand. It was eerily quiet. The hooded crows were circling above the valley beneath Beit Hakerem. 'The club is under a cloud,' Kornfein said.

Beitar, league champions only three years before, were now outcasts. The club was living hand to mouth and waiting for help from anybody who was mad enough to get involved after Gaydamak didn't put a shekel into the club. 'We were an exciting team and the fans loved it,' Kornfein said, 'but we couldn't persevere with it. The management was not sophisticated and was based on friendship and donations, without a real managing operation. Although we had political support it never led to turning the club into a professional organisation.'

Kornfein was the man trying to save the club. He had many meetings with potential buyers but to no avail. Beitar, again, were looking for a saviour. Guma Aguiar came and went in a personal tragedy, before two Jewish-American businessmen promised to buy the club and start a new dawn in 2011. They came to Bayit Vagan, got a Beitar kit and ran with the players, although one of them was clearly out of shape and short of breath. The players did very well not to laugh in their faces. That was the end of that promising regime as they disappeared, only to star in every list of 'The most bizarre Beitar owners' since. 'I should have been more suspicious when I found out one of them came on an EasyJet flight and slept on the sofa at a friend's home,' said Kornfein.

But maybe there was more to it. I was told by a club insider:

> Beitar is a club with a big fanbase; history, stadium, in the capital city but no Jewish billionaire, and there is no shortage of them, agreed to come close to the club. There were two guys from Los Angeles, and the first meeting with them went smoothly and they showed lots of interest. In the second meeting they told Kornfein, 'You are not a football club; you are a hate organisation.' Their lawyers told them they are out of their minds to even think of it.

Kornfein says:

> The loss of identity came in phases. It began with Gad Ze'evi's team and the big money. Players without any link to the spirit of Beitar came and ran away once the money run out. Maccabi Haifa got stronger and Beitar fans had to make do with poor reality. And then came Arcady with a lot of money, excellent players and the fans got used to attractive football and success and winning became more important to them than identification with players. We have a core of homegrown players but the fans are still unhappy. Racism is an acute problem; people are not willing to take it anymore and nor are we. As far as we are concerned this thing has no place. There are fans that refuse to bring their kids to such an atmosphere. People want to come and have a good time. With the team not doing so well and the nasty atmosphere, people are turning away from Beitar.

Kornfein is a man with a calm voice and a Pep Guardiola-like pensive look, but he was adamant in 2011:

> We say it as clear as we can. There were times when we used to pussyfoot around it but now we take a clear stand against racism. We take part in an education programme at schools as well as cooperation with police against the leaders. We have no intentions of giving up and at the start there was no dialogue with them but now there is a will to understand and work together. The leaders [of La Familia] sat here and were told that racism will disappear sooner or later. I have no illusions; it will take time but we will insist on it and we need the help of the police, the Ministry for Education and the IFA.

'When you met them, what did they say?' I asked, to which he replied:

> They have no logical explanation. 'That's Beitar, that's how it has always been,' they said. We try to tell them our true ideology is respect for others but to no avail. There is an attempt by Kahana members to join and incite the young fans. It's got nothing to do with Beitar or football, just an attempt to manipulate young and careless fans.
>
> In the past Beitar has suffered immense harm to its image and that's not counting the many games behind closed doors that we were punished with. People don't want to be affiliated with us and I'm talking about potential owners and big national companies. Such firms don't

want to be associated with such fans and we have great difficulties recruiting sponsors from outside Jerusalem.

My old friend Yossi Gabay fulfilled his longheld dream and became the marketing director of the club during that time. He saw at first hand the fight against racism:

> Itzik sued them and the court sent us for mediation and I was there with the lawyer. You see kids, teenagers, and they and their parents are begging you that it was a mistake. The parents with tears saying he is just a child. You see how easily influenced they are. Stupid and influenced that they want to make what they see as an important thing when they are 16 but can't handle the consequences. The leaders are smart, we know who they are but they pull the strings from behind. They half talk, half threat but no matter how many agreements you reach with them they will break it.
>
> It is a battle against them and if we don't win it the club will be in serious problems.

And so it was.

* * *

The 2012/13 season had a twist in the tale. Out of the blue the disgruntled Gaydamak showed a renewed interested in the club and started attending matches. The team also surprised everybody. After a slow start, the local young group built on a low budget gelled and started winning, making it to fourth place and playing good football after some very dull years. The atmosphere for most of the time was good, and the fans came back to the stands. It felt a bit like the old Beitar. La Familia hadn't gone anywhere but both sides could enjoy the team for a while. However, it was the last days of a ceasefire that Beitar would enjoy for a long while.

More unexpected events were to follow. In January 2013 Beitar announced a match against Terek Grozny, in the Russian Muslim republic of Chechnya. Recovering from horrific war, Ramzan Kadyrov, the leader of the republic from south Russia, became a business associate of Gaydamak and arranged a match between the two teams, hoping somebody in Moscow would like it. Beitar were treated like kings during the brief tour to the troubled Caucasus republic, which took place amid extremely high security. Kozaks danced to Hebrew songs, the players were guests of honour at a feast and a 0-0 result was arranged so everybody would be happy. 'It was a good trip,' said Gaydamak.

\* \* \*

Eli Cohen is a veteran coach with a great memory. He won the title with Beitar in 1997, then lost it with Hapoel Tel Aviv due to the 'Shoelaces Game'. He can recall results and scorers but when we spoke about that period his defence mechanism kicked in. After talking about the first half of the season I asked about the Chechens. 'Ha ha, I forgot all about it for a second,' he said. Trauma does that to you. Cohen continued:

> It killed our season. We were in a good position in the league, four points from the top and suddenly I see Mr Gaydamak at a training session after two years in which he didn't show up. He said he wants us to go there and I wasn't thrilled about it

but he said we will return in a private jet and we went, we played and won the next game in the league. No harm done. I thought of bringing in a Croatian player in the winter window that could have made us title contenders but then he told me there is no money for it and I have to pick up players from Grozny. I understood he wanted to get in business with the leaders there and to get close to Putin so I said I would like to get the striker Zaur Sadayev. He told me to take another one so he would have company here and that was Dzhabrail Kadiyev.

When the news broke one Saturday morning, the pandemonium began. The La Familia intifada. Everybody expected some kind of revolt and bedlam but what engulfed Beitar for the next four months shocked Israel and made the news around the world. That day Beitar played against Bnei Yehuda. La Familia had fired the opening salvo in the civil war that would bring shame on the club.

Yossi Gabay explains:

I had a sponsorship deal with a burger chain for a season and a half, very nice deal. One game was played after the signing and I invited him [a representative of the burger chain] to Teddy for the VIP box, with plans for cooperation. Everything was going very well. It was the game against Bnei Yehuda. It started and then the banner 'Beitar forever pure' was spread. I saw him standing up and leaving the stadium with his delegation. I ran after him downstairs and asked him what's wrong. He told me let's talk tomorrow in the office but it's not for him. When we met, he said he didn't want to become a sponsor, it doesn't suit him. Whatever we told him he wasn't interested anymore. He said, 'I come from a position of goodwill, not of racism. We wanted to do social campaigns, work in the community and it all went wrong.' I left and called Itzik and asked what to do. He said we can't force him; we should respect his wishes. He paid for the two games only.

'Beitar forever pure' wasn't a new banner. It has also been around for long after the Gaydamak years but went under the radar in the general wretchedness of La Familia. This time it was different. The eyes of Israel were looking for the reaction and the country was aghast. The meaning was clear, it needed no explanation. The Nazi connotations were revolting. 'As Jews after all we have been through, we can't accept such a thing,' said Kornfein to Maya Zinshtein. She was part of a TV crew that followed the two players for a while for Israeli TV. Zinshtein, a Russian speaker, got permission from Kornfein for full access to the team during those months. The result is *Forever Pure*, a documentary from the heart of the disgrace and an unnerving watch.

A press conference was called with the mayor. Ariel Harush, the 23-year-old goalkeeper and captain, is seen looking pale and with a tremor in his voice saying, 'I welcome the two players who joined the team. We will welcome them the best way possible and we'll give them the best feeling in the world.'

Harush, one of a small number to come out of the affair with his reputation intact, did that. As a captain and human being he welcomed them. He didn't say anything political, didn't confront anybody. He just said he welcomed the two

players and asked the fans to do the same. That was enough.
He was called a traitor and made a scapegoat.

Coach Cohen stated:

> I knew that they are Muslims but I didn't think
> it would cause such a shock. The fans didn't let
> us breathe from that moment. The first training
> was chaotic, the fans tried to hurt us. I'm a strong
> man but it was hell. The players feared for their
> lives. They received threats. I saw phones full with
> threats. Kornfein told a player to go to the police
> and he begged us not to do it. The team fell apart.

The player was Kobi Moyal. He was on the pitch when Zaur
Sadayev made his debut. Hamizrahi ordered him not to pass
to the Muslim player, it was reported in *Haaretz*. 'Kobi, bring
us his leg' and 'Kobi, if you pass to him you are done with us'.
The Beitar fans started supporting Moyal in response and he
gestured his thanks towards them. That was enough to make
him another traitor. He was bombarded with threats and
messages and received a post from one of La Familia's leaders
on Facebook: 'This is for you, dear friend, Mr Kobi Moyal
– you see what I write and I must tell you are a hypocrite
and grovelling joke of the media. I gave you my heart but
I found your real face you nobody bootlicker of the media
and Kornfein.'

Bait Vagan saw some of the most revolting scenes.
Hundreds of fans came to a small valley to curse, spit, attack
and vilify anybody who wasn't on their side. 'Kornfein, you
have ruined the team,' they shouted with foaming mouths.
The irony was lost on them.

Beitar couldn't win a match and a civil war broke
out. Teddy was divided between east and west. The west

supported the players and the team, and the Mizrahi were on the attack against anybody who dared to stand in their way. A knife was put to the belly of a fan who dared to support the team. 'Next time we will puncture you' was the message.

'One game I was on pitch level and Kadiyev got up to warm up and I could see the whole western stand rise up and cheer him and the whole east stand curse him,' says Gabay. 'It was odd. Like two rival teams. It was civil war but the fans on the western didn't stand a chance against the violence.'

Harush suffered horrible abuse during matches and training. Other players were ordered by the fans not to show any support for the club or the two players, and they complied. The media gave non-stop coverage to the Beitar shambles, while Sadayev and Kadiyev were counting the minutes until the end of the season. Sadayev, 23 and built like a boxer, seemed to take everything in his stride and played some good football, while Kadiyev, only 19, looked overwhelmed and bewildered by the hate. In a heart-breaking scene his mother visited Israel to find that her young boy was pilloried and abused just because of his religion. She watched a match in which he was attacked physically by a Maccabi Tel Aviv fan and received a red card. What would she make of Israel after that visit?

A key moment in the battle arrived on matchday 25 against Maccabi Netanya. La Familia spent the match showering Gaydamak and the two Chechens with a torrent of abuse. At the start of the second half Sadayev was sent free on goal and slid the ball past Netanya's goalkeeper. It was his first goal for the club. The Argentine Darío Fernández jumped on Sadayev's shoulders and celebrated with him, pointing at the scorer, but the reaction in the crowd showed how bad the rift was. On one side the supporters celebrated the goal, but, at the La Familia end, hundreds walked out in protest. When Sadayev was replaced, he received a standing ovation from the La Familia-free stadium. A rare moment of joy for the decent fans.

'These poor boys came to help us so why do they have to have all this shit?' said an angry Fernández in the film. Together with Harush and Moyal, they were the only players to show any support for their fellow team-mates from Chechnya.

As Harush was made a target for the scorn of the ultras, another player, Ofir Kriaf, 22 at the time, became their hero. He was a regular at the Mizrahi as a boy and grew up to be a mediocre midfielder. Never a big star, he made his name when he posted support for La Familia during the crisis. 'It is not the same without you,' he wrote. He was suspended for a week but was crowned as the ultras' idol. 'Make him the captain,' they chanted at every match.

More shame was to follow. In an arson attack in February 2013, the Beitar offices at Bait Vagan were hit and the little club museum was burnt. The history of the club, established in 1936, was erased in this highly symbolic act. 'One morning we woke up to an arson attack at the club,' says Yossi Gabay. 'It is something you can't comprehend. The smells, the sights, the feeling. Try to imagine somebody trying to burn your home. You open the door and it is burnt. Your most intimate place. The memories, the cups. You can't understand, you can't contain it. I felt like we are all alone.'

Two La Familia members from the south of Israel, 21 and 23 years old, were convicted and sentenced to 15 and 10 months in prison, respectively. The old Gashash sketch/prophecy came true: the fans demanded to pick the players and when they didn't get their wish, they burnt the club to the ground. It wasn't a crazy one-off episode; it was a process. Violence, and benefiting from it, were part of Beitar's history, from intimidating rivals at YMCA, to Bloomfield riots. The fire was bound to scorch Beitar at some stage.

They stopped at nothing. A group of La Familia members stood outside Kornfein's house every day, chanting vile sexual threats. The leader was David Mizrahi, a well-known figure at Teddy who had dozens of children around him, chanting in unison about raping Kornfein's wife and daughter. 'The magnitude was extreme,' says Kornfein. 'People stood two metres from me and told me to my face, "We will rape your daughter." When you run a football team the purpose is to bring joy and if a bomb squad comes to your home to check if there is an explosive device under your car, it is clear that things are out of control.'

Following the bad results, Beitar could have been relegated as the last match of the season finally arrived. Of all the fixtures in the world it was Sakhnin away. Sakhnin's ultras fantasised about delivering the ultimate humiliation and sending Beitar down a league, but in the end it was an anti-climax. A 0-0 draw suited both teams in a match that saw Sadayev sent off, to the warm applause of the local fans to add a final touch of Israeli surrealism to it all. Results in other matches went Beitar's way in any case so they weren't at any real threat of relegation.

Everybody was just waiting for that season to end. At the end of the match both Sadayev and Kadiyev said their goodbyes and went directly to the airport to the huge relief of everybody.

They never opened up about their personal nightmares. One can only guess what they must have thought of Beitar and Israel. It ended with visits to Al Aqsa, one goal, two red cards and a stain on Beitar. That one goal against Netanya proved to be crucial in the end. Had Beitar lost that match, avoiding relegation would have been much harder.

'What doesn't kill you makes you stronger,' said a much-relieved Cohen to his players on the bus after survival. He was wrong; it nearly killed Beitar and made them weaker. The club had become a pariah, an unwanted toxic brand.

According to Gabay:

> People had done deals with us but then asked for it to be terminated. They told me, 'We understand you have worked hard so put my board in a place that it can't be seen easily. Put it in a corner so it won't be on TV. We have built the brand for years and in the end people associate it with racists.'
>
> There were times when big companies, the biggest in Israel, stood in line to become sponsors. We used to get big sums and it's gone. Only small offers from small organisations, which wasn't right for a brand like Beitar. Adidas left us, which for me was a personal blow. We couldn't get a sponsor for the season, just for single games. Nobody wanted more than that.

* * *

It was Gaydamak's parting shot from Beitar and Israel. The man who took over by storm left with the feeling that he had been fleeced in Israel and treated ungratefully by the fans to whom he gave so much joy. 'It's a big relief not to be in Beitar anymore,' he told Maya Zinshtein. It starts at the Wailing Wall and ends in wailing.

'Did you think the reactions would be so tempestuous?' she asked.

Gaydamak's reply was:

Well, yes of course, it was obvious that was the purpose. I don't know if the reaction was that tempestuous but of course that transfer was organised for this reason. Not because they are good footballers. I have no idea if they are any good. I assumed there would be a big reaction. I did it to show this society as it really is, expose its real face.

Kornfein's point of view is different. He told me in 2020:

When the owner asks to have a game in Chechnya you do it, no question. From here to there a situation developed where we could bring players. It was Arcady's idea with the agreement of Eli Cohen's and myself.

Mistakes were made, they weren't good enough and we weren't ready media-wise. If you go for such a move, you pick very good players and they weren't such. You need to bring very mentally strong players and not young ones. We didn't manage the crisis right and we should have brought in experts for crisis management. We should have received help and support from city hall, police and government. The whole thing had an impact not just on Beitar and the city but on the reputation of the State of Israel. I met the highest officials but they moved on and left us to deal with the situation all alone. We knew that there would be a big reaction but we didn't think it would cause such noise around the world. It is, however, an important chapter in the history of Beitar and it should be remembered.

'Do you think it was an act of revenge by Gaydamak?'
I asked.

> I don't think it was revenge or trying to expose
> anything. He thought it would help him for
> financial cooperation with Chechen companies.
> The main thing is that the move has utterly failed;
> we didn't predict the levels of aggression and it put
> a mirror to our faces. In the future there will be
> an Arab player in Beitar or there won't be Beitar.

The fact that the two weren't world-class players was used by
objectors such as Ofir Kriaf and La Familia to justify their
behaviour. Yes, Gaydamak had done it for the wrong reasons,
for his own benefit, but would the result have been very
different had he brought Karim Benzema instead? I doubt it.

It didn't end there. In the first training session of the
2013/14 season, Harush and Fernández were attacked again.
Harush wouldn't play again for his boyhood club. Kriaf
wanted to become the next captain and was honoured years
later with a big banner made by La Familia. It displayed Uri
Malmilian and Eli Ohana, the two greatest players of the
club with him, a player who wouldn't make it to a list of the
100 best Beitar players.

Harush left as a proud man. He told *Haaretz*:

> If you grow up in a house that does not teach
> hate, you won't do such a thing. I grew up near
> Beit Zafafa and always met Arabs on the pitch.
> Growing up in Jerusalem is not like growing up
> in Tel Aviv. A bus exploded 100 metres from my
> house that shook all over. You grow into hate, that
> all Arabs are bad and try to kill you. But when

you get older you understand the other side. Here people attacked players who came from Chechnya to help the team just because they are Muslims. I would do it all over again. Without thinking for a second. Yes, the same, without fear, although I knew what is the price. I wanted to send a message and I paid the price but I feel that I've done the right thing.

'The biggest mistake is to call them Beitar fans,' says Yossi Gabay. 'They only do harm to Beitar. They are La Familia fans. When you describe them as Beitar fans you actually blame the club and not them.'

* * *

I saw *Forever Pure* at a Jewish film festival in Swiss Cottage, London, in 2018. Behind me sat a group of expat Beitar fans who couldn't resist the temptation to join in with some of the 'clean' songs. After 82 minutes of Kornfein you son of a whore, Gaydamak you son of a whore, Harush you son of a whore, Kadiyev you son of a whore, Sadayev you son of a whore, everybody son of a whore, death to the Arabs, fuck you this and fuck you that, I will rape you, hundreds of fingers and hand gestures, a whole thesaurus of Hebrew and Arabic cursing and Jewish supremacy, the house lights went up. 'It's a beautiful country, Israel, very nice, you must go and visit,' they said with bitter sarcasm that didn't cover their deep shame, to the visibly shocked non-Israeli and probably Jewish viewers.

Later I went to cover England's under-17s playing against Israel's under-17s in Chesterfield. The Israeli team was a mix of Jews and Arabs of all classes from all over Israel with wonderful relationships between all players and parents.

As usual there were anti- and pro-Israel demonstrations. The anti-Israeli group from the BDS movement (Boycott, Divestment, Sanctions) looked like a typical Jeremy Corbyn fan club, with the usual Palestinian flags and 'Boycott Israel' routine. 'Do you know that many of the players in the team are Israeli-Palestinians?' I asked. No they didn't nor did they care. Like La Familia they called for the boycott of any cooperation between Israelis and Palestinians.

They handed out flyers with a photo of the east stand where a Kahana flag was visible and a long list of claims, most of them wrong. However, that's what Beitar had become – a tool to attack Israeli football with. A means for Israeli haters to try to hurt one of the most successful spheres of cooperation. I don't think it will mortify any of the La Familia members; on the contrary, they would like to have Arab-free football but it won't happen. Arab clubs and players are an important part of Israeli football and make it to the national team on a regular basis. They're respected by most football lovers in Israel but La Familia have caused unimaginable damage to Israeli football. They'll not leave one stone unturned if they can get their way; the menorah spreads darkness due to their acts.

On the pro-Israeli line one woman looked different from the rest of the church ladies from Sheffield. 'For Zion's sake I will not hold my peace,' she said and told me her life story:

> I used to be a prostitute in Manchester, doing crack and stealing from the clients. One day when I was at rock bottom, I had sex with a vicar and stole his very expensive Bible. On my way to sell it I just had a random look and opened it where it describes when Mary Magdalene washed Christ's feet with her tears. I felt like I saw the light, a

bolt struck me, like Christ redeemed me. I was a sinful and wicked woman but today when I'm going back to the crack dens in Manchester people can't believe I made such a change in my life. I'm happy to defend Israel as part of my new life.

Beitar are world-famous now for the wrong reasons. The sinful and wicked have won. A group of several thousand people was enough to bring shame on this club and Israel. Just a year after the Chechen affair, government minister Miri Regev wrote: 'I'm a Beitar Jerusalem fan. I try to go to games and then I enjoy sitting with La Familia and walk around the fans.'

Not just a handful of football hooligans then.

# 18

# Repent

DEEP IN the Muslim quarter in the Old City stands Torat Haim Yeshiva, a Jewish religious settlement in the very heart of Palestinian Jerusalem. The place has a fascinating and complex history. At that location stood a yeshiva from 1894 until the riots of 1936 when its people fled the Old City fearing for their lives. In 1967, after the Six-Day War, an Arab man surprised a delegation of Israeli generals and handed them the key to the yeshiva. All that time he had kept the holy books and furniture of the institute behind a wall and hadn't let anybody inside the place.

At another place near the Old City there's a water fountain in memory of 'person', a tradition in Islam where every time somebody drinks from it the late person is rewarded in heaven. Attached to it there are notes in Arabic and Hebrew that say, 'Hey, every thirsty person may drink cool kosher water.' 'In memory of my father, Abu Majer, may his memory be a blessing, that during his life he gave to anybody without discrimination: Jews, Christians and Muslims.' 'And I, Majer his son joins his will: love your fellow human!'

Jerusalem is a place that will never cease to surprise you. Every Ramadan the area around Damascus Gate is filled with food sellers and among them one can spot the favourite bread to break the fast: challah bread – the traditional Jewish sweet white bread for the Shabbat. Living together in a mixed city brings unforeseen results.

Even when you have good basic knowledge and understanding of how basic it is, the Jerusalemites will show you how very little you know. Taking a taxi in the city can get you out of your bubble. I once took a ride from the west of the city to the important Rockefeller Archaeological Museum by the north-eastern corner of the Old City walls. It's an important museum situated in a magnificent white limestone edifice with a tower and lovely court opened in 1938. It was quite a long drive going through the Haredi areas, listening to the radio. The driver erupted at some insignificant piece of news regarding President Rivlin, who had fallen out with PM Netanyahu. 'He is not my president! He is a left one,' he called one of the Likud elders, Beitar through and through. Then in a bragging, Jack-the-lad tone of voice he moved on to tell me about his sex life, adding that he regularly drove two Haredi women to their Arab lovers.

'Really?!' I asked. 'Isn't that dangerous? Why do they have to go to East Jerusalem?'

'Ffffff, no, no, no – YOU don't understand,' he harrumphed, capturing beautifully in the one 'you' all his dislikes – Ashkenazi, secular, middle class, presumed Tel Avivian, lefty with a bit of a strange accent and a wee bit of outdated Hebrew. 'Listen brother, they can't have Jewish men to fuck them because that will make them spill their seed. Understand?'

You learn something new every day.

Once I had a short ride with an East Jerusalem driver to the central station. Passing near the Knesset, another driver overtook us recklessly at the big menorah outside the parliament. Some hand gestures were exchanged and the Palestinian driver was consumed with rage. A dangerous chase began in front of the police and security forces. 'Leave it, it is not important,' I tried to say. 'YOU don't understand,' he replied. 'In my culture if somebody insults me, even in his mind only, I have to defend my honour.'

I was left speechless, pondering some of my old beliefs. We made it to the station safely, where I sombrely took the bus to Tel Aviv.

It shouldn't surprise me, however, that the most defining trait of the Jerusalemite is their resolve. They don't give up easily. With so many wars, conquerings, sieges and daily struggles you can't make it in this territory if you don't fight for what's yours. The Palestinians call it 'sumud' – to cling to the land. The secular communities of the city retained their numbers in recent years and were willing to fight for their rights. Hapoel Jerusalem fans know all about it. In 2006 they reached breaking point after relegation to the wilderness of the third league. On the first day of the new season, the fans couldn't get into the stadium after the owners hadn't bothered to hire stewards.

Uri Sharedsky, my old colleague, was one of the fuming fans. In desperation, after his son asked him why he had to support such a team, he called his fellow Hapoel fans to unite and to buy the club from its owners, two local businessmen named Victor Yona and Yossi Sassi. He suggested a model where the fans would be the shareholders.

He edited the sports section in the local paper, so he wrote:

I'm willing to buy the first five shares if that will keep my team alive; if you are willing too, email me and we will see. Spread this email address to

everybody you know. If by Monday morning we
have more than 500 commitments to buy shares,
the story will go ahead.

The following week he received emails from all over Israel
and abroad from other long-suffering Hapoel fans and he
decided to give his embryonic idea a go. Soon it became
clear that the club wasn't for sale. The main emphasis of the
owners at that time was to fight each other in court and in the
local press, so they decided to stay put and together oppose
the new initiative. They became the laughing stock of Israeli
football after selling stars for pennies and declaring that one
of them was actually a Beitar fan, amid sheer incompetence.
But there was no way to get them out now.

The other option was to form a new club in the hope
of taking over Hapoel one day. The founders obtained the
rights of Hapoel Mevaseret Zion, a small club from the city
suburbs around the Castel, and added the name Katamon
(Hapoel Jerusalem's old stadium). The inspiration came from
AFC Wimbledon and FC United of Manchester, which
had caught the imagination of many disillusioned football
fans in Israel. With unusual national media coverage for a
fourth-tier club (a semi-amateur regional league), enough
shares were sold and the new Hapoel Katamon was formed.

With the Katamon name and the old socialist Hapoel
badge of a hammer, sickle and a boxer, plus Che Guevara
flags, the message was clear. Hapoel Katamon was formed
as a reaction to the demise of Hapoel but just as much as
a challenge to Beitar, at least ideologically. 'It is not just
about saving our team,' said Sharedsky. 'We want to give
the feeling that you can still live in this city and there is
something to stay for. The old Hapoel has sunk without a
fight and maybe that is why people were so eager to join.'

Joining the club from Mevaseret was a mistake. The shortcut didn't work culturally and personally, it was forced and contrived. The Katamon and Mevaseret union was fraught with tension and it felt wrong. Like when the original Wimbledon club was transferred to Milton Keynes to form MK Dons, Katamon decided in 2009 to start all over again, this time as Hapoel Katamon Jerusalem in the fifth league. It meant playing in god-forsaken places in front of hostile crowds (when there was one) that resented the big and famous media-savvy visitors. But the fans stayed on and the journey back to the top leagues had started.

TV presenter Jonathan Cohen said to *Israel Hayom*:

> The beginning was awful. I can remember going to a game in Tel Sheva [a Bedouin town near Beersheba], where we stood on the hills, between donkeys and camels getting hammered. It was a slap in the face, the coach picked players from wherever he could. One got back from a trip of several months to India, one was brought from the Knesset Guard and a third from the Arminean Quarter. And all that time we remembered better days at Bloomfield and Haifa with old Hapoel Jerusalem.

After seven years Jerusalem saw its first Hapoel derby, Hapoel vs Hapoel Katamon. Two sets of fans took over the western and eastern stands at Teddy with an overwhelming majority supporting the new project, about 80 per cent to 20 per cent according to people in the know. 'It is hard, this rift, it tears us apart,' said Mishel Dayan, a star of the old Hapoel who stayed loyal to the dysfunctional regime. One Katamon fan was filmed crying and saying with quivering lips, 'We play against my team, love of my childhood, love of my life. How did we get here? This is hell.'

Others found it easier to channel their animosity, especially after Katamon scored a 90th-minute winner. 'Jump if you hate Beitar,' the fans chanted as they celebrated the historic victory.

There were other victories. Eitan Perry is a director and chairman of the shareholders' conference:

> There is a new thing at the schools in Jerusalem. Suddenly it is cool to be a Hapoel [Katamon] fan. It is a respected thing. In every class you can find a big number of Hapoel fans. We have youth teams all over the city, kids celebrate their birthday at our ground. You can see our stickers on cars and you can find people of all walks at our home matches.
>
> Everybody said that our model can't work but this is the future. When you are willing to fight for the things you believe in, take responsibility and to work in the community, not just in football, it is a meaningful act.

Dr Amos Noy, an expert in folk culture, is a fan with a sharp, critical eye. He feels that part of Katamon's appeal is a nostalgia about the old days of liberal Jerusalem and Labour party hegemony, but he adds:

> What makes Katamon into a radical team are two things: total rejection of any kind of racism and violence and the social activism. Not feeling pity for us but taking action and changing history via struggle. There is a sense of the team as a community and this is a political stand against

the view that a club is an asset of the owner, or a charity work of a generous patron. Katamon is political by its model, by the work it's doing around the city, by making the stadium a safe place for women and children, by joining other right causes.

If Beitar are governed by exclusion, Katamon's motto is an inclusive approach. Arab players and fans are part of the club as well as the ex-Beitar skipper Aviram Bruchian. They played using rainbow corner flags in support of the gay and lesbian community, a brave act in a city where a young girl, Shira Banki, was stabbed to death in the last Pride march by an orthodox believer. The girls' team is named after the murdered Banki. 'We have kids from settlements coming together with Arab players from East Jerusalem,' says Perry. 'We had one occasion where the parents from the settlements didn't want their Jewish kids playing with the Arab kids – but the children told their parents, "We want to play, and they're our friends."'

In 2017 Hapoel were relegated to the third league and Katamon became the leading Hapoel team in the city. In seven league matches between them Katamon won three and Hapoel two, but that would be the final score. Two years later Hapoel didn't register for the season and in February 2020 the club was shut down by a court order. That summer Katamon bought the rights for the name Hapoel Jerusalem and after a long discussion changed their own name back to that. The journey had been completed, but not before tedious fights between the Katamon People's Front and the Front People of Katamon, who didn't like the change. A few Katamon fans felt betrayed and some old Hapoel supporters couldn't make the emotional step, but now there's one functioning Hapoel Jerusalem, a great success story of a club saved by its fans.

Katamon left another mark on football life in the city: they inspired the disillusioned Beitar fans. Drip by drip, provocative songs about Rabin's murder and physical attacks meant more and more Beitar fans had had enough and felt that they weren't welcomed anymore or they couldn't support what the club had become. The Chechen affair was the tipping point. The supporters who couldn't stomach the racism and nationalism anymore and refused to cut Beitar from their lives looked to Katamon for inspiration. It started the same way as with Katamon, when devoted fans felt the team they had grown up on had deserted them, that Beitar had been hijacked, and they didn't feel safe there anymore. A new team, Beitar Nordia, was formed as a fan-owned alternative.

It started after the first training session of the 2013/14 season. Ariel Harush and Darío Fernández were attacked and abused for their support of the two Chechens the previous season. Social psychologist Itsek Alfasi couldn't take it anymore and posted his frustration on Facebook, calling for the establishment of a fan-based alternative called Beitar YMCA Jerusalem. Very soon they found out that the C stood for Christian and that they couldn't use YMCA for legal reasons anyway, so they went for Nordia, the name that the national Beitar movement used during the 1947–48 British ban.

Alfasi says:

> I sat with them for many years on the Mizrahi so I know the people well. As a young man it was fun; non-stop singing, banners, confetti, etc., but at one point LF became too dominant and you

could see bullying on the terraces. They were well organised and showed their strength to the club. Towards the end of the noughties I had a season ticket for the Mizrahi. I could see first-hand that the situation was dire, it was not just the media, the territory was theirs and people were afraid to speak up at the stadium. If you didn't comply somebody would have taken care of you. He didn't have to punch you, just stand near your face and ask what is your problem. You get the message.

The breaking point was the arrival of the Chechens. I knew LF and I knew what to expect from them, they behaved by the book, their book. There was one half-time when Dzhabrail Kadiyev warmed up with the rest of the subs. Usually you don't pay any attention to what happens during half-time but this time they did. The subs exchanged passes and each time he touched the ball they booed him. And I thought to myself what a lack of humanity. Okay, you hate Kornfein and Gaydamak and who knows what else but here we have young kids who don't know anything about the conflict and just want to play and it is so important for you to hurt him? I studied in England and thought: how would I have felt if any time I opened my mouth they booed me for being Jewish?

What broke me was the sane majority that just disappeared. They went home hoping the storm would pass instead of making a clear stand. One game one of the bullies summoned me to a talk. It was only a talk and an interesting one. He said, 'You are supporters of Kornfein and you want an

Arab player and, if that happens, we will be just
like any other team.' I tried to explain that these
are not the values of Beitar but for LF this is what
made Beitar singular. A taboo.

Where does he thinks it comes from?

It is an identity thing. Each team has an identity
and Beitar's is a right-wing one. I don't have a
problem with it, I grew up in such a household
and I feel close to the right values. But for
them it means no Arab player and this is the
difference between patriotism and nationalism
and I'm a patriot and not nationalist. There
is also the dynamic of the Likud and the
Israeli right – from a liberal movement they
have changed into a nationalistic movement.
Jabotinsky was a liberal who believed in
equality, he was a democrat and [Menachem]
Begin followed that route. Now I can't vote for
the Likud, which is unthinkable.

Alfasi sent an email to the Israeli FA and asked how to
register a new club. They replied with a list of things to do,
including getting recommended by two clubs. One of them
would be Katamon. Alfasi adds:

I was never ashamed to admit that Katamon had
a big part in founding Nordia. Without them we
wouldn't have thought it was possible. Katamon
was the model for work in the community as well.
While it was clear that we wanted to promote
Zionist values they had universal values in their

322

mind but the aim was the same – to use sport as
a tool to make a better society.

They started playing in the fifth division in 2014 at the
bottom of the football pyramid. According to Alfasi:

> We played in little god-forsaken moshavs
> [agricultural cooperative associations], a dune
> with two goals, places I never heard of. A game
> in torrential rain in Rahat [a Bedouin city near
> Beersheba], the pitch was a huge puddle but the
> referee insisted so we played. But it is romantic.
> You are not just a fan, it is yours, you built it with
> ten fingers. I don't have kids but this is the nearest
> thing to a child I had.

There's footage of fans carrying a mobile stand at an away
match. That moment was the ethos of Nordia, in a remote
place, away from the media or the big money of the top
league; the fans were doing it for themselves. While Beitar
was ruled by racist thugs who lynched Arabs in the streets of
the city for fun and attacked other fans, Nordia had family
activities. Supporters brought food and drink, the drummers
beat, and the fans sang their hearts out.

Noam Bitton, a journalist and a spokesperson for the
club, says:

> We have all kinds of fans, from left and right,
> religious and secular, some Arab fans as well, local
> people and ex-Jerusalemite. All of everything.
> Maybe in five years we will have a mass of fans
> but for now Nordia shows that there is a hope
> and cure for the Israeli society. People can play

together instead of fight each other and people can make a difference. Becoming a Nordia fan is not changing loyalty, we are Beitar the way Beitar should be.

The reaction from the general public was positive while those from Beitar fans were acidic. Alfasi says:

LF said, great, we got rid of the lefties, while the sane ones said you deserted and should have stayed to fight from the inside. The most famous Beitar fan, President Rivlin, showed his support, saying, 'Beitar Nordia Jerusalem is a welcomed project with great value beyond sport.' This is a proper answer to the outrageous behaviour in the eastern stand, which has been going on for years. Sadly, the current Beitar Jerusalem can't pretend to represent the values of the Nationalist movement and its founder Ze'ev Jabotinsky. I give my blessing to Beitar Nordia Jerusalem.

\* \* \*

There used to be times when David Mizrahi led the singing among Beitar fans and much more. He was a key member in La Familia, always happy to shock the mainstream media with well-spoken racism. He led the protest when Beitar dared to sign the Muslim players and was one of the people responsible for actually turning Beitar into the racist club of the country.

These days you won't find him among La Familia's yellow-clad minions. While some of his former friends were convicted for the attempted murder of a Hapoel Tel Aviv fan, Mizrahi's life took a different route. He still attends

Beitar's home matches but stays away from the people who once adored him and now despise him. It's one of the most remarkable turnarounds in Israeli football; the messenger of hate has become a man of peace. The fan who used to lead manhunts of Palestinians in the streets and alleys of Jerusalem is spending his time in the city's schools preaching understanding and tolerance.

Mizrahi was born in a West Jerusalem neighbourhood to a poor family, son of handicapped parents who lived off state benefits and street begging. He was sent to a religious boarding school in the south of the city in the hope of him finding meaning and discipline; instead he found Beitar. He says:

> I was 12 and I jumped over the fence of the boarding school, I put my kippa [skull cap] in my pocket and went to the nearby stadium. It was Beitar against Maccabi Haifa, 20,000 people singing in unison, in love, passion, with flags and drums. I felt immediately that I found a family. I started going to all the home games and then away games as well. Every shekel of my allowance went on games. Coming from such a poor background, Beitar gave me a warm hug, sense of belonging, an anchor to life. As I advanced, I felt that I could lead people, that I could have control over them, that they were listening to me and that I have presence.

Two years later, when he was 14, Mizrahi linked his love to the club:

> Other people dream of being a football star, I dreamt of being a famous fan. I asked my father

for money to buy shoes, a man without a shekel in his pocket, a father that sometimes had to choose between medicines and food, and went and had my first tattoo to symbolise my love for the club. It shows the club crest of menorah and the words, 'Beitar Jerusalem, I was born for you, I will die to serve you.'

Mizrahi served the club as a prominent fan. He became a dominant figure in Hamizrahi, and was involved in attacking Hapoel Tel Aviv fans as well as Arab citizens in his home town. Only 18, he already had five convictions:

I was one of the leaders of the protest against the Chechens. I was troubled by the fact that they are Muslims and I decided to lead the call against them. We abused them at training; we didn't support the team during games. We cursed and fought until they left. The fans were divided; there was civil war, violence against the fans that still supported the team. We threw things at them. It was war in the stands.

Mizrahi, with a group of loyal devotees, took the fight outside Teddy and settled in front of Kornfein's home, shouting horrific sexual slurs against the chairman, his wife and kids. It went on for weeks:

I cursed his wife and kids in a terrible way that I can't repeat. He sued me for 380,000 shekels [about €90,000] and I didn't even bother to come to court. I took it lightly, put the court papers in a drawer and didn't think much of it. And suddenly

I saw on the internet that I have to pay it. It shook me to the core, it brought my marriage to an end, and these two, the divorce and the fine were the worst moments of my life. These days I regret it not just because of the fine; he [Itzik Kornfein] was a great goalkeeper of the team and I was implosive. Nobody set me any boundaries and I said things no one should hear.

But a lot of good came out of it. It was Yom Kippur [Day of Atonement] and I realised it was all my own doing, that a man is responsible for his actions. It was a moment of lucid clarity. I had to have a good look into my actions and go on a soul search. Eventually it was also a good thing for me. Without it I would now have been behind lock and bars. Without that slap to the face you could have not talked to me right now.

When the fine was reduced to 60,000 shekels and Mizrahi went to work in order to pay, it was the second moment that changed his life:

I started working in a date-packing plant in the Jordan Valley and it was the first time that I properly met Arabs and talked to them, although I grew up in a mixed city. From an early age I used to see every Arab as a terrorist. I spoke to a guy called Abed about his family. He has four kids and he earns 70 shekels a day while I'm making 300 for the same hours. Why? Isn't he a human being too? Later that week an Arab bus driver helped my mother and gave her a cold drink on a hot day and I realised that they are not the

monsters I thought they were. People want to
live, not to die, they are looking for hope, on both
sides, for a better future for their families. As a
kid I never had guidance or tools and I chose the
wrong way. Today, with my experience I want to
help boys in schools and give them the right tools
to make the right decisions.

As a prominent leader and media-loving guy, his previous
actions are all over YouTube, including a meeting with
Muhammad Gadir, then in 2013 a star player of Sakhnin.
Mizrahi refused to shake Gadir's hand or drink at his house
and spewed hate at his host with his soft Jerusalem accent
with echoes of his religious education in his rich vocabulary.
Gadir, who believed that the invitation could lead to a
change of heart, was visibly shocked at Mizrahi's venom.
Mizrahi says:

He opened his house to me, that was my first
meeting with an Arab but I came all blocked
because of my prejudices. I said some harsh things
like that he is second rate and left the place. The
problem was that after such negative action I got
warm reactions, people came and said 'well done'
and I thought – I did well. When I watch the
video today, I feel that I was implosive. I lacked
respect. What's the point of all this hatred?

Mizrahi's change of heart became the talk of the town. He
became the most hated figure among La Familia members,
some believing his life was in danger, while others were
sceptical about his motives. He works now at schools, talking
about tolerance and respect for others:

My grandfather told me that he got along with the Arab neighbours in Iraq and we should reach out for the weak population, give our hand in peace. They respected each other in Iraq but over here the incitement is just getting worse. People from both sides need to meet each other more, and an alley cat like me who made all the mistakes and learned from it can help. Only last week a child told me that he stopped throwing rubbish on the floor for the Arab cleaner to pick it up after a talk I gave.

As expected, he isn't welcomed at Teddy anymore:

I love Beitar but I take a pounding there. I can only go to the western stand, the moderate one. I can't get to the east one. People there physically attack me, abuse me and spit at me. They call me a traitor just because I changed my views. I grew up with them, I am the enemy?! It hurts. They say that I betrayed the country, the club and La Familia, but I am not a traitor. I am a man who loves his team and believes that a real fan should concentrate on supporting his team. If you get in a problem and your parents see you handcuffed, is that support? I get calls from people who are looking for a change but unfortunately Beitar is hijacked by those people. The ultras became more important than Beitar Jerusalem.

\* \* \*

The Orthodox Church of St George in the city of Lod is a church built over a ruined 12th-century Crusader structure and shares space with the El-Khidr Mosque, which is also associated with the same saint. It holds the tomb of Saint George, the famous patron saint of England, Georgia, Catalonia and many other places. Legend has it that Saint George tamed and slayed a dragon that had demanded human sacrifices.

Not far from there at Or Yehuda, on the other side of Ben-Gurion International Airport, I saw in late 2019 Beitar Nordia Jerusalem play in the third division. The club, which had stood up against its own dragon, was slowly moving up the leagues. It was a night match; bats, moths and aeroplanes filled the cool air, and the local stadium was full of local and visiting fans. Not huge numbers but a good showing and an excellent atmosphere for this league. The small one-stand stadium felt right, not too small or big, with people walking from home to see their team, although Tel Aviv and the big teams were a very short drive away.

Nordia were well organised off the pitch. They set up a little drop-leaf table and sold the best merchandise I've seen from an Israeli club, even the big ones. Shirts, socks, notebooks and Beitar's official book. It was original and with the iconic roaring lion of Melnikov from Tel Hai everywhere. It was all the things Nordia aspire to be: a link to the old Beitar but better, with attention to detail and understanding of symbolism. It looked miles ahead of Beitar's clichés and with much better graphics.

Alfasi wasn't among the fans. He parted ways from his child about a year earlier. Momi Dahan was the sponsor of the team but they couldn't find a way to work together so Alfasi left. 'At the third division you need more money and the people who put it up want to have more say, which is legitimate. They want to decide and then you start having arguments about everything so it was a mutual decision,' Alfasi says.

Alfasi, a kind and gentle man, seemed hurt. He called the Nordia fans 'lefty hipsters', which turned into a bitter debate between friends. 'Maybe I shouldn't have written that but Nordia have a problem with the Beitar identity,' he says. He wanted Nordia to be more political with Jabotinsky as a role model, but most fans didn't feel this way. For them Uri and Eli without the racism is the best ideology. Most of them don't feel very close to Jabotinsky, he reckons. 'I guess most fans are more left than right since most people who object to racism are left-leaning naturally and for me as a right-wing person it is sad because racism isn't a left v right issue,' he says aptly.

'We have 500 kids in teams all over the city,' says Dahan. 'We don't charge them. We work in the community, promote coexistence and preserve Beitar's history. We see the benefit of the education of our children, and people want to be part of it. We are investing in what is important to us and have made a mark already.'

On the synthetic pitch things didn't go as planned. Nordia fans made most of the noise but it also felt synthetic; non-stop drumming, too many flags with an image of Jabotinsky having a pint of beer and not enough reacting to the action. A bit like the monotonous noise of vuvuzelas at the 2010 World Cup and not a real football soundtrack. Or Yehuda led 1-0 when Yossi Asayag, Nordia's leading scorer for three seasons and on the back of 28 goals in the previous season, a star with a star salary in this league, missed a sitter. Towards the end of the match Or Yehuda scored their second and that was it. Nordia seemed to have missed their chance.

Nordia have a problem – Beitar hasn't fully gone away. It's still there, poor and deformed, an empty shell of its former self but it won't go away and die like the original Hapoel Jerusalem did. Nordia have a niche as a community club but couldn't find their place as a football one. The COVID-19 pandemic was around the corner, and with its slashing of budgets came more reflection and doubts. Still, it's a brave and encouraging statement on a personal and public level.

\* \* \*

On 30 April 2021 thousands of Hapoel Jerusalem fans made the pilgrimage to Teddy armed with flags and bottles of bubbly. After a not-so-tense 90 minutes Hapoel Jerusalem were part of the top league again after 21 years of suffering. 'How many people in Israel who suffered from abuse took their own fate in their own hands and made it from start to finish?' said one happy fan. Beitar supporters tweeted a picture of a press card under the headline 'Katamon's Season Ticket'. How both sets of fans missed this spark of nostalgic hate.

Although Beitar thrashed Hapoel 3-0 in the first league derby, Hapoel tasted a sweet victory in the Toto Cup, a pre-season tournament. Adjusting to the top flight is hard but getting there is an example for all football fans. Nordia, though, are struggling in the third division. Their budget is at its lowest level for years and relegation is a possibility. There's talk of cooperation with Beitar again, mainly as a community club, but the constant chaos at the mother club isn't helping to reach a common way.

Both Katamon and Nordia fans can get smug and sanctimonious but this is nit-picking. All of them did something brave, arduous and emotionally excruciating. They also made a contribution to the public sphere, giving a voice to alternative ways of running and supporting a club. It's no mean feat in Jerusalem, where the extremists are the loudest.

I was wrong. Jerusalem doesn't choose who can become a Yerushalmi. This harsh city tests and rejects any moderate citizens. It encourages bigotry and resentment. To stay in the city and contribute to it, by example, is an act worthy of great respect.

# 19

# The Passion of Beitar

*'History never repeats itself,*
*but it does often rhyme.'*

Mark Twain

IN DECEMBER 2019 I went back to Jerusalem and stayed there for a week. I stayed in Nachlaot, the lanes quarter by the market. It was in a lovely stone house with a courtyard built by the owner's grandfather, 101 years previously. A perfect location to explore the city again and to feel the pulse. I went to Jerusalem on the new train line, not as spectacular as road number 1 but fast and efficient. On arrival I put down my bag and went to Morduch to have my kube soup fix. As good as ever.

The city has changed dramatically since I lived and worked there in the 1990s. The scars and traumas are accentuated and the pain and fears are palpable. Everything and everywhere is a battlefield, between Jews and Arabs, secular and orthodox, reason and piety. Pictures of women on buses and billboards were covered with paint. It didn't matter if they were five years old or 85, if it was a model or a football player, poet or a Holocaust survivor. The fear of women, their bodies and their effect on men is very much part of the landscape.

I took a bus to Givaat Shaul for a trip down memory lane. From the market the bus goes by the old Lemel School where my grandparents used to teach, now an Orthodox school, and from there to the Me'ah Shearim, the Haredi area's main street. The walls were covered with pasquil, a wall poster often containing polemic text. It was hard to understand who was against who with all the internal fighting but it was clear that the smartphone is the worst thing that can happen to a virtuous man. 'Happy life only without internet!' screamed one poster. The COVID-19 pandemic, soon to hit this population harder than any other, spread the use of the smart abomination, to the horror of the rabbis. Knowledge was available in their palms after generations of ignorance. In a kosher book shop an anatomy book was sold: 'The liver is the centre of spirituality'.

Everywhere there were shops for disposable plates and cutlery. Big families use them instead of washing, and government plans to reduce this caused some anger. According to some it's no less than anti-Semitic persecution of religious and Haredi families by first-class Israel. It never ends.

By the time I reached my destination in the western outskirts of the city I was the only secular person on board. Everybody else was Mizrahi orthodox; all the men with black suits, white shirts and the same kind of kippa.

On top of the hill stands a psychiatric hospital, where the village of Dir Yassin used to stand. Inside, some parts of the village are ironically preserved better than almost any other Palestinian village. Even an old bus stop remains among the beautiful, cobbled alleys, although the place has been closed to the general public for many years.

Around it, dozens of Mizrahi Yeshiva boys were playing football and basketball on the pitches nearby – they're not as strict as the Ashkenazi religious boys, where sport is a 'Hellenic activity'. On the high ground you can see some of Dir Yassin's houses, the Castel, road number 1 beneath, Nabi Samuel from which guns shelled my mother's house in 1948, and vast parts of West Jerusalem. It all connects.

I looked for the old *Shem Hamisehak* office but it's now long gone and, in its place, is a new building. The local papers have also almost disappeared. Once feisty and critical, now a shell of their former selves. In 2021 you could hardly find a word against La Familia in them.

It was an opportunity to meet old friends, the few who had stayed in the city. I had lunch with Yulie Chromchenko at the Ishtabach restaurant near the market, where we had lovely shamburaks, a Kurdish pasty, with a variety of not so traditional but tasty fillings. Waiting for her at the market's tram station, I saw Yehuda Keisar, the guitar hero of Mizrahi music, setting up his red Gibson and amplifier. 'Ah, serendipity!' I said to myself.

At the start of the season he had played the national anthem at a Beitar match. Sadly, he wasn't in the mood for a free gig; he just strummed a few chords and riffs and looked bored.

I told Yulie that everywhere I go I see memorials for the dead. Everywhere. 'Of course,' she said, 'it's all part of the battle of narratives. It's done for a purpose.'

'It must be a burden to see it all the time,' I said.

'You don't see it,' she said. 'You walk like a horse and look only forward.'

I kept hearing it: 'I live in a bubble', 'in an aquarium', 'in my own little place'. People build walls around themselves as a defence mechanism.

Yulie's children go to a bilingual school where they study in Hebrew and Arabic with pupils from both sides of the city. 'I want them to speak Arabic and didn't want them to grow up thinking they belong to a superior race,' she said.

Not far from there on Jaffa Street sat a Haredi man with a grotesque puppet of a mini-me orthodox Jew on his lap. The puppet looked right out of Nazi Germany, hooked nose and all. 'The Jews are stars, they light up the night,' he sang and pulled the strings.

In 2014 the bilingual school was targeted in an arson attack by a group of Lehava members. Lehava is one of the neo-Kahanists' most visible groups in the streets of Jerusalem and Teddy's east stand. After his release from prison, one of the arsonists was a guest of honour on Channel 20, a channel dedicated to Judaism and tradition but in fact another propaganda channel for Netanyahu and the Israeli right. It was all fun and games at the studio.

The hit on the radio and stadiums was a ghastly contrived 'We are the World' kind of Hasbara song, called 'A Tribe of Brothers and Sisters'. It was sung by 31 performers. Not so much wallpapering over the cracks of fragmented society but more a psychology text book demonstration of denial (and a money-making product).

I met Shalom Yerushalmi in a café on Jaffa Street near my old flat on Heleni Hamalka Street, where I noticed two things: the tram has transformed Jaffa Street from an ugly and polluted road to a lovely and quiet street and the city is now much more mixed. In a little space, not far from Zahal Square and the imperious walls of the Old City, sat Israelis, tourists, Russian priests and Palestinian students. One young woman had a gold pendant in the shape of the territory of Israel/Palestine from the Jordan River to the sea. She looked like the other students from the opposing table. 'It's a good thing that it is so mixed now,' said Shalom. 'It means that no suicide bomber will come here and blow us all up.'

The tram changed the city's texture. The tracks go from Mount Herzl in the west, the sacred heart of secular Israel, to the new neighbourhoods in the north. The route passes near the market, the centre and then dramatically follows the north side of the Old City walls (sit on the right side for the best views). At Damascus Gate it takes a sharp turn to the left along the old green line. There are no walls, no signs, no fences but everybody knows – this is the border. On one side the Haredi zone, on the other Palestinian East Jerusalem. The carriages are usually mixed by now with Israelis and Palestinians, and you can feel the tension. There's always a woman reading psalms or *The Road Blessing* and a young man with a special text to redeem his sins of the night before. In 2021 a mini religious war started on this stretch of land.

The light railway follows the old border to Ammunition Hill, the place of a major battle in 1967, and goes up north to Arab Shu'afat and finally to Pisgat Ze'ev, a bland disputed neighbourhood on the West Bank, but part of Jerusalem. It's worth taking the whole route, seeing the different parts of the city, architecture, people and landscapes. Be warned though, some of the new zones are unbelievably ugly, crimes against Jerusalem and aesthetics. Jerusalem stone is still mandatory but it's only a thin covering to modern buildings. Google the Holyland Project: it's not just an eyesore but a testament to municipal corruption and massive overbuilding.

The light railway goes back and forth in time as well as distance, from the British Mandate to Israel's first years and current times, via Ottoman and the first days of Islam in the city. It goes over wadis and history and on the way back it glides towards Damascus Gate. The gold Dome of the Rock is rising slowly over the roofs and towering over the Old City in a majestic vision.

Nir Hasson is the author of *Urshalim: Israelis and Palestinians in Jerusalem 1967–2017*, the best book on modern Jerusalem. He's a Jerusalem correspondent for *Haaretz*, one of the great positions in the journalism world. Between the wars, he had the pleasure to write about archaeological discoveries and local stories such as the outlandish tale about the missing head of Flinders Petrie, the great Egyptologist (do visit the Petrie Museum in London) who died in 1942 and is buried at Mount Zion. He donated his head to the Royal College of Surgeons, but after being stored in a jar in the college basement, its label fell off and no one knew who the head belonged to. It was eventually identified and is now stored, but not displayed, at the Royal College of Surgeons.

The tram changed the city together with the separation wall, Hasson says. It created a daily meeting place between Jews and Arabs and connected Palestinian areas to Israeli Jerusalem. The colossal cement snake that's the wall also transformed the city. It's piercing the hills, mountains, neighbourhoods and the tissue of East Jerusalem with unforeseen results. Hasson explains:

> The populations are mixed much more than 20 years ago. There are long-term dynamics, which were escalated in Jerusalem because of the wall. You feel that you live in a mixed city now while a few years ago you hardly met Palestinians. The wall has cut East Jerusalem from the West Bank and now the people have to integrate more in West Jerusalem. They go to work in the west, learn more Hebrew, they study more at the Hebrew University, have days out at Sacher Park, shop

at the Malha shopping mall and marry Arab-Israelis. They are Palestinians but much more involved in Israeli life now. The Israelisation of Jerusalem's Palestinians is making things even more complicated.

The Palestinians of Jerusalem have a unique status, which makes things even more complicated. Palestinians who live in Jerusalem have an Israeli ID, which gives them some privileges, but they're not citizens.

Hasson says:

It's a kind of limbo. Israel has divided the Palestinian people into sub-groups and each of them has received a whole package of carrots and sticks. We want to integrate the Arab-Israelis, Gaza is locked behind the fences, getting hit or receiving supplies when there's a need. Each part of the West Bank gets a specific treatment and the only section for which Israel doesn't know whether to swallow or to vomit is in Jerusalem. These sections are part of Jerusalem and Israel doesn't want to give them any section of it and on the other hand there are 320,000 people who will vote for Arab parties if they become Israeli citizens. It's an anomaly; we talk about a united city but 40 per cent are not citizens. It is a mad situation but if you go and ask Jerusalemites, nine out of ten wouldn't know about it. It is a blind spot in the Israeli discourse. In the Israeli mind.

And there are the islands on the other side of the wall, still part of Jerusalem but blocked by the wall and not part of the Palestinian Authority. Around 100,000 people live in anarchy without any law and nobody cares about them. They're just Palestinians behind the fence of Israel. Living in unsafe buildings, burning their garbage, living near raw sewage and in constant fear of gangs of criminals. Israel doesn't do anything about it, just ignores it, until it's no longer an option.

For most Israelis, East Jerusalem means hummus in the Old City and little else, but within a five-minute drive, sometimes walk, you can get to a whole different city. You can spot in a little grocery shop a Nakba map with all the places that were demolished in 1948. You can see the impact of the wall that severs communities, houses and even one school. You can witness the actions of the Israeli army. The one I remember most is a huge boulder of Jerusalem rock that blocked the only road leading in and out of a village on a hill slope. It was there for no security reason. Just because.

'There are unsolvable problems in Jerusalem,' says Hasson. 'There is no way to solve the issues of Al Aqsa and Temple Mount. It is a threat that is always there and you have to live with it.'

These days Israelis meet more Arabs in the big cities of Israel and in Jerusalem, the media and football. When a Beitar fan goes to a match in Teddy they'll probably see Arabs on the way to the ground. The fear and hate are different now. 'If we let an Arab into the team we will be like the rest,' say self-imposed Beitar purists, and in their bigoted way they have a point. Beitar could have local Arab players and fans, people from Jerusalem who live near the stadium. They could make Beitar an authentic club of Jerusalem instead of a club of a fictional notion of the city with only 14 per cent of season ticket holders from within it. The potential is there. This is their nightmare.

'I would love that to happen,' says Itsek Alfasi.

\* \* \*

After Arcadi Gaydamak's departure in 2013, Eli Tabib became the new owner of Beitar. Tabib, who had previously owned Hapoel Kfar Saba and Hapoel Tel Aviv wasn't Jerusalem Syndrome material. He didn't take over for the spiritual meanings of the city and he didn't get carried away. He meant business. With a keen eye for talent, he believed he could make money by transfers and sales. He was at the helm for five years, during which La Familia became even stronger and the gap between Israel's top teams grew bigger.

After the 2013 victory, La Familia were running the show. The organisation became larger and more violent and in 2016 they attacked Hapoel Tel Aviv fans in south Tel Aviv and almost killed one of them in a horrific hammer strike. Following a police crackdown, the attackers were sent to prison, but the organisation re-emerged soon after. The offences of the terraces go unpunished. The song about the attack and maiming a person is a fan favourite.

Tabib's best season was the most farcical one. He hired a puppet of a manager named Benny Ben Zaken, an unassuming and weak person who received direct orders from Tabib before and during matches. In one case Ben Zaken was short of fit players and wanted to play Yossi Benayoun. Tabib vetoed it for some reason and Ben Zaken ordered Benayoun, a legend of Israeli football, to sit on the bench while a bunch of nobodies started in the first XI. Beitar were again the butt of jokes but somehow the team did well. They played ordinary football but with great goals scored in every match – a disproportionate number of the goals from outside the box. It was clear that the anomaly couldn't go on forever but after two rounds Beitar were just behind Hapoel Be'er Sheva, the back-to-back champions of the previous two seasons.

With few matches until the finishing line, Beitar fans dared to dream: if they won their remaining matches they would win the double. They had a match against Be'er Sheva at home and also the cup final in South Jerusalem. Unfortunately, Be'er Sheva hit their purple patch in the last round of the season and crushed their opponents, while Beitar's luck and energy ran out. The team was shattered and spent.

They still had a fighting chance after leading 1-0 against Be'er Sheva at half-time in the vital league clash, only to be steamrollered in the second half as Be'er Sheva won 4-1 and went on to win a third title in succession. Four days later Beitar got back to Teddy for the cup final. Tabib started with a shocking line-up, missing key players with whom he had fallen out due to contract disputes. A 3-1 defeat to Hapoel Haifa ended their miserable week. By the end of the season they had dropped to third place, 12 points behind the champions from the Negev.

Still there was one burning humiliation in store for Beitar. Tabib, sensing his time was up, tried one last desperate move. He announced that Beitar would change its name to Beitar Trump Jerusalem, in honour of the American president who had moved the American Embassy from Tel Aviv to Jerusalem. It was a 'Bibistic' move; patriotism as the last refuge. Nobody fell for the empty gesture and it never got off the ground. By the end of the summer, Tabib was out due to the fans' pressure.

That season demonstrated how bad the damage was that La Familia had done. Even as title contenders the attendances were usually around 6,000. For the big match against Be'er Sheva, Beitar had around 20,000 fans and the visitors 9,000. Beitar were a huge distance behind Maccabi Tel Aviv and Maccabi Haifa now, and miles behind Be'er Sheva and their near-16,000-capacity crowd. For Beitar not to get even near their allocation of 29,000 tickets for the title decider was the price of the years of decay of club and city.

All over the city there were magnificent posters of Uri Malmilian and Eli Ohana for a Beitar exhibition. The fine event was in Holon, south of Tel Aviv. The historical Beitar and Irgun posters, the state cups, burnt boots of Ohana, and a banner with Eli, Uri and Ofir Kriaf, told Beitar's story in an honest way but the location was also part of the story. Beitar is viewed as Jerusalemite by history, importance and sense of national duty but no longer by its fans.

* * *

In the summer of 2018 one tweet was sent from the Luzhniki Stadium in Moscow before the World Cup Final. It showed a group of Hapoel Be'er Sheva fans with the red-and-white flag of the proud champions of Israel. There was nothing unusual about it; Israelis go to big matches in massive numbers. But by the end of the summer the picture looked odd when one of the guys holding the flag brought Beitar Jerusalem from the brink.

Moshe Hogeg was born in Beersheba in 1981, played for the youth teams of Hapoel and Beitar Be'er Sheva and was a big fan of the former. He made his money in cryptocurrency and was the sponsor of the club in the 2015/16 season. For him to become the owner of Beitar Jerusalem was puzzling to say the least.

Hogeg, a nebbish-looking, sanguine and highly likeable man, is an avid collector of superhero memorabilia. He arrived without a cape to save the club after another cycle had ended. As the saviour he was greeted as a hero and enjoyed the support of the fans as he tried to dismantle Beitar's main problem. As a businessman he could read numbers and he understood that Beitar needed to change their image.

A man close to religion, Hogeg went to the Kotel on his first day in office, brought rabbis and met La Familia leaders during the honeymoon phase. He told them that he intended to bring in an Arab player, who was loyal to Israel, and foreign Muslim players. The rabbis explained that racism was forbidden by Judaism and called for the fans to love their neighbour. Hogeg promised them unprecedented support and also threatened to sue individuals who sang racist songs and harmed Beitar's image. La Familia, in response, ordered their loyal personnel not to sing the offensive songs and chants anymore. Results were poor but Hogeg had the biggest support any owner had received since the Gaydamak heyday.

In the summer of 2019, Hogeg put La Familia to the test. He signed Ali Mohamed, a midfielder from Niger and a Schrödinger's cat of ethnicity, with a Muslim father and Christian mother, and who chose to identify as a Christian. La Familia protested at first and disrupted a training session, then said they would accept him but only under a nickname – Fabregas or something like that. The move went through and a barrier was broken. With a player called Mohamed and much better behaviour in the stands, Beitar's image was starting to heal, slowly.

\* \* \*

I met Yossi Gabay at a pub in the market during my stay. It was close to midnight and the place was buzzing with people drinking, eating and flirting. Never underestimate the Jerusalemites and their resoluteness. 'I want you to come to dinner at my place tomorrow evening,' he said generously.

'I can't, I have a game tomorrow,' I said.

'Which game?'

'Beitar Jerusalem? Your team?'

'Really? That goes to show you how much I care about them today,' he laughed.

And so I went to see Beitar Jerusalem at Teddy against humble Hapoel Hadera. The VIP stand and boxes were closed for renovation, so the press box, well four tables, was moved to the top of the west stand. Around it there were about 5,000 better and cleaner seats but still a fan was sitting there. It wasn't a problem; there were only two other journalists.

Around 6,000 fans inside a dusty and windy Teddy saw a routine 2-0 Beitar victory in a lacklustre affair. The east stand was in good voice and singing mainly about Hapoel Tel Aviv. Beitar are probably the only football club in the world with a biblical fan song. The godly command from the *Book of Deuteronomy*, 'You shall blot out the name of Amalek', is directed at the most hated of enemies – Arab teams or Hapoel Tel Aviv. La Familia members, however, kept their word; they sang for most of the time with no racist songs, chants or special treatment for Arab players.

The best Israeli player on the pitch was 21-year-old Mohammad Abu Fani, a defensive midfielder on loan from Maccabi Haifa to Hadera. In 2021 he was the backbone of the title-winning Maccabi team, ending a ten-year drought and earning a place in the national team. Jock Stein, the great Scottish manager, used to say that if he had the choice between signing a Catholic or Protestant player to Celtic, he would take the latter knowing that Rangers wouldn't accept a Catholic player to their ranks. There's a lesson there for Beitar. Until they resolve this issue they'll always be behind in signing the best Israeli players available.

It was an underwhelming event. Teddy looked too big for the team, and the atmosphere was decent but a pale shade of the past. 'It is because it's cold and because of traffic and parking problems,' I've been told. Hogeg himself raised the issue of low attendance, and the answers were the same: traffic, parking, cold winter and prices.

All correct but missing the point. Had people come from Jerusalem to the match, driving and parking wouldn't have been such an issue, but when only 14 per cent of them live in the city, you have a problem. Many of the fans wore kippas and some were Haredi but the Haredi community in general don't go to football in large numbers. Jerusalem is a poor Haredi and Arab city with one decent entrance from the west and no train back to the Tel Aviv metropolis after the match. For all the big talk, the city is suffering from years of neglect. The fall of Beitar reflects the status of the much-lauded but poor capital city.

And there are more issues. The club demands not to play on the Shabbat for religious reasons but it's much harder to get to the city on weekdays. Instead of enjoying the free day, having a nice time in the city and getting back home early, the match starts late and people can't use public transportation. Well, you can't eat your challah and still have it. You can't refuse to play on the Shabbat and complain about how hard it is to get to the city on a Monday night – but they do.

And there's the biggest issue: La Familia drove away moderate fans, made it almost impossible for non-far-right fans to enjoy the matches and made it inappropriate for children. They shoved the conflict, racism and hate into people's faces. Even after they cleaned up their act, they still sang about sticking a hammer in the skull of a rival fan. People chose to stay away for all these reasons. So, it's not because it's cold, even though it can get cold and snowy. Oh no.

Shlomi Barzel, my former editor at *Haaretz*, told me:

> I'm not a Beitar fan anymore. It ended in 2013.
> I went through chemo and I don't have Beitar in
> my blood anymore. I was at the semi-final in 2018
> and I had tears in my eyes and Eli Ohana noticed
> it. 'Yes,' I told him. 'It is part of me. Beitar was my
> team and I did love them and I loved the fans but
> I'm not there anymore. I'm not a Beitar fan now.'

There was one positive point. Ali Mohamed played well and was received respectfully, just like any other player. You couldn't tell that there was something special about him playing in front of this crowd. Could it be that Beitar were on the right path?

'Racism cost the club dearly,' Hogeg told me. 'Even after my second year some potential sponsors were still afraid of the racist image. The club is known for the wrong reasons, not for great football or success but for a small bunch of racists who cause damage to it, to the city and to Israel.'

For two and a half years the relationship between Hogeg and La Familia was tense, and you could sense that things would come to a head. It always comes to a head. The football, despite finishing an improved third in 2020, wasn't great and Hogeg's credit was running low. The eccentric owner, more a hyperactive kid with wacky marketing ideas every other day than a sound owner, went for a big, bold move. Following the Abraham Accords – a peace deal between Israel and the UAE and Trump's USA – Hogeg signed a deal with Sheikh Hamad bin Khalifa of the UAE to become a partner.

First Hogeg met Rabbi Chaim Kanievsky, the 93-year-old leading authority in the orthodox society of Israel. Hogeg asked for the rabbi's views on a ground-breaking deal. 'I asked him if it is allowed to have a Muslim co-owner for Beitar Jerusalem; are there any stipulations and can we get his blessing,' he said to me. 'We were asked not to play or train on Shabbat and we were told that there is no problem with having a Christian or a Muslim partner. Sometimes it is even better to have a non-Jewish partner for the parts of the business that have to operate on Shabbat. Thankfully, the rabbi gave his blessing.'

When Hogeg declared that Sheikh Hamad, a distant member of Abu Dhabi's ruling family, would buy 50 per cent of the shares, it was global news. The film *Forever Pure* made Beitar famous worldwide and now this surprising news was televised to the world. The fans hoped for a Manchester City kind of deal that would propel the club to success and glory, not just in Israel but in the Champions League as well. Bringing in Bin Khalifa looked like a masterstroke – getting money and getting rid of the racists. Beitar seemed to be on the border of legitimacy again.

Most fans reacted happily. 'I hope that we fall into a well of money,' said Moshe Ziat, a well-known supporter. Over social media fans supported the move, while La Familia reacted angrily. Graffiti against Bin Khalifa, the deal and the Prophet Muhammad were sprayed on Teddy walls. The two sides clashed on a Friday morning during a training session at Bait Vagan. Support outnumbered the objectors, a few pushes and shoves were exchanged, but the outcome was clear: an Arab owner was welcomed warmly into Beitar. 'It was moving,' says Ziat, who was one of the organisers of the show of support. 'It was the first time that our side, the silent majority was heard. We are not silent anymore. You can't change an image overnight, but our way now is out in the open.'

'They don't understand what the soul of Beitar is,' Hogeg said about La Familia. 'They are ignorant. They don't have a clue. There is no logic to them. The deal is good for the whole Middle East, the peace was achieved by PM Netanyahu and the UAE is a country that took our side. It is in the true spirit of Beitar. I will work with the police and I'll sue the heads of LF and we will win this battle.'

'I will go to the first game when fans are allowed so I can show my support, we need to be present in the stadium this time,' said Itsek Alfasi. 'It's a different situation, this time people are dreaming about the Champions League and fans won't let LF destroy it.'

On 7 December 2020 the deal was signed in Dubai and the underwhelming details were published. The level of expectation dropped sharply. Sheikh Hamad bought 50 per cent of the shares for about 300 million shekels ($92m), which will be paid over ten years, including a return of Hogeg's investment so far. These aren't sums unheard of in Israeli football, where Maccabi Tel Aviv and Maccabi Haifa have had budgets of over 100 million shekels per season. The big money, promised Hogeg, will arrive via sponsorship deals.

The plans according to Hogeg were far from exhilarating. Investing in infrastructure and building a youth academy were top priority before marquee transfers. 'We will be the Borussia Dortmund of Israel; we have even got the same colours. We will buy young players and play attacking football. The money won't be used to inflate players' salaries, this time we will be building for the long term,' he told me.

It felt strange and I had my doubts. When you strike a deal with one of the richest families on earth and you have a football club in trouble, you don't just talk about the long term. The image of Beitar had improved overnight but now it was time to save this season, give the fans some hope for the future. Sign an Arab player for huge money, make a statement. He talked about social change this and social change that, not about becoming Israel's number one club again. Something wasn't right and I didn't believe a word. 'Be careful what you wish for,' I wrote after the interview when other fans were still jealous of Beitar.

Then came the facts. Both Sheikh Hamad and the Israeli businessman who helped mediate the deal had changed their names in recent years and the sheikh's website had been built amateurishly only six months previously. Doubts started spreading but Hogeg kept saying there was nothing to worry about.

More worrying news came when the Israeli liberal newspaper, *Haaretz*, revealed that Hogeg had a contract with a convicted Israeli fraudster to get a potential loan with a shocking interest rate of 12 per cent. Hogeg mentioned the value of Beitar players as his assets. He didn't use the loan in the end but the alarm bells kept ringing louder and louder.

Another bombshell from *Haaretz* followed. It turned out that Bin Khalifa wasn't as rich as he claimed to be. According to *Haaretz*, a business intelligence company reported:

> One was concerned about the possibility that the Emirati was actually a front man. The investigators found that he owned dozens of inactive companies and that there were large discrepancies between the valuation presented in his formal list of assets to the soccer association and their actual value. In addition, information was presented regarding the

sheikh's connections to people who have been tied to fraud and money laundering.

The most bizarre finding was about the true value of the Bin Khalifa fortune:

> The sheikh informed the IFA that his net worth is an estimated $1.6bn. His main asset, as listed in the declaration of assets, was Venezuelan government bonds, whose value he estimated at about $1.5bn (i.e., 95 per cent of the valuation of his full assets). But these bonds were non-tradable, and because of the deep economic crisis in Venezuela, the payments on the bonds were suspended by the government. The assumption is that these bonds will never be paid off and in the best case scenario they may be worth one-tenth of their face value.

Bin Khalifa was asked to show the Israeli FA transfer committee, the body that approves any ownership of a football club, an official UAE Police certificate proving he had no criminal record. It was a mere formality but when he failed to do so the deal fell through. Hogeg was furious, at first blaming the FA and the media for derailing the deal and saying that rival fans were behind the negative news. The latter part was correct. Months later he admitted that things looked odd. When I spoke to the source of the information that scuppered the deal, he predicted that Hogeg wouldn't start the 2021/22 season as Beitar's owner. There were problems beyond the sheikh's shambles, he said.

Hogeg soon had to deal with more troubles. Two of his personal friends, Roee Bruchiel and Eran Okashi, sued

352

him for 18 million shekels ($5.5m) in a civil suit. Bruchiel was a childhood friend of Hogeg's, and Okashi served as a bookkeeper at Hogeg's Singulariteam Venture Capital fund. The plaintiffs alleged they were owed money by Singulariteam after they invested in several of its failed projects. The defendants were accused of creating fictitious and inactive dummy companies, which they used as a front to raise money from unwitting investors before allegedly removing the funds from these companies, leaving them bankrupt. 'After the funds were raised for those ventures, the defendants began plundering the coffers, and funnelled the money into their own private pockets,' said the plaintiffs. The two submitted a transcript of a recording of Steven Kruger, Singulariteam's legal counsel, in which he told one of the plaintiffs that Hogeg had stolen from them and other investors and could end up in prison. Hogeg denied the allegations and said the lawsuit was an attempt by disgruntled employees to extort him.

Beitar fans reacted angrily and said that the TV reporter on Channel 13 was a Hapoel Katamon fan but after a period of bereavement they crowned Hogeg as the worst owner Beitar has ever had, and that's some competition. Never in the history of Beitar has an owner had such vast support, so much patience from the fans, who even defended him with their bodies against the thugs. All to be squandered over shady deals that didn't make it past the first hurdle.

The truce with La Familia was over by now. Hogeg was targeted at matches and on social media; anything from a red camel due to his Be'er Sheva background, to sickening chants about his wife and children were aimed at him. He called La Familia 'a cancer that has to be eliminated', which wasn't unusual. 'Cancer' is the most common way to describe La Familia by normal fans and with good reason. It's not an infection from a foreign virus but something that grows from within the body, knows it very well and is extremely hard to eradicate. The gentle souls of La Familia were offended. They wrote: 'To call our organisation, which does so many good deeds like helping sick kids and supporting the poor, cancer is incomprehensible!!'

\* \* \*

Momi Dehan is the man behind Beitar Nordia and has Beitar Jerusalem close to his heart. He was a main sponsor during the glory days and worked with Itzik Kornfein during the worst of times. Like many Nordia people, he felt closer to Beitar during Hogeg's time and he knows the ins and outs of the club:

> La Familia stole the club from everybody. They ruled and took over since the end of the Arcady regime and during Tabib's time. They control the agenda. When they want, it is peaceful and when they need, it will be back to their old ways.
>
> We found that the best way against them is to sue them personally. We sued people who burnt chairs, threw bananas or called racist chants. It was an act that brought them to their knees. When it hit them and reached their homes it looked different. But then Eli Tabib took the club and he told me that he is not going to sue because he does not want a war with them. They are the customers and he will hug them. At that point I knew that Beitar is dead because sooner or later, the monster will turn against you. It is like Hamas; it may be quiet for a time but then they decide there will be a rocket attack.

What can Beitar do? I asked. The IFA punishments of fines and closing Teddy don't work at all.

> You can bring an Arab player or ignore the problem and say that there is no good enough Arab for Beitar or that no Arab would want to come to the club. It is fine now in the stadium but the racism is still there. The problem will return.
>
> It cost Beitar dearly. Beitar is not a huge club anymore. They may have between 150–200,000 fans but in the run-of-the-mill game they have 7,000 or less. Maccabi Haifa even during a poor seasons has 20,000 season ticket holders. They are fans but at home. They don't like Teddy; it is unpleasant there. The sane people with wives and kids don't come to Teddy and not because of a parking problem. I don't bring my children and grandchildren to Teddy – they have to get rid of the disease that is La Familia.

\* \* \*

Between April 2019 and March 2021 Israel went to the polls four times. The only question was Netanyahu, yes or no. He lost four times but only at the fourth attempt did the 'no Netanyahu' majority manage to form a coalition, thanks to Islamist party support. Netanyahu no longer had anybody left to lie to in the Knesset. This could only happen after Netanyahu gave the Arab party Raam a kosher stamp when he first tried to get their support.

Knesset member and former minister Bezalel Smotrich wasn't happy: 'This historical event is equal to the decision to give the Arab-Israelis the right to vote for the Knesset. It was an irreversible step the let them in the democratic field forever.'

It ended a year of demonstrations outside Netanyahu's official residence in Jerusalem. He was standing trial on four charges, including breach of trust, accepting bribes, and fraud, and the protestors called for his resignation. Every Saturday night thousands of them gathered there, clashed with police and in some cases with La Familia members. During the time of pandemic, when football was played behind closed doors, La Familia had more time for political activity. When a female left-wing protestor sat half-naked on the menorah in front of the Knesset they sprang into action. They felt the supposed desecration of the Jewish state and the Beitar symbol couldn't go unanswered and they clashed with leftist protestors in the streets of Jerusalem.

'Thank god we have come to the holy city to make it clear: if you defile our symbols, all things that are holy to us, we will be there to protest,' wrote Moshe Mothada, one of the top leaders of La Familia. 'You wrote that we are a terror organisation? I'm proud of our people, the only men in this country. While right-wing supporters are only keyboard heroes, we are out there showing that we care.'

In the spring of 2021 Jerusalem was simmering again. The new coalition was taking shape but the old conflict was making the rounds. The cause was the eviction of Palestinian families in and around Sheikh Jarrah to the north of the Old City. Then short clips of Arab youths attacking orthodox Jews and humiliating them during a ride on the urban train appeared on TikTok. For some Israelis it was reminiscent of old Holocaust footage. The 'TikTok Terror', screamed the media in a typical over-reaction. It was followed by clashes and harassment on the streets of Jerusalem by both sides. During Ramadan, for some unknown reason security forces decided to close the plaza in front of Damascus Gate. It felt like somebody in power wanted it all to escalate.

Ehud Olmert, the former prime minister, didn't pull any punches, writing in *Maariv*:

> Netanyahu needs a wave of terror to create a false impression of an acute national emergency that will require the forming of a national government with his leadership. Netanyahu doesn't strike the match, Lehava people will do it. He gives them the matches. He wants a crisis, if possible, in Jerusalem – this is the place you can gather more solidarity and agreement with right-wing people.

On 7 May, Israeli forces clashed with Palestinians inside the Al-Aqsa Mosque. It was like somebody wanted it to catch fire. From there it was hard to stop: Hamas fired rockets from Gaza and violent clashes erupted on the streets of the mixed cities of Israel. Haifa, Acre, Lod, Ramla, the Negev, Jaffa and Jerusalem turned into battlefields. The Arab-Israeli population reacted with violence and vandalism all over Israel, burnt synagogues, destroyed roads and property and killed civilians. The far-right organisations, including La Familia and Lehava, went on a rampage. Live on Israeli TV, Jewish rioters attacked Arab-owned businesses and lynched an Arab-Israeli on Bat Yam promenade, south of Jaffa. They hit the helpless man with an Israeli flagpole in a highly symbolic act. Citizens were mortified and Israel looked doomed. It wasn't the Jewish militias of the West Bank going on the weekly pogroms against Palestinians, it wasn't the Bedouin gangs putting fear into the people of the south. It was the centre of Israel, the cities, the core of the country. For a short time it felt like Yugoslavia on the eve of its war.

The impact of La Familia was clear. The songs from the stands trickled on to the streets. 'May your village burn' and 'Shu'afat is on fire' echoed all over the burning cars. On La Familia's WhatsApp group, missions were organised. It was clear that La Familia had become not just a political force but also a brand name for many far-right groups.

When one of the rockets fell in an Arab town, a reporter on Channel 20, the channel for tradition and political propaganda, said on air, 'Unfortunately there are no massive casualties here.'

While they're only a small group compared to Yeshivas and armed Jewish militias in the West Bank, it was obvious that years of hate and nationalism spewed by some Beitar Jerusalem fans hadn't gone unnoticed. It was amplified by the acoustics of Teddy, it was broadcast live on TV every week, it inspired people. Football clubs are important social institutions, for good and bad.

Over Twitter famous footballers made their voices clear. #SavePalestine tweeted Zaur Sadayev. Paul Pogba of Manchester United was very subtle: 'The world needs peace and love. It will soon be Eid, let us all love one another. Pray for Palestine,' he posted.

That was enough for Hogeg, still in charge, to go on the offensive, posting:

> The Arab-Israelis can't sit on the fence. If you support Hamas, you should say it so we can help you cross the border or arrest you for treason. If you are against hurting civilians, you should grow balls and condemn the terrorists. A word about Beitar: as long as I'm in Beitar no person who disrespects Israel and Jerusalem will set foot here. Even a Christian footballer that supports the

attack on Israel will not be in the club even if he
is as great a talent as Pogba.

You could sense his time was up; these shows of patriotism
are usually valid indicators of other problems.

It subsided after a few days, as did the conflict with
Hamas, but it can't be forgotten. It showed how easy it is to
unravel the tapestry of life in Israel. How the integration can
change direction in a flash and friendships can be lost. Still,
there's no other choice, everybody still has to live side by side.

In June 2021, a strange government was sworn in, a
jumble of liberal left and soft-right parties, one Islamist
conservative party and all led by Naftali Bennet, of a small
right-wing party. Netanyahu was out at last. The Israeli right
had been taken over by Netanyahu's personality cult but now
deep in it there's nationalism, messianism and Kahanism.
Looking at the history of Beitar can send warnings of where
this is heading to.

In September 2021, Hogeg announced that he was
stepping down from running Beitar and that the club was for
sale. Another tenure had ended in wailing and the search for
a new saviour was on again. Before the start of the 2021/22
season, Ali Mohamed was transferred to Maccabi Haifa.
He couldn't wait to get out of Beitar, according to the Israeli
media. La Familia were back to their old ways during the
season with the old racist songs and chants. Hogeg came and
went and nothing has changed.

Uri Levi is the founder of Baba Gol, a website for Arab
and Asian football and not the big leagues of Europe. He's an
expert of the Middle Eastern game and grew up in Jerusalem.
He's a Hapoel Jerusalem fan.

He was there during the bad times, avoiding a bus
explosion by two stops, and knows the city inside out. Levi

speaks fluent Arabic and has seen football matches around the city in places most Israelis have never heard of. He says about Beitar:

> It is a sad situation. The club is an economic and political tool for so many people. Most of my friends are Beitar fans and most of them would like to have the best players and they had had enough of the situation. It is very convenient for the society, media and politicians to dismiss this bad ugly boy who is all that evil. It is the same regarding Jerusalem's place in society. It could have been the best place in the world, open and inventing people from all over the world. Jerusalem is a bar of gold, when the tsunami will cover Tel Aviv Jerusalem will still be there on a mountain, holy for all. Jerusalem has it all but the State of Israel uses the city in order to preserve its status as a victim.

\* \* \*

The horrible events of May 2021 put Israeli football to the test. On the day of clashes on Temple Mount, before the fire engulfed the land, Munas Dabbur, the Arab-Israeli striker of Hoffenheim and Israel's national team, posted on Instagram a picture of the Dome of the Rock and a quote from the Koran: 'Do not ever think that God is unaware of what the wrongdoers do. He only defers them until a day when the sights stare.'

It made him an object of hate, and after discussions with the Israeli FA he took a break from national duties. Before Israel's crunch match against Austria in Haifa in September 2021 he was summoned back to the team and had long talks with his fellow players. He published a clarification, saying, 'I'm all for tolerance, mutual respect and coexistence.'

Knesset member and Kahana successor Itamar Ben Gvir called for fans to protest against Dabbur and other non-Jewish players. During the match a lot of the fans booed every time he touched the ball while others supported him. When he scored a crucial goal for Israel, he was hugged by all the Israeli players, most of them politically right-leaning, in a show of unity. Yes, footballers can't speak up on political subjects, and Dabbur was in fact silenced, but Israeli football again showed that it could lead by example, that it's a place where citizens can live and play together despite tensions. It was far from perfect but they understood and compromised for the good of the team. Beitar stands out in acting the opposite way until they're cured of their malaise.

Beitar foretold the story of the underprivileged, the rise of the Likud and gave Mizrahim a voice. Like the Israeli right it became consumed by racism and hate until the realisation that it must change. Dabbur and his colleagues showed that this should be the direction of Israeli football and society, understanding the differences but working together. Without underestimating the colossal problems of the Israeli-Palestinian conflict for a moment, it's a tiny ray of hope and it can make life in Israel better. This is why the story of Beitar Jerusalem is important. The club has to keep fighting its cancer and must join this direction or it will continue to struggle under the spell of La Familia, neo-Kahanists and politicians.

'Beitar wants a messiah' is a banner displayed at Teddy by a Hasidic cult. They think it's the solution but actually it's the cause of their problems.

# 20

# Apocalypse

ON THE Mount of Olives, watching the Old City, is the Roman Catholic church, Dominus Flevit – 'The Lord Wept' in Latin. According to the 19th chapter of the Gospel of Luke, Jesus becomes overwhelmed by the beauty of the second temple and, after prophesying its future destruction, he wept openly:

'The days will come upon you when your enemies build an embankment against you and encircle you and hem you in on every side. They will dash you to the ground, you and the children within your walls. They will not leave one stone on another, because you did not recognise the time of God's coming to you.' Luke 19: 41–44

The unique church on this site dates to the 1950s and was designed by the celebrated Italian architect Antonio Barluzzi. He strove to have the form of each church he designed reflect the essence of the relevant scriptural passage commemorated. Accordingly, Dominus Flevit is a small chapel with a high pointed dome that's meant to evoke the shape of a tear. The altar contains a modern mosaic of a hen protecting her chicks, a reference to a related prophecy uttered by Jesus earlier: 'Jerusalem, Jerusalem, you who kill the prophets and stone those sent to you, how often I have longed to gather your children together, as a hen gathers her chicks under her wings, and you were not willing.'

\* \* \*

On Boxing Day 2021, Beitar hosted the derby at Teddy. I was planning to be there and write my impressions in my room at the beautiful Salesian Sisters Pilgrims' Home in Musrara after a morning of hummus by Damascus Gate. The idea was to travel from London to Israel, watch the match, feel the pulse in post-Bibi Israel and tie up all the loose ends in this tale. But plans and bookings were all disrupted by the Omicron variant, red list countries, quarantine, PCR tests, isolation and practically a travel ban in December. Argh! Mustn't complain though, as I'm healthy, vaccinated, boostered up and with, I hope, a healthy immune system. All you definitely can't say about Beitar and Jerusalem. The club is sick, struggling and fearing for their life and can't fight infections, viruses and tumours. Beitar Jerusalem is on the brink again, at risk of going bust and being relegated. Everywhere you look you see the results of years of neglect, corruption and racism. Hogeg may have killed the club but it was just the final act in years of decline.

After the sheikh debacle, things got worse. At the start Hogeg was angry at the Israeli FA and media for not approving the deal and for their revelations. Later he admitted that things looked fishy, even to him. In September 2021 Hogeg announced that he was stepping down from running Beitar and putting it up for sale. He stopped pouring money into the club, put a trustee in to run it under a tight budget and was looking for a buyer. Without one the club faced major financial difficulties from February 2022. A flurry of weirdos came and went, enjoying hardly 15 seconds of fame. Not one serious offer was submitted to save the stricken club.

Finding a buyer, given Beitar's toxic reputation, was hard enough but in November 2021 it became near impossible. Hogeg was arrested by the Israeli police for a jaw-dropping list of misdemeanours. He's alleged to have committed fraud involving hundreds of millions of shekels in cryptocurrencies, as well as theft, conspiracy, aggravated fraud and violating money-laundering laws. He's further suspected of drug-related offences, false corporate record-keeping and intentional concealment of income. The suspicions are that most of his companies were just a way to get investors' money, which he used for his own lavish lifestyle.

Hogeg was also investigated for trafficking and underage prostitution. The owner of the Beitar club is suspected of carrying out indecent acts, sexual harassment, operating a location for the purpose of prostitution, invasion of privacy and bringing an individual into prostitution, the Kan public broadcaster reported. He's also suspected of supplying drugs and alcohol to underage girls. Hogeg is believed to have filmed many of the sexual encounters, some without the knowledge of the women or teens involved.

It's suspected that Hogeg paid to have a well-known model have sexual relations with potential investors whom he was trying to convince to invest in his business enterprises. It's also suspected that he then used the investments to pay for sexual relations for other investors and for himself. In exchange, Hogeg allegedly gave the women jewellery, luxury handbags, clothing and mobile phones at a total value of hundreds of thousands of shekels.

Channel 13 News also reported that Beitar received a loan from Hogeg's main company. It meant, so it was reported, that any potential buyer would be exposed to future claims for millions of dollars. He also signed a contract giving his permission to build at Bait Vagan and in return received flats and money. It seems that Beitar wasn't his priority.

Hogeg vehemently denied the accusations and was released on bail in January 2022. But with his assets, including Beitar, seized by the police, any sale became much more complicated. Every move had to be approved by the courts and a possible buyer might face demands by the state. It was no wonder that no deal materialised.

In January, however, Beitar released a statement: 'Beitar Jerusalem is happy to announce that a French Jewish businessman, Stephane Melloul has signed the declaration of understanding to buy the club from his current owner Moshe Hogeg.'

'Happy to announce', no less.

'Thank god', was the first reaction of the fans. It lasted for about 30 minutes. It turned out that Melloul had hardly any digital footprint; companies under his name had dodgy-looking dormant websites, other companies were inactive and his major asset, Koshalal, a meat products company for the kosher and halal market, didn't look big enough to allow him to buy Beitar. All was revealed after half an hour of googling.

More was to come when Melloul gave a barrage of interviews in broken Hebrew saying that he would make Beitar one of the top six clubs in Europe with a budget of $100 million. He would get the money from selling TV rights to Fox USA and selling Beitar shirts worldwide. Social media had a field day and the lasting impression of Melloul was a bizarre TV interview in which Eyal Berkovic said in his usual understatement to Melloul via Zoom, 'Enough, enough, you have stung us for 15 minutes of air time … Thanks, what a ride you have had on our expenses.'

Still the club issued daily updates that actually nothing had happened, and they were still waiting for the down-payment from him. Anybody could see that nothing would come out of that farce but Beitar were still 'happy to announce'.

Later, it turned out, according to *Yedioth Jerusalem*, that the statement was all Hogeg's idea. Eli Ohana, now the chairman and the trustee, could see that nothing good would come out of Melloul and that Beitar would once again become a laughing stock. Yet Hogeg insisted.

The local media also reported that a group of Jerusalem-loving evangelists were looking into buying the club. That would have made a perfect ending for this book. A doomsday church from the Bible Belt, praying for the apocalypse, rapture and the mass conversion of the Jewish people, getting hold of a sensitive symbol in a hazardous time. Evangelists have been active in Jerusalem since the latter parts of the 19th century. Just think of Trump-adoring ultra-Zionist Bible nutters setting a policy for Beitar. Sitting with La Familia leaders before a match against Sachnin, crossing their fingers under the table, hoping that the Third World War will start thanks to a football war. Come Armageddon come!

It hasn't happened yet. Four years of a Bibi–Trump alliance was bad enough, thank you very much. The apocalypse is getting nearer, but just Beitar's one. As the city was covered in heavy snow on 26 January 2022 time was running out. Beitar needs to find a way to survive this season.

\* \* \*

After Netanyahu, Israel is slightly more 'normal'. This odd government is trying to rule first and not act for the benefit of the Netanyahu family, his court case and his ongoing fight against the justice system. His attack on democracy was foiled by the skin of their teeth, thanks to just enough members of the Knesset, but the coalition is fragile. The Likud and the neo-Kahanists are trying to destabilise the country by continuous attempts to raise the tension between the Arab citizens of Israel and the state, hoping that Raam, the Islamic party, will leave the coalition. In the West Bank, the nationalist religious militias have been seen going on pogroms against the Palestinian population on a weekly basis with the support of some religious and political leaders. Itamar Ben Gvir, now one of the most televised members of the Knesset, called for the assassination of Israeli-Arab citizens in Ramle and Lod.

As the Netanyahu court case is ongoing, the Likud is turning into a radical party. One Knesset member wrote: 'We need to establish an alternative parliament. A parliament that will discuss, observe, legislate and truly represent the people until the replacement of this vile government.'

Another one screamed during a debate: 'You don't understand what an earthquake is about to hit you! We are on the tip of a volcano! I'm standing on the lava and warning – the situation where a Jewish Zionist majority is oppressed won't continue! We are millimetres from setting this land on fire!'

Another Likud MK announced: 'The Arab-Israeli representatives should only speak about the Arab-Israel public. Period.'

Dudi Amsalem, a former minister, said: 'A Bolshevik dirty gang took over the country, Government of Palestine, spineless rags. Bunch of kids that Mansur Abas, the arch terrorist is running around.'

It went on for two hours with threats to Ashkenazim, liberals, judges, the high court and anybody who's not part of the Bibi cult.

The Israeli right is more racist and violent than Beitar Jerusalem now. The Likud has become a political La Familia. At least Beitar are trying to clean up and move in the right direction, only to find out how hard it is to get rid of racism.

Jerusalem stinks to high heaven these days. Night after night this city is simmering in hate and violence. Haredim clash with police, settler youths are protesting in the Jewish part, there are clashes on the Arab side too, and the security forces keep using the skank, a foul-smelling water cannon. There is a metaphor there.

On the pitch and in the stands, things haven't been much better. Beitar spent most of the season near the wrong end of the table and played dismal football. I mentioned in the Introduction that in September 2021 Hapoel Tel Aviv hosted Beitar Jerusalem, where both sets of fans pelted their rival keepers with items but it was the brutal attack on a young woman that made the news. The 23-year-old Beitar fan with a physical disability was attacked by La Familia fans because she supported her own team despite an order from the mob not to do so.

This was purely because La Familia considered it unacceptable that Kamso Mara, a Guinean Muslim, was in the team and was warming up on the sidelines.

It turned out to be the much needed tipping point. The masses of regular fans had had enough of the racism and fear and openly attacked La Familia's leaders and its foot soldiers on social media. Every post of La Familia was answered by hundreds of negative comments. The fans who had feared to say a wrong word at Teddy and on Facebook were now calling La Familia 'cancer' and telling them to get out of their club. Eli Ohana didn't mince his words and called them 'haters and enemies of Beitar'.

The next home match saw the biggest crowd of non-La Familia fans, who came to support the team and the rising up against the racists. It became an ongoing civil war between the fans, which once again split the club. Not as violent as the 2013 uprising, but still Teddy isn't a nice place to visit.

La Familia are still there despite this. They're not afraid to show their strength and won't go away. Beitar and the decent fans asked for the help of the police and courts but to no avail. La Familia members, even those who were caught on video abusing Mara, can still attend matches. They're back to their old habits, singing their racist filth, but something has to change.

Mara played and was a part of the team. Some fans booed him but for the majority he was a Beitar player. It's a big step forward since the Chechens' persecutions and one psychological barrier has been broken. You don't have to bring Muslim players of the calibre of Karim Benzema or N'Golo Kante for them to be accepted by most fans. You don't even need a popular owner to pass such a move. Hogeg is almost out, and while Mara isn't that good, on that front Beitar and the fans did achieve something important.

For the derby though, the civil war was put aside for one night and the fans came back to Teddy in droves. Beitar need every point to avoid relegation, Hapoel Jerusalem are a direct rival in the relegation scrap and the last haven of pure hate. The three Jerusalem clubs are having a torrid season and all face the threat of relegation. After 58 matches (not including the derbies), the Jerusalem trio have won only eight in total. With Hapoel Tel Aviv and Sakhnin having a decent season, Beitar fans find themselves every week hoping for them to defeat their own rival teams from the foot of the table and cheering their goals in self-loathing. The derby is all they have now, a rival they can hate and beat. Reading the tweets before the derbies you would think it's the year 1982 all over again, with the class and ethnic tensions. Hapoel fans weren't too shy either and spread a provocative banner declaring: 'The hammer, the sickle, the international – the red shirt the hate to the menorah!'

The match was a poor one and Beitar led 1-0 through a goal scored in the first half by Richmond Boachi. But in the second half the Czech, Ondřej Bačo, scored an equaliser, which led to one of the most bizarre events in the derby's history. All Hapoel's foreign players celebrated it wildly, while the Israeli players looked bemused. Hapoel fans started taunting the Beitar fans but were answered in mockery rather than rage. They already knew that Beitar would be awarded the three points following an embarrassing error by the Hapoel manager, who in the 77th minute had brought on the wrong sub. Each team in the top division is allowed to have six foreign players but only five of them can play together during matches. Hapoel had six non-Israelis on the pit

ch and Beitar were awarded the three points and a 3-0 victory a few days later. The players had a raucous but pathetic celebration near the east stand with the fans; it was their first win in ten matches.

Hapoel the ever 'schlimazel' were humiliated and may live to regret the error during their survival battle. For Beitar it was a rare moment of joy in what's becoming their *annus horribilis*. Beitar are known to have nine lives but for every minute that passes it looks as if they may have used all of them.

Relegation, administration, points deduction – all look a possibility. The club has enough fans and donors to start again but the big question is how. It needs to go through a painful Via Dolorosa of fighting the racist and nationalistic cancer. It's not just La Familia – it started well before them.

Without change, it will be only a matter of time until the next collapse.

Mara was one of the first players to be released from Beitar in January in order to save money. His contract was terminated in a move that will probably reach court one day. He did leave a legacy though: it will be much easier for Beitar to sign a Muslim player from now on. However, the big question of whether an Arab player will be welcomed to the club is still open and critical to its future. Hogeg caused more damage to the club than any other owner but I want to believe that he tried to fight racism for the right reasons and not just to get support from the fans and media.

## Hearts of Darkness

'I hope that this bad period will pass soon because the fans and the club deserve it,' said a teary Ofir Kriaf after another match in which Beitar were easily put to the sword. As captain he's one of the few who gave his best on the pitch but he should ask himself how Beitar got here. What's his part in it? Beitar never recovered from the winter of 2013, the 'Forever Pure' banner, the Chechens, the La Familia triumph. Kriaf became associated with the resistance to the Chechen move while other players such as the keeper, Harush, were vilified for welcoming the two. I'm sure Kriaf doesn't sleep well at night knowing that his club may be relegated or worse but can he see the connection? Can he identify the cause that kills his beloved club, beyond that one despicable owner?

Another day and more news: the Museum of Tolerance, a big white elephant in the centre of the city, a non-active museum built on a Muslim cemetery and financed by an American billionaire close to Netanyahu, will give Beitar a loan to keep them going until they find a long-term solution.

Beitar? Tolerance? It lasts barely half a day before Hogeg says that the museum people were deterred by the connections to La Familia. It's hard to know which are lies, spins or straws deparately clutched at.

Another week passes with enough headlines for a month. Each day is slow torture for the fans. Below the Hogeg penthouse in Tel Aviv, the fans are protesting, but only La Familia members after they issued a warning to other organisations not to show up. American buyers are back in the frame but are weary of future claims now that Beitar are listed as a Hogeg asset. The Israeli FA and the league are bending over backwards in looking for a solution, including a long-term loan from a broadcaster. Other clubs in this position haven't received such help but Beitar, despite all the problems, mean big away crowds, nice viewing numbers and a buzz in a league that sometimes is not that interesting.

They may go under or may win some time, but the tale of Beitar is clear.

They rose because they were a political football club and gave a voice to the voiceless. They had their nasty side but for years they were an important club in the social success that's Israeli football. But they declined when they crossed one border too many – when they let the Likud use them, when they gave the racists the right to become the voice of Beitar, when they didn't fight it when it was possible. Beitar were a valid foreteller of Israeli society for years and Israel can learn from them or follow their way to disaster.

# Acknowledgements

MY SINCERE thanks to all the people quoted in the book who generously gave me their time, insight and knowledge, and to all my interviewees over the years as well as those who guided me to them. I have used many of the articles I've written in the past about Beitar and Jerusalem; many thanks to the editors for commissioning them. Uri Sharedsky and *Shem Hamisehak* staff, Jonathan Wilson from *The Blizzard*, Uli Hese and *11 Freunde*, Josimar, *When Saturday Comes* and the old *Kol Ha'ir*.

I'm hugely grateful for the people who help out with time, wisdom and better grammar.

Thanks to former prime minister Ehud Olmert, aunt Shlomit Evans, Yossi Gabay, Doron Adar, Yoram Aharony, Itsek Alfasi, Shlomi Barzel, Beit Ariela Library, Noam Bitton, Yulie Chromchenko, Assaf Cohen, Eli Cohen, Jonathan Cohen, Ruth Cohen, Momi Dehan, Ronny Deon, Omer Einav, Amir Fuchs, Yair Galily, Eyal Gil, Amir Goldstein, Noam Gur, Gabriel Haydu, Alon Hadar, Nir Hasson, Moshe Hogeg, Tom Holland, Haim Kaufman, Itzik Kornfein, Uri Levi, David Luxton, Yossi Medina, James Montague, Jonathan Northcroft, Anshel Pfeffer, Aviad Segal, Akiva Segal, Avishay Sela, Benny Tavory, David

Winner, Shalom Yerushalmi, Michael Zandberg, Moshe Ziat, Maya Zinshtein.

Special thanks to Vivian Osrin and Paul Thomas for their enormous help and support throughout the long journey.

# Bibliography

**Books:**

Nir Hasson, *Nir Hasson Urshalim: Israelis and Palestinians in Jerusalem, 1967–2017* (Books in the Attic)

Ron Amikam, Ronnie Deon, Meir Gabay, *I Love You Beitar* (Media 41, Tel Aviv, 2007, in Hebrew)

Haim Baram, *Red Yellow Black* (Maariv, Tel Aviv, 2004, in Hebrew)

Haim Be'er, *This is the Place* (Am Oved, Tel Aviv, 2017, in Hebrew)

Elon Amos, *Jerusalem City of Mirrors* (Flamingo, London, 1990)

David Kroyanker, *Jerusalem Architecture* (Jerusalem, 1998, in Hebrew)

Simon Sebag Montefiore, *Jerusalem: The Biography* (Weidenfeld & Nicholdson, London, 2011)

Moris Benny, *The Birth of the Palestinian Refugee Problem Revisited* (Cambridge University Press, Cambridge, 2004)

Amos Oz, *A Tale of Love and Darkness* (London, 2005)

Amos Oz, *In the Land of Israel* (Vintage, London, 1984)

Daniel Rubinstein, *The Battle on the Kastel* (Books in the Attic, Tel Aviv, 2017, in Hebrew)

Elisha Shohat, *100 Years of Football* (Elisha Shohat Publicatuions, Tel Aviv, 2006, in Hebrew)

Eliezer Wiztum and Moshe Kalian, *Jerusalem of Holiness and Madness* (Modan, Ramot Hashavim, 2013, in Hebrew)

**Film:**

Zinshtein Maya, *Forever Pure* (Tel Aviv, 2016)

**Articles from:**

*Shem Hamisehak, Haaretz, The Marker, Yedioth Ahronoth & Ynet, Walla Sport, Maariv, One.co.il, Israel Hayom, Makor Rishon, The Blizzard, Sport 5, Hair, Kol Ha'ir, Hashulchan, Encyclopedia Britannica, The Great War ... I was There, Yisca Harani's Database,* National Library of Israel, Ben-Gurion Institute, Israel Democracy Institute

**TV:**

Channel 11, Channel 12, Channel 13, Shiur Moledet (Gum Films), Sport 5

# Index

157, 173, 206, 316–320,
322, 332, 353
Hapoel Petah Tikvah 58, 82, 95,
99, 130, 134–137, 158, 168, 222,
227, 230, 267
Hapoel Tayibe 218–221,
226, 250, 254
Hapoel Tel Aviv 11, 23, 39–41, 58–
59, 62, 68, 96, 104, 113, 130–131,
155, 158, 168, 179–180, 182, 200,
204, 207, 218, 227–232, 235, 237,
269, 274, 289–290, 295, 300, 324,
326, 342, 346, 368–369
Harani, Yisca 44, 376
Harush, Ariel 302, 304–305,
309–310, 320, 371
Hazan, Almog 231–233
Hebron 51, 101, 128, 215, 219, 292
Hinkis, Shimha 51
Histadrut 39–40, 92–93, 95, 131,
140, 182, 200
Hitler, Adolf 62, 144, 224
Helena (Empresses) 43–
45, 47, 50, 102
Herut (party) 66
Herut (paper) 52, 54, 66, 92,
95–96, 119–120, 122, 130, 133,
156, 182–183, 215
Holland, Tom 245, 373
Holocaust 22, 26, 62–63, 81, 91,
102, 107–109, 117, 144, 146–147,
174, 192, 223–224, 290, 334, 356
Holy Fire 187–188
Horn, David 55, 67, 113
Hunt, William Holman 88, 135
Hummus 47, 178, 192, 217, 226,
277–279, 341, 363
Hussein, King of Jordan 20, 127

Husseini, Abd al-
Qader al 72, 74, 78–79
Husseini, Amin al 35, 62
Husseini, Hussein 32–33

I
Intifada 193, 247, 249, 254, 301
Irgun 55, 64, 66, 69, 79–80, 83–85,
92, 94, 96, 118–119, 182, 207, 344
Israel 13–15, 18, 23–26, 28–29,
31, 34, 37–39, 44–45, 54, 61–62,
64–67, 76, 80–83, 85, 88–89, 91,
93–94, 96, 101–107, 109–114,
116–117, 120–122, 127–129, 131,
133, 137–139, 144, 147, 149–158,
161, 163–164, 168, 171–175,
177–178, 181–183, 185, 189–193,
195–198, 200, 202–205, 210–211,
213–215, 218, 221, 223–225, 227,
231, 236–237, 239–240, 242–244,
247, 249–257, 260–262, 264–265,
267, 277–281, 284, 290–292, 301–
302, 304–308, 310–312, 316–317,
332, 335, 337–338, 340–342,
344–345, 348–351, 355, 357–361,
363, 366–367, 372, 375–376
Israeli FA (IFA) 262, 298, 352, 355

J
Jabotinsky, Ze'ev 52–54, 66, 120,
322, 324, 331
Jesus 12, 19, 22, 44–46, 48–49, 88,
108, 140, 187–188, 246, 253, 362
Jerusalem 11–16, 18–23, 25, 28–35,
37–39, 41–43, 45–51, 54–55, 57–61,
64, 66–68, 70–75, 77–83, 86–89,
91–92, 94–101, 103–110, 112, 117,
120, 123–125, 127–128, 130–131,

# Also available at all good book stores

9781801500470

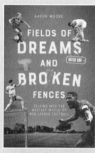

9781801501002

9781801500586

9781801500876

9781801500906

9781801500913

9781801500968

9781801500975

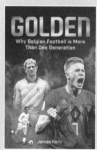

9781801501057